MW01389012

RestlessTribes.com

SALTLICK FOR WANDERING MINDS

Restless Tribes

Travel Stories
1989-2003

by Stephen Ausherman

Judy says read this... and start a book club

S. Ausher—

RestlessTribes.com

A SALTLICK FOR WANDERING MINDS

Published by Central Avenue Press
Albuquerque, NM

Copyright © June, 2004 by Stephen Ausherman

All rights reserved

Requests to reproduce of any part of the work should be mailed to the following address:
Central Avenue Press 2132-A Central SE #144
Albuquerque, NM 87106

Publisher's cataloging-in-publication

Ausherman, Stephen.
   Restless tribes : travel stories, 1989-2003 / by
Stephen Ausherman.
   p. cm.
   LCCN: 2003114028
   ISBN: 0-9715344-3-8

   1. Ausherman, Stephen – Travel 2. Voyages and
travels.   I. Title

Similar incarnations of these essays have been published in *The Sun, Outpost, Grand Tour, The Korea Times, The News and Observer, Weekly Alibi, The Independent, MENZ* and *Travelers' Tales China.*

Cover design and photography by Kyle Zimmerman

www.centralavepress.com
(505)323-9953

Printed in the United States of America

for my father, one of the last great travelers

(Egypt notwithstanding)

Contents

HONDURAS: The Last Good Weekend	1
ALASKA: Eating with the Old Dogs	15
THE PHILIPPINES: Spell of the Filipino Bubble Men	23
IRAQ: Facing the Enemy	43
CHINA: Habits of Flying	63
KOREA: Bearing Witness at the DMZ	85
VIETNAM: Wishing Away the War	93
INDIA: In The Eyes of a Stranger	109
TANZANIA TRILOGY	
Interview with the Witch Doctor	135
The End of the Earth	151
Ghosts of Africa	163
VENEZUELA: Honeymoon in Caracas	175
IRELAND: Nothing Will Kill You	201

Restless Tribes

Restless Tribes, an introduction

I sometimes suffer a longing for belonging, a people to call my own. But if I've ever found comfort in a tribe, it was a restless one, a transient culture that finds temporary purpose in a foreign land, then moves on before a sense of place can root us in.

Yet a sense of place is often fleeting. Sometimes it gets more slippery the longer I stay in one location. I spent two formative decades in Chapel Hill, North Carolina, submerged in Southern indoctrinations that don't wash out easily, before realizing I'd long exhausted my purpose for being there. So I severed those ties, and I've since heeded one Carolina native's most memorable warning: You Can't Go Home Again.

I've lived in New Mexico for more than seven years now and I still can't quite explain why I'm here. I exist in a state of perpetual, sometimes frantic dislocation, and it's not all bad. It's a feeling many a restless traveler still wearily seeks, because in that state we somehow become disarmed and more open to knowledge. Or perhaps we simply panic enough to grab onto anything that might ground us, if only for the moment. Yet later, safely back at home, we may find that we never truly let go. Sometimes we shelve these experiences inside, like souvenirs for the soul. Sometimes they come back to us at unlikely times, like karmic postcards we'd sent to ourselves from a long lost weekend.

So it shouldn't be surprising that the pieces I kept the longest were those found in unlikely places. In lands trampled under the unbridled hostility of war and religion, I found inexplicable hospitality. I gleaned wisdom, gracious and otherwise, from the most unlikely people—particularly the agents of war and religion: Marines and missionaries, colonels and clerics, war heroes and witch doctors. But while both friendships earned and lessons learned were sometimes short lived, I retained pieces of them within me. These are the pieces within this book, the experiences that paradoxically warn and assure us that more are waiting to be discovered elsewhere in the world.

Finally, my apologies to those places that couldn't be included. Nigeria, Egypt, Jordan, Germany, France, Holland, Belgium, Wales, England, Portugal, Spain, Mexico, Canada, Thailand, Borneo and the United States Virgin Islands, we had good times, and you each deserve a heartfelt chapter of your own.

As for Japan, Switzerland, Scotland, Kenya, Texas and peninsular Malaysia—well, maybe next time we'll try harder to understand each other a little better.

The Last Good Weekend

HONDURAS: 1998

Three U.S. Marines stationed in Honduras planned my trip through La Tigra, a 200-square-mile cloud forest and the nation's first national park. The trip was my idea. I left the details to them partly because they had the gear and vehicles, and partly because I figured that when U.S. Marines make a plan in Honduras, nothing can go wrong.

That line of reasoning is not a demonstration of my ignorance of the region's history, but rather a testament to the obscene amounts of alcohol we consumed prior to the trip. Understand that I had no intentions of a ten-day binge with our servicemen in Central America. I'd gone only to attend my cousin's wedding. But as Sergeant Jeff became increasingly tied up in the red tape of international matrimony, he had no choice but to leave me in the care, or at the mercy, of his former coworkers, the U.S. Marines.

My cousin had warned me about Honduras with tales of stray grenades, random gunshots and various assaults that helped this nation earn one of the highest rankings in the Western hemisphere for violent crimes. He'd been attacked by a local with a box cutter outside a bar. In a show of goodwill, local police responded within a matter of seconds by blowing off the assailant's kneecaps. Because Marines were often the target of street violence in Honduras, he told me it would be a good idea not to look like one. But I already did, mainly by virtue of my haircut, and there wasn't much I could do to change that.

Their presence in Tegucigalpa was small—about ten—all assigned to the coveted embassy duty, but they lived larger than glorified frat boys. While soldiers in Honduras' voluntary armed services earned about seven dollars per month, U.S. Marines earned well over a hundred times that amount, plus accommodations. Their house came equipped with widescreen, surround-sound satellite TV, and the most popular show among them was *Dawson's Creek*. They also enjoyed video games, a weight room, private bedrooms and baths, a swimming pool and full bar. They had drivers at their disposal twenty-four hours a day, as well as a van called "Dogcatcher." I had a hard time picturing them doing anything more strenuous than lifting a beer.

Drinking was an intense activity. My first night out among the few and the proud took me to no less than five nightclubs. Many resembled daycare centers, with all their favorite Warner Brothers cartoon characters plastered on the windows and walls. One drink could cost a day's wages for the average Honduran. I'm fairly certain that we drank several into an early retirement.

Another popular pastime involved watching girls, but it rarely amounted to anything beyond that. Language barriers and rules against bringing locals into the house complicated matters. So it surprised me to learn that most Marines there didn't fully appreciate the one women who already lived in the house. She was the token on the team, and the others referred to her as "the waste." It was not a personal attack, one Marine explained, but a comment on the inefficiency of female Marines in general. This after she lost an argument about where to aim when shooting to kill. Apparently the correct response was the right ventricle. Her answer, which I never heard, earned such derision that she stormed out of the bar.

Dogcatcher was our transport between bars more than a block apart. Sirens and blue lights helped facilitate speedy travel to the next disco or strip joint. Even well past midnight when the streets neared emptiness, the Marines aboard found the sirens necessary, or at least humorous. In a city where few can account for our many missing grenade launchers, I often felt we were a highly visible and noisy target. But my bigger concern was for those in the residential areas.

As the sirens wailed and blue lights strobed, I turned to a soldier named Joe and asked: "What would you do if soldiers from a foreign power came blasting and wailing through your hometown at two a.m.?"

He thought for a moment, then said, "Yeah, I guess this could make us look really bad." He then ordered a younger Marine in the front seat to take the light off the roof. Soon the interior of the van lit up with blinding blue pulses that bounced off the windows and windshield and rendered the outside world invisible. Joe said, "Don't tell anybody about this, okay?"

Joe and I often ventured into the Juan Pablo II area, a nightclub zone so prone to violent outbursts that it was declared off-limits to the Marines. To avoid unnecessary attention, we'd bail out of Dogcatcher three blocks away from the main strip. However, nothing seemed as dangerous as Joe had promised.

Drunkards eyed us with suspicion and kids sniffed glue at an age where they should've been eating paste, but both groups left us alone for the most part. Though gunshots were near and frequent, we never had to dive for cover under a hail of bullets. Street fights and barroom brawls rarely broke out. And though the streets and sidewalks sank in a stew of mud and muck, the rains didn't fall hard enough to drive hoards of rats into the bars. It was a slow week, Joe explained.

I tried to ignore the urban squalor, which seemed to take on epic proportions. Even the mayor, César "El Gordito" Castellanos, recently described his city as "ugly, dirty, noisy, polluted and foul-smelling." I couldn't argue with such astute observations.

Earlier in the day, I'd noticed evidence of vandalism that was particularly disturbing. The victim was Tegucigalpa's patron saint, Archangel Michael. He stood near City Hall in his usual statue form: heroically brandishing a spear, thrusting it down to keep Satan pinned to the ground. In this case, however, vandals had swiped his spear and amputated a sizable chunk of his right arm in the process.

Satan now appeared free to rise and run amok in the streets of Tegucigalpa.

Ever wary of the demon, I followed Joe to an outdoor café, where we ordered a beer and took a bench in the back, away from the street. Vendors gravitated to our table. One boy offered a shoeshine, one man had bags of salsa, another sold cane liquor in containers that looked like ping pong balls, a girl offered gum, another had cigarettes, a third said she had nothing but hunger. A man with a machete dangling from his belt reminded us this area wasn't safe, and offered his services as a bodyguard, while two teenage girls offered the services of their bodies. Finally, a toothless gentleman with a ventriloquist doll offered to put on a show.

Everyone in Tegus was trying to make an extra lempira, and understandably so. In terms of national poverty in this half of the world, only Haiti was worse off. But in Tegus, even the consular general from Switzerland was not immune to moonlighting. The sign outside his office read: DRY CLEANING and Swiss Consulate.

After a solid week of drinking and dancing until dawn, I declared that we should set an early curfew for the night before our march through La Tigra. We agreed to retire at the decent hour of 4:30 a.m. so that we could snag two hours of sleep prior to the hike. We'd need at least that much, I figured, because of last-minute changes. One Marine had backed out upon hearing that the Honduran government prohibited firearms in the forest. Unfortunately, he was also the one with the four-wheel drive vehicle. Another Marine, Tim, almost bailed out as well. He didn't seem like the adventurous sort, and often spent his evenings on-line with a distant girlfriend rather than going out with the rest of us. And he didn't seem too enthused about going into the forest unarmed.

Even though we'd have to leave the guns at the embassy and take a bus to the forest, Joe said not to worry: With three of us remaining, we'd be safe enough. Most of the people who disappeared in La Tigra were traveling alone. Whether they got robbed and murdered, fell down a mineshaft, or just lost their way was anybody's guess. In this mountainous forest four times the area of Boston, all that seemed certain was their bodies would never be recovered. So as an added precaution, Joe strapped a couple of Rambo knives to his hip. There in the embassy locker room, with a world-class arsenal at our disposal, Joe's knives seemed about as threatening as a spork.

At 6:30 a.m., the call came in over his radio, a signal designed to wake soldiers for combat. We slept through it. I don't know what prompted us to wake at 8:15, but we did and hit the ground running. Not that it mattered. We'd long since missed the bus.

Joe summoned Dogcatcher shortly after nine. Two hours later, we were halfway to La Tigra. However, Oscar the driver determined the road was too hazardous for Dogcatcher. He was right. Seasonal rains caused several small landslides along the way. Cabin-size chunks of mountain spilled onto the road. Worse, the way it twisted and climbed, this rutted, muddy track could easily pitch over the top-heavy van. We wondered how a bus could handle it, since most buses in Honduras were nothing more than our second-hand school buses. In any case, we had no choice but to walk from there, an estimated seven miles from the park entrance.

Not five minutes passed before I began to struggle under the weight of my pack. Close to an altitude of 7000 feet, clouds rolled over us and I felt their moisture soaking into my sleeping bag. To make matters worse, dogs attacked us in the village of Los Jutes. Or maybe Los Limones. We weren't sure where we were, only that four mongrels charged from behind, barking and snarling and lunging for our legs. We scared them off by hurling profanities and imaginary rocks.

Soon after, as a karmic reward for not throwing actual rocks, a pickup truck stopped and offered us a lift. Joe and Tim congratulated themselves on this stroke of luck; but as the truck strained up the mountain, often pausing or sliding backwards towards fifty-foot drop-offs, I offered the following consideration: "We're hitchhiking on a remote road in Central America, making no effort to not look like U.S. Marines, and we're heading for a forest where several foreigners have already been attacked, gotten lost for days or simply vanished. Yes, this seems great now; but if anything happens to us, the first question people will ask is: 'What the hell were they thinking?'"

It was merely a cautious reminder, a paraphrase of vague warnings from guidebooks and the State Department, but it put a damper on the moment. For the rest of the ride we scanned the trees for snipers and regarded everyone we passed with suspicion. It didn't help that they all—men, women, children—carried large machetes.

We arrived at the gates at noon. A sign warned us that, for our own safety, we were not permitted to enter the park without a guide. A guard on duty informed us there was no guide, and signed us in anyway. Then we began our journey into the damp, dark world of moss-covered trees, bromeliads and ferns, uncertain of the trail we'd chosen.

The map suggested we were entering a large area defined as Bosque Nublado. I told Joe and Tim that this meant "the Forest of Imminent Danger." It was a reasonable translation, but the more accurate one is simply "cloud forest."

This particular cloud forest was placed under national protection in 1971 primarily because it's the source of nearly half of Tegucigalpa's water supply, so we would have to do our best to preserve the natural integrity of these soggy woods. However, the first leg of the hike was like climbing out of hell, an ascent approaching verticality with intermittent log stairs apparently designed to trip us up. I sucked in air that smelled of rotting wood, ripe musk and monkey piss. Though a cool mist filtered through the trees, I felt a week's worth of tequila and beer bleeding out my pores, and sleep deprivation began to weigh me down. After about an hour of this, we arrived at an old mining road. Joe and Tim dropped their packs.

At this point, I'd lost track of time because my watch was stuck on noon. The others didn't think to bring a timepiece, or a compass, flashlight, first aid kit or most of the standard camping paraphernalia. Joe had his Rambo knives, two gruesome blades made from Filipino car parts. He also had a radio, but we were way out of range. We rested on the roadside and devoured the first of our MREs (Meals Ready to Eat).

Minutes later, while I was still trying to force down my dessert, Joe and Tim retreated into the forest and took turns vomiting like high-school girls on prom night. All that loud retching was sure to scare off any pumas, ocelots, agoutis, tapirs, pacas and peccaries in the area, and that pissed me off, even though I wouldn't recognize half those animals even if they bit me on the ass. At the same time, I felt a sense of triumph, seeing how this day was damn near killing two young Marines, while I was only slightly nauseous.

But then, on the second leg of the hike, they decided to run. The trail took an abrupt downhill twist, as steep as the first part, and we picked up a momentum that made me weak in the knees. As an excuse for falling into third place, I reminded them that I was the only one carrying expensive camera equipment. They didn't slow down. Above the quickening thuds of their combat boots, I heard a distinct tearing sound behind me. My backpack was beginning to disintegrate as we hurdled fallen trees and tangles of ancient roots.

The accelerated hike and all its noise dashed out any remaining hopes I had for seeing just one woodland creature, but that didn't matter anymore. While trouncing over mossy rocks and splashing through rivulets, I sensed delirium setting in. I heard noises in the trees, what certainly sounded to me like late-hour cocktail chatter. I called for a cigarette break so we could all pause to listen, but all they heard was a gush of running water. I heard that too, but there was something else above it. There was a party in the forest, I was sure of it.

"Hard to tell," Joe said. "My ears are still ringing from last night's disco."

As we continued jogging down the trail, the whitewater roar grew louder, but didn't drown out the voices I heard. They didn't stop until the trail ended at the base of a waterfall that was at least five stories high. Clouds obscured the top and spilled over like graveyard fog in a B-movie; the water seemed to be pouring out of the sky.

Joe and Tim immediately scrambled for vantage points where they could assume heroic poses for my camera. In crossing the stream, however, Tim slipped on a log and dropped into a foot of water. He landed like a cat, on his hands and feet, but the momentum of his pack quickly followed, flipping over his head and forcing his face into the water. The shoulder straps kept the pack firmly in place on the back of his head, and he remained stuck like that long enough for Joe and I to wonder out loud if he just might drown. Worse yet, we were completely unable to rescue him, as we were rendered powerless by convulsive laughter. Tim the brave Marine had to save himself. He dropped to his knees, splitting a shin over a rock, then heroically crawled ashore.

The third part of the trail kept us within reasonable variations of altitude. We kept our pace up as the air thickened with mosquitoes. We'd also long since lost track of time. We could scarcely see the sky through the canopy of branches, but it had darkened several times already as clouds passed over like low-flying zeppelins. We figured we were near the trail's end when we reached a series of abandoned mine shafts.

Silver mining began in this region in the 1580s, but all we saw were the remains left behind from the Rosario Company of New York, which assumed operations here in 1877 and effectively ushered in a new era in U.S.-Honduran relations.

The United States, slowly learning that an aggressive policy of Manifest Destiny would not be enough to coerce Central American nations out of their sovereignty, began employing a unique brand of Free Enterprise that would at least allow access to the reigns of Honduras, the strategic and geographical epicenter of the Central American isthmus. By 1900, the Rosario Company controlled about ninety percent of the nation's metal exports. Meanwhile, other U.S. companies, such as Standard Fruit and United Fruit, devoured banana plantations. By 1918, they'd taken over seventy-five percent of Honduran banana lands and turned the nation into the original Banana Republic.

Despite constant instability—Honduras has endured nearly 300 rebellions, coups and civil wars since independence from Spain in 1821—U.S. fruit companies kept a steady hold on power and influence. When rebellions brewed in 1911 and 1912, threatening to upset U.S. investments in Honduran bananas, President Taft responded quickly and decisively: He sent in the Marines.

Today the economy of Honduras is still revolves around the export of bananas, and the Honduran banana industry is still governed largely by U.S. interests. The mines, however, shut down in 1954. Now their narrow tracks, half buried in weeds and vines, stop short of the gaping black craws of this lush green mountain. Joe and I ventured inside a muddy shaft with cigarette lighters held above our heads, but the small flames only magnified the void.

Shortly after reemerging into daylight, I heard music—percussion mostly—but I wasn't sure if it was coming from underground or up above.

"Anyone hear music?" I asked.

They listened for a moment. "Maybe," Joe said. Then: "Wait . . . nope, don't hear a thing."

I convinced myself that what I heard was nothing more than aural hallucinations spawned from exhaustion. Or perhaps Tegus' tinnitus-inducing night clubs were still reverberating in my head. Anything seemed more plausible than the idea of social gatherings deep in the forest; though in my delirious state, visions of dancing *chupacabras* couldn't have been too far off.

We followed the mining road to the ghost town of El Rosario. The wooden houses built on stilts and steep hillsides resembled those in any West Virginia mining town. Few buildings in this community built for a thousand were still inhabited, though hundreds of bats found refuge in the train depot. Surrounding coffee and banana plantations made the town seem that much more lonely and out of place. Even a U.S. embassy, the first in Honduras, stood here in anonymous quietude.

We took a room in a hospital that had been converted into a dormitory. I unrolled my sleeping bag over a bunk and found a small and disoriented scorpion inside. It ran in frantic circles before I smashed it with a shoe.

Meanwhile, Joe braved an incoming storm to find beer in the ghost town. Miraculously, he returned with a case of Nacional. A nearby kiosk was well stocked, he informed us. He'd even bought rounds for the men there. As the night progressed, we could hear their voices and music rising above the storm. Both were hauntingly similar to what I'd heard in the forest.

Music and voices rose through the air the next morning as well, but they were far more distant, drifting in and out with changes in the wind. I was eager to head back into the forest to investigate, but Joe and Tim complained of muscle aches and insisted on continuing downhill toward the next village, San Juancito.

This nineteenth century mining town nestled in a deep

crevasse was visible from the road just outside of El Rosario, and it remained in sight for most of the hour it took for us to walk there. Along the way, the voices and music grew louder, and soon it became apparent that the whole village was engaged in celebration.

"Can you hear what they're saying?" Joe asked.

I stopped and listened to one voice amplified above the rest, then replied: "She just said it's 'El Dia de los Gringos Muertos.'"

Joe stopped in his tracks and translated for Tim: "Day of the Dead Gringos." For a moment, they actually believed me.

In truth, it was a children's fiesta. We didn't have to get much closer to recognize the oversized cartoon characters dancing in the plaza. The local police welcomed us into town, asking if we enjoyed our hike through La Tigra, and their chief showed particular interest in the two knives strapped to Joe's hip.

They talked about their village with a tone of pride, but we couldn't understand much of what they said because of their heavy accents. The conversation faded until Joe, in a spontaneous show of goodwill, presented his knives as a gift to the chief. He received them with enthusiasm, and said something along the lines of how useful they would be in La Tigra. Then he showed us his knife, a small bayonet from an old rifle, made in the U.S.A. It looked like an antique, probably worth much more than Joe's knives, so I was glad that he immediately refused when the chief offered it in return.

We sat with the police on the front porch of their station, a good vantage point for observing the village. We didn't talk much, just admired the place. It was like no other I'd seen in Honduras, or any other Third World country. Despite the fiesta, the streets remained clean. Landscaping around the buildings showed an attention for detail. Red tile roofs were in good condition and most walls seemed freshly painted. Folks acknowledged us with a smile or a nod rather than the usual clusters of stares and circles of yelling children. We didn't stand out so much there because blond hair and blue eyes were not uncommon—a genetic legacy of foreign miners.

Despite its proximity to the cloud forest, San Juancito did not cater to tourists. Aside from the U.S. ambassador, who happened to cruise by us in a caravan of two white Chevy Suburbans, we were the only foreigners in town that weekend, perhaps longer. Still, the government had declared it a historic place with a rich cultural past. During the mining years, San Juancito had theaters and dance halls, and in 1910 it introduced motion pictures to Honduras with the first movie house in Central America.

Now plans were underway to open museums, restore hotels, and even build a cable car to El Rosario. All they needed to get these projects underway was money. In a way, I hoped it would never come. It was a selfish thought, I know. But there were so few places like that left on earth, and tourists could trash this one within a year. I made a silent promise not to mention this place in any articles until after its magic was gone. I had no idea how soon that would happen.

We remained so captivated by San Juancito we nearly forgot that we had no transportation back to Tegucigalpa. When this problem finally surfaced in our conversation, no one seemed too concerned about it. Then, in a sudden burst of energy, Joe said, "Let's just hump it over to Valle de Angeles and catch a bus from there."

The chief told us the valley was no more than six kilometers away. But after ninety minutes of hiking a winding road out of San Juancito's crevasse, we suspected that his estimate was as the crow flies. Sun-scorched, aching and hungry enough to dine on MREs again, we dropped our packs by the side of the road. Halfway through our lunch, Joe figured that the high altitudes had caused the bags to expand, drawing in air and spoiling the food. Still, my cold meatballs with barbecue sauce seemed fine. The chocolate cake was delicious. And when Tim and Joe started to throw out their food, I offered to eat it for them.

Stuffed now, I flagged down the first truck that came along. We climbed into the back and barreled down the mountain toward Valle de Angeles. Twenty minutes later, we arrived and found it in depressing contrast to San Juancito. A declared tourist zone, the valley contained a handful of hotels and dozens of souvenir emporiums. Every other store sold irrelevant carvings and overpriced leather goods, while folks wandered the streets pushing ceramics and baskets. We needed to find the fastest way out of there.

As fate would have it, two white Chevy Suburbans sped down a narrow street, passing us at what might be considered terminal velocity in the slow-paced town. Joe radioed one of the drivers and requested a ride. The ambassador responded, saying he'd be happy to take us along, but first would we join him for a beer.

In sunglasses, a baseball hat and casual attire, the ambassador claimed he was traveling incognito. So maybe it was the Suburbans and armed escorts from Honduras' elite Cobra division that tipped off the locals. Everyone at the hotel café seemed to recognize him. Food came free of charge, and the hotel manager and his family greeted us with enthusiasm. When introductions were exchanged, which was several times in the course of an hour, the ambassador referred to Joe, Tim and me as "three Marines." A wink in my direction indicated he knew I wasn't one, that he'd said so only for the sake of brevity.

Prior to my trip, I would've more likely envisioned myself ensconced with the Peace Corps. I couldn't have imagined fraternizing with the Marines for more than ten minutes, figuring instead they'ed be too busy nuking rougue banana plantations in an effort to protect U.S. interests.

Now, a week or so later, I understood why they were so few and proud, and their Santini-style hijinks were as much fun as they were obnoxious. Still, there was this nagging guilt by association, this lingering moral dilemma.

Our military actions in Honduras have rarely been honorable. When I was Joe's age, the Reagan administration used Honduras as a base to launch covert wars against Nicaragua and El Salvador. Our military trained tens of thousands of Contras and Salvadorian refugees and Battalion 316, the death squad responsible for the "disappearance" of hundreds of leftist activists. And in all likelihood, given the history of our relations, some equally insidious act of intervention was probably going on that very moment.

But considering the fuss Joe put up to keep me entertained in the absence of my cousin, a protest would have been impolite. So instead I sought diplomacy and told the ambassador that I didn't mind being introduced as a Marine, just that maybe it wasn't fair to the others. After all, I'd done nothing to earn the title—aside from drinking tremendous amounts and holding up with two of them on a hike through twenty-odd miles of Honduran countryside. And in the end, all it really earned me was a Marine T-shirt, which Joe presented with a minimum of ceremony that very night in the Marine house.

My first few days back in the States, the voices I heard in the forest faded in and out of my mind, along with the music from San Juancito's fiesta. Then one day, nothing but silence. I didn't think too much of it until I began to notice reports of Hurricane Mitch pummeling the entire region and reducing it to a haven for more misery and disease than most folks care to name. I tried for days to e-mail Joe and others I'd met there, but most of my messages just bounced back.

Two weeks later, after both the hurricane and the news reports subsided, I got e-mail from Joe. He apologized for the delayed reply, explaining that the clean-up efforts were keeping him busy. He also wrote: "Remember San Juancito? It's gone! Mudslides took it away. You should see the carnage down here, it's unbelievable . . . . I tell you man, we had the last good weekend this country's going to offer for a while."

The last good weekend. It was a great weekend. But looking at the photos, I could only imagine that steep crevasse channeling a wall of mud past the ghost town and upon the village of San Juancito. I looked at the police on their front porch minding a children's fiesta and thought of how quiet it must be now. I wanted to imagine their pride and their determination to rebuild, but it was difficult. Joe never said if anyone survived.

He did describe the rescue efforts in Tegu. He told of pulling survivors from collapsed buildings and plucking the dead from tree limbs where floods had crested. Mostly, his stories focused on blowing debris dams out of the rivers to prevent further flooding. No one else in Honduras had the munitions expertise to do that, he said.

In short, they did more for the initial recovery effort than any relief agency in the world. And for a moment, I actually wished I could have been there—as a Marine. Hell, they even rescued a few hopelessly stranded Peace Corp volunteers.

I scarcely heard from Joe again in the following weeks. All the while the official count the of dead and missing crept closer to 15,000. Among them was mayor César "El Gordito" Castellanos, who perished in a helicopter crash while surveying the damage.

Finally, after many months, I started getting firsthand reports from San Juancito. The first came from a Red Cross volunteer, the second from a Baptist missionary. Details varied, but both agreed that, ironically, the mines that had created the town were instrumental in destroying it. They'd filled with water; and when they reached their limit, they channeled a debris flow through the town in the crevasse.

The missionary's report contained the best news. He said that the people of San Juancito had been aware of the impending catastrophe and evacuated the area in time. He also seemed more optimistic about recovery efforts.

Later reports would prove him right. The town did recover, in a manner of speaking. It rebounded with new handicraft centers modeled after those in Valle de Angeles. New accommodations sprouted up to supplement the dormitory in El Rosario. Even Pepsi joined the renovation efforts by sponsoring a hotel and a visitors center. Transportation services have been added so nobody needs to walk to the park entrance. And tourists herded through today, they don't seem to notice that anything is missing.

Eating with the Old Dogs

ALASKA: 2001

The huskies are brawling over some bitch. Snarling and barking and gnashing their fangs, they drown out Dario Daniels' every word. That's unfortunate because Dario, an Iditarod veteran, is instructing me how to mush. It seems like something I should hear before stepping on the rails of a dogsled for the first time.

He pauses for a break in the clamor, but there are about a hundred Alaskan huskies up here on top of Godwin Glacier, and they're all riled. The dog team I'm about to drive lunges forward, ripping their anchor from the ice, and piles over the team on Dario's sled.

He says, in his German accent, "We got some females in heat, so obviously it gets everybody a little excited."

While his assistants break up the fracas and secure the sleds, Dario explains the most important thing to remember: "Rule number one, two and three of dog mushing is . . . ."

Apparently, the dogs don't want me to hear it.

Then he says something about leaning and something about brakes. I can't hear that either. The ASTAR helicopter that whisked me up here is taking off, adding much percussion to the husky chorus.

Still, I find my place on the sled. It's tethered behind another sled with Max Warren at the helm to drive twelve dogs. That's about 600 pounds of dog under the direction of one seventeen-year-old Junior Iditarod musher. My job, it seems, is to keep the rear sled from tipping over or crashing into his sled.

Max yanks up the anchor and commands the dogs to run. They bolt out over the ice. Rule number one, two and three suddenly becomes clear: Hang on.

I've been warned about driving a team with a bitch in heat. Former mushers Ralph "Darby" Darbyshire and Robert "Bob" Ernisse detailed the hazards in Fletcher's tavern back in Anchorage. Bob was not a subtle man. His voice and posture suggested he could hold his own in a shipyard brawl, yet he managed Fletcher's and tended the bar, serving the upscale clientele with familiar ease.

Meanwhile, Darby held down the third stool from the end and savored wines of selected vintages.

We were discussing the Iditarod, "The Last Great Race on Earth" or "The Idiot Ride," depending on who you talk to. Bob yanked down two ale taps and told me: "I can go out and start an Iditarod, and all my dogs are healthy. But then you get to Yentna Station and you get a dog that's coming into heat. And you go, *Oh my God*. And by the time you get to Skwentna, which is another thirty-five miles down the trail, every female you got on your team is coming into heat. Then you got problems. Major problems."

Darby nodded in agreement. "The real problem is because when they're in heat, you got to take care of them. Somebody's got to go out and fuck those females."

Bob confirmed this with an uncertain, "Yeah."

"You've got a mess on your hands," Darby continued.

"Every time you pass a team, all males on their team want to get in your team and screw your females," Bob explained. "You put your females out in front, you're fine."

"As long as you got me at the tail," Darby said, laughing enigmatically.

Bob shrugged him off. "But then all of the sudden, they want to get laid, so they turn around on your team." He leans over the bar and states emphatically: "There is nothing more aggravating than having sixteen dogs in a ball, fighting and fucking."

"Fighting and fucking," Darby repeated, shaking his head.

"Oh my God, you're trying to get them untangled."

"And they're biting you."

"It's not fun sometimes," Bob concluded, draping a bar rag over his shoulder.

The air is warm at the top of the glacier. The only reason I keep my sleeves rolled down is to protect from sunburn. Max seems comfortable in a T-shirt. He shifts his footing to the right rail as the sleds bank to the left on a sloping curve. I do the same, watching the snowy blur beneath my boots.

The rail I'm standing on isn't more than a few inches wide, but it's topped with black rubber, like a piece of a shower mat, providing good traction. Confident in my footing, I pull out my digital camera and shoot the dogs as they plow over the arctic landscape. The snowy expanse seems unlimited, save for flanks of rocky peaks on two horizons. It's hard to imagine that we're racing over ice millenniums old and hundreds of feet thick, in constant motion and prone to splitting into horrifically deep crevasses.

More confident still, I reach for my slide camera, the one that survived countless jolting journeys across Asia, Africa and the Americas. For some reason, it's not responding well in this environment. The telephoto lens is jammed at 70mm. As I mash the buttons to coax it out further, I notice the rope in front of me going slack. Max is braking. Common sense tells me I need to brake as well. I stomp down on the spring-loaded bar. Its metal teeth bite into the ice and spit up snow. The rope goes taught again and the sled grinds to a halt.

Max says I need to let someone else drive for a while.

The Iditarod is the only reason why dog teams survived the age of the airplane in Alaska. Iditarod mushers are to dogsleds what the Amish are to the horse and buggy. But since the application of dogsledding changed, the dogs had to change as well. They are still Alaskan huskies, but they are of mixed breeds and reduced size. Today's dogs, being much smaller than the earlier dogs, can run much further, much faster than the old dogs could. They can run 120 miles a day, take a short nap, get up and do it again for twelve days on end.

But few people truly understand the capabilities of the old dogs. Colonel Norman D. Vaughan remembers. Norman is the sole surviving member of the First Byrd Antarctic Expedition (1928-1930) and the first American to drive dogs in the Antarctic. He also raced at the winter Olympics in 1932, the only year the Olympics featured dogsledding as an event. He's rescued downed aircrew in Greenland and led 209 sled dogs to the Battle of the Bulge. He's raced in thirteen Iditarods, most recently in 1992. Two years later, three days before his eighty-ninth birthday, he summited Antarctica's 10,302-foot Mount Vaughan.

With his dog team, he crashed President Carter's inaugural parade, (but was invited to Nixon's and Reagan's). And on a plexiglass-enhanced, bulletproof sled, he taught Pope John Paul II the basics of mushing.

The list goes on.

If you ever want to feel as though you've wasted half your life, just compare your résumé to his. Even when he worked as a janitor at the University of Alaska, he did so as the proud owner of a Congressional Medal of Honor, and the University later awarded him with an honorary doctorate.

Norman and I met for lunch at Fletcher's, where he's eaten everyday for the last two years and more than occasionally over the past twenty-five. He moseyed in, aided by a pair of Extreme Sierra 3 walking sticks, and eased up on his reserved stool at the end of the bar.

I'd anticipated tales both heroic and harrowing, but he seemed more preoccupied with future plans—"upcoming trips to Maine and Czechoslovakia," for example—as well as his current dilemma over what to order for lunch.

I tried to steer him back to the past, asking, "What's the biggest problem you've ever run into on the trail?"

His answer was as immediate as it was succinct: "That would be myself."

"Have you ever been afraid for your life on a dogsled?"

"Many times."

"For example?"

"Going out there. Period."

This was not going as well as I'd hoped. And he bristled when I asked him about his idea to use dogsleds to retrieve wounded Allied soldiers from the frontlines at the Battle of the Bulge.

"We tried to do what we could, but we didn't really accomplish anything." He sipped his iced tea and poked at the clams in his bowl.

"It was Washington's fault," he went on, "because they took thirty days of fiddling around down at the Pentagon wondering if this was a good idea or not. So on one day, they sent a wire to General Patton and asked, 'Do you want the dogs to come?' He just sent three words back: 'Send the dogs.' He did it the same day he got the message. And we left that same day because I had everything all keyed up. Every dog all ready to go. Their harnesses were packed, sleds were ready. Everything was ready."

By now, a small crowd had gathered around his end of the bar. He didn't seem to notice them. He continued speaking softly, forcing them to lean in closer. "Just as Patton welcomed the dogs, rain and melting snow and hot weather came. The snow that we had turned into slush and the roads that were there turned into mud. And the men were dying and they weren't getting back from the frontline. They were dying out there."

Ultimately, the mission was a failure. But Norman is a man of many maxims, the most popular of which challenges: "Dream big and dare to fail!" He even has it printed on his business card, along with a recent photo of his jovial, white-bearded visage, and his stunning list of achievements.

Early into our lunch, he warmed up to a more light-hearted conversation and transformed into the affable man I'd heard so much about. It seemed he just wanted to tell a story he hadn't been asked to tell a hundred times before. Forget the 425 dogs he led on Air Force Search and Rescue missions. Never mind the thirty-six consecutive hours he spent spotting icebergs from a crow's nest. He had something better to say. I could tell from the way his eyes lit up when Bob urged him to divulge the Granola Story.

The Granola Story is one I try to suppress during my debut run on a dogsled. I need to stay focused on the adventurous chronicles of man and dog scoffing at elements known to induce hypothermic seizures in lesser creatures.

Halfway through the three-mile loop, I recline in Max's sled, leaving the driving to him and others on the tour. A dozen husky butts bounce before me as their wide paws beat down the trail. They may run this route a dozen times a day, and they seem maniacally happy about it.

Admittedly, I am equally full of crazed enthusiasm. Of the many tours packed into my Alaskan press junket, the Godwin Glacier Dog Sled Tour is by far the most breathtaking. The thin dry air and austere surroundings conspire to collapse my perception of depth; I have no way to gauge the size or distance of the nunataks hedging the snowfield. These black mountain peaks spiking up from the stark white ice create a landscape completely alien to me, at once serene and hostile.

The dogs' labored breaths and the crunch of compacted ice fold around me. And then, for one brief moment, I hear Jack London calling. I see visions of Norman Vaughan and Admiral Byrd fleeting over the tundra. I am Nanook of the North.

I am kidding myself.

With stories of true dog driving stuck in my mind for comparison, I can't help but feel that my experience here essentially amounts to little more than a pony ride in the park.

Damn those Iditarod mushers.

But not every musher tale is fit for legend. The Granola Story, for example, involved a recent road trip in a friend's truck, where Norman mistook a plastic bag full of ashes for a serving of granola. And having never enjoyed dry granola in his long, long life, he unwittingly choked down what was once his lead dog.

He told the story at length and in great detail, bringing rounds of laughter to his end of the bar. But for those of us who expect tales both harrowing and heroic from legends like Norman, it was a bit of a letdown.

Ask him for a more meaningful narrative and he'll respond with the Underwear Story.

We forget that he's endured spells of normality throughout the past century, that his foreboding maxim—"The only death you die is the death you die every day by not living!"—applies to himself as well. He's served his time cleaning lavatories and selling ad space in magazines. He's gone weeks without bus fare or any other means of escaping cities he hated.

It's not fun sometimes.

He's no stranger to shortcomings, such as getting cut from the Harvard football team, placing tenth at the Olympics and not once winning the Iditarod. He still knows humility, particularly when potential sponsors shy away from funding his next adventure, unconvinced that he'll survive it. No one can say that Norman hasn't tasted the average life. On some levels, we can identify with him.

He's not so tough. Bet he wouldn't last three rounds in a boxing ring with me. On the other hand, Norman plans to spend his 100th birthday ascending once again the Antarctic mountain that bears his name. On some levels, he hardly seems human, and we can only applaud his bravery and endurance.

Or we can damn the old dog for setting the bar too high.

Once Norman and I finished our steamed clams and grilled scallops, Bob nodded me aside to tell me one last story, one about his rookie race in 1992. It was twenty-two degrees below zero, the coldest start in the history of the race. "And it never warmed up one day," he said.

I settled in for what promised to be another saga of lunatic bravery.

He leaned across the bar and locked me into his steely gaze. He said, "I was getting ready to take a nap at the Skwent Roadhouse, and Norman Vaughan came walking in." Dramatic pause. "He started talking about the old days. And I can remember lying under the table with my head up. I forgot about sleeping because I was listening to Norman's stories. And the reason I was running the race, I realized it was happening right now—to hear Norman's stories."

That's it?

I, too, have heard Norman tell his old stories. True, that in itself is an experience. But it didn't require dogs dragging me hundreds of miles through Godforsaken frozen wastelands. Maybe that's my own loss, though I could die at peace without ever knowing for sure.

"Only the bold brave the cold!" is another one of Norman's sayings, as if the brain-wilting sun down south of the Yukon has rendered us all slack-jawed cowards. Ha! Give me military juntas, venomous snakes and malaria. Pass the full-body sunscreen and the Swahili phrasebook. Let the bold brave the cold. My call of the wild still beckons from more tropical climes.

And yet, as the helicopter swoops down toward Seward, I am filled with doubt and wonder. A bald eagle circles below, stalking prey. A moose emerges from a beetle-ravaged cluster of spruce. The unyielding glacier grinds through the final stronghold of the Chugach Mountains, where snow melts into cascading ribbons that plunge their way to Resurrection Bay.

In the midst of all this, Norman's last words to me occupy my mind: "Come back in the winter and have a big taste of dog mushing. I know you will like it so much you might move here permanently."

Chilling thought, but I can't shake it. I've got to experience this place in the winter.

In memory of Bob Ernisse, 1948-2003

Spell of the Filipino Bubble Men

THE PHILIPPINES: 1995

The second time I met President Gerald Ford was at a small Carolina college in 1986. He sat a few feet away from me in the parlor of Elon College's Holland House, frowning and looking too big for his overstuffed chair. I edged closer to the fire and thought about Ferdinand and Imelda Marcos sunning their fat asses in Hawaii. Why did we let them in? I wanted to ask Ford. I was there when you met them. Don't your remember what scum they were?

Instead I turned to him and said: "Last time I saw you was more than ten years ago. We were in Manila. I didn't know exactly what you were doing there because I was only in the third grade. But I do remember sensing some hostility towards Americans. Did you get the same feeling?"

A gaping smile spread across his face. He laughed and said, "I don't think I knew what I was doing there either." His smile subsided as he added, "But yes, I did get that feeling."

Twenty years have passed since my six-month stay in Manila, yet some days will always remain clear. Like October 1, 1975. Our whole class, even the teacher, left school early to go to Irfan Pabany's house and witness a historic event on TV. Irfan was my best friend, and the event was "The Thrilla in Manila: The Ali-Frazier Fight of a Lifetime."

And no matter where I am, the smell of burning trash always reminds me of our home on the Saint Luke's Hospital compound. Our apartment was near the incinerator. They'd fire it up nearly every evening; and cats that had come to feed on medical waste would be trapped inside, their yowls filling the air thicker than the smoke they soon became. Then, sometimes, night would bring the desperate screams of maniacs. Our apartment was near the mental ward as well.

But some memories are losing texture, too many details are missing. I'm hoping my return will bring them to life like some ghost of Christmas Past, but that seems unlikely. It's Christmas Eve, 1995. I've been in Manila for a day and nothing seems the same.

My first glimpse from the plane struck a familiar chord: the wreckage of a China Airways passenger jet, its logo visible despite their attempts to white it out under chalky paint. But then again, I've seen this at a half dozen other Asian airports.

From there, Manila grows less familiar. Sure, it's as filthy as I remember, its sidewalks paved with soggy cardboard. And the jeepneys are still here, styled like the one I rode to school every day, all gussied up in shiny tassels and chrome ornaments, pinup girls and dashboard saints. But they look bigger, even feel bigger on the inside. In fact, the whole city feels bigger. Its sky looks huge, and dark, heavy clouds take up the greater part of it. Rain has already devastated much of Luzon and other provinces, and the winter forecast has threatened that worse will come.

Christmas is perhaps the most dangerous time to be in Manila. The papers are filled with reports of revelers "setting off highly explosive fireworks and wrongly discharging firearms during the traditional birthday of Christ our Lord." Military units are on alert, while many National Police members have been ordered to surrender their weapons until the festivities are over.

Even the Communist Party of the Philippines is "keeping in the spirit," by declaring a cease-fire so that rebel troops can "visit their families without fear of being attacked by government forces." Meanwhile, the radical Muslim Abu Sayyaf group has acknowledged the season by stepping up threats of terrorist attacks against Westerners.

The entire nation is preparing for Christmas in ways I've never imagined, and it's making me feel like Ford did: I don't know exactly what I'm doing here. So I leave Manila without visiting Saint Luke's, my school, or anyplace else I might recognize.

Instead, I decide to go to Siquijor, a remote southern island of about 70,000 residents, most relying on fishing and farming for their daily bread. Forty miles of roads connect its six towns, all encompassed within sixty-five miles of shoreline in the Mindanao Sea. The beaches and scuba diving here are said to be among the best in the region.

However, I'm more interested in its witchcraft. Throughout the Philippines, traditional practices evolved along Catholic lines during the 300 years of Spanish rule. And while Catholicism and witchcraft continue to flourish nationwide, Siquijor's reputation stands above the other 7106 Philippine islands as a hotbed of sorcery.

Even the early Spaniards, the first arriving in 1561, noticed a strange aura about the island. Observing it from their galleons, they claimed that it glowed eerily in the night and dubbed it *Isla de Fuegos*, or Island of Fire.

In recent years, its notoriety has grown with reports of political candidates visiting its sorcerers, presumably to put a curse on their opponents or for protection from such curses. When questioned, however, most claimed that they were simply seeking a cure for some strange ailment. Imelda Marcos, for example, reportedly suffered from an unidentifiable skin disease until she sought help from a Siquijorian healer.

Spellbound with such stories, I board a plane bound for Dumaguete on the southeastern edge of Negros. By Christmas morning, I'm on the docks, edging down a slick, bucking gangway onto an outrigger pump-boat, where I find my place among thirty or so other passengers seated on wooden planks. There's room enough for half of them to sprawl. An engine near the back belches to life at a decibel level higher than a cement truck, rattling the entire wooden hull.

As the boat wobbles out to sea, its bamboo pontoons alternately submerging and resurfacing, I climb upon the roof to join a group of college students from nearby Cebu. They're all Seventh-Day Adventists out on a caving expedition, one tells me, eagerly inviting me along. When I decline the offer, he asks why I'm going to Siquijor. Not wanting to offend his SDA sensibilities, I don't mention my quest for sorcery. Instead, I tell him, "I hear it's a magical place."

He nods. "Yes. They use much black magic." He adds in a conspiratorial tone: "They can make something from cloth, something to look like you. And when they put the pins in it, you can feel something bad."

"We have that in America," I tell him. "We call them voodoo dolls."

"Voodoo! Yes. It is what they have on Siquijor." He pauses, phrasing the English in his mind before speaking again. "In America also?"

I nod, though wondering with considerable doubt how this African-Caribbean practice was introduced to a small Filipino island. I ask him, "Can you tell me more about the island?"

He shakes his head. "I've never been there before. Only Pastor Campo. He knows the caves." He points out the pastor, a short, muscular man with a short-sleeve shirt and hairy arms. Earlier I mistook him for a deckhand. "But I think you have been there already."

"Actually, no."

He looks surprised. "Then you must know someone there?"

"No. No one."

His eyes widen more. "I think you must have much faith in God." I suspect he's about to launch a religious discussion on behalf of the SDAs, but all he has to add is this: "To travel this way, so many things can go wrong."

The boat docks in Tambisan, where several tricycles (Honda pedicabs) are waiting. None of the drivers, however, is willing to take me to the resort at Paradise Beach, about thirteen miles away. No one's even heard of it. I point to its approximate location on a map of Siquijor. Three drivers study the map for nearly five minutes before coming to the conclusion that what they are looking at is, in fact, a pictorial representation of their island.

"Yah! Siquijor!" one gasps. The revelation is followed by a lengthy discussion in the local dialect.

"Paradise is too far," Pastor Campo explains. "Would you like to come with us?" When I hesitate to answer, he puts his expedition on hold for the next twenty minutes, until he can convince a driver to take me for a fair price. All that trouble (though he insists it isn't any) and he doesn't even know my name.

The driver, Rudy, is a balding, clean shaved man, except for a slight mustache. He has an alert look in his eyes, and he leans forward whenever I speak. His English is easy enough for me to understand, though it's clear early on that he doesn't quite follow much of what I say. I can't be sure if it's my American accent or if a daily dose of engine noise has impaired his hearing.

His tricycle, christened the Sr. San Rogue, is a powdery shade of lemon drops with Biblical scenes hand-painted on every flat surface. He drops me off on a perfectly deserted stretch of beach where the only manmade structures in sight are a rusted barbwire fence with five-foot cement X's for posts, and a storm-gutted shack with the painted message: NO SAND HAULERS, punctuated with a skull and crossbones.

"The Paradise is that way," he says, pointing down the empty beach.

"Where is everybody?"

"People are afraid to come here anymore," he says with a shrug. "We had bad typhoons this year. And the NPA is kidnapping and killing so much now."

"Are they here?" I ask.

"On Siquijor? No." He forces out a laugh, then adds as a further assurance: "They came many years ago, but nobody was interested in them and they had no good place to hide. They did not stay long."

I would later read that sorcerers drove them away with spells and hexes.

But I'm not worried about the New People's Army. This guerilla division of the Philippine Communist Party is a greater threat in urban areas, where they operate in assassination squads called "sparrow units"—not exactly the kind of name that ices the heart with fear. Besides, I was never scared of communists.

I'm more concerned about the Abu Sayyaf group. These Muslim separatists operate primarily in Mindanao, the island directly south of Siquijor. Hellbent on carving an independent state out of Islamic toeholds in the southern Philippines, the Abu Sayyaf's favored forms of persuasion include hurling bombs at Christians and kidnapping foreigners. The perceived financial incentive in the latter activity attracts many otherwise reluctant rebels to their cause, giving them the manpower to step up threats of terrorism during the holiday rush. In short, Siquijor is about as far south as I can travel without overtly volunteering myself as a terrorist's bargaining chip.

"What made you come here?" Rudy asks.

"I'm on a witch hunt."

His eyes widen. "There are no witches here!"

"No? I heard there were lots."

He smiles and shakes his head. "Those stories you hear about witches eating people, they are not true."

"I haven't heard those stories."

"Anyway, they are not true," he insists. Then, after a long hesitation, he adjusts his seat and offers this: "There was a man who was a witch. Some people tried to shoot him, but the gun wouldn't make any noise. So they put him in a sack with some big rocks and threw him in the ocean." He says 'sack' so it sounds like 'sock', and I imagine a giant Christmas stocking writhing and sinking to the ocean floor, a torrent of bubbles streaming away. "Anyway," he continues, "that happened long ago. I was only seven. Now we have no witches. But I think you can see the *Mananambal*. The healers."

"Do you know any?" I ask.

"What is the particular reason?" he says, looking concerned. "Is something wrong with your body?"

"No. I just want to talk to them."

He seems to understand. "Ah! I think you are very curious. Anyway, I can take you tomorrow if you want."

"Yes, that would be great," I say. "Do you ever visit the healers?"

He tucks his chin close to his neck and shakes his head briskly. "No. Never."

After a ten minute hike down the beach, I arrive at the Paradise Beach resort. The hostess runs out to greet me, all the while balancing a pot on her head. Her name is Alfreda, and she's near tears with joy to see me. "So long I have prayed for guests," she says. "And today God brings you to me. It is my Christmas present! Are you hungry?" And not waiting for an answer, she takes the pot off her head and says, "I have your dinner ready. It will be my Christmas present to you." I catch a whiff of what's in the pot. Fish and rice, I'm guessing. I detect coconut and some kind of curry as well. Whatever it is, it sets off hunger pangs in my belly.

She escorts me into the dining hall, a hardwood house with bamboo floors that sag under my footsteps. The thatched-palm ceiling soars up to twenty feet. The place is big enough for six dining tables, a bar, a souvenir counter and a stage. A small library is stocked with romance novels, bootleg action videos, and a stereo with cassette, CD and karaoke functions.

However, except for a jar of instant coffee and three homemade postcards, the bar and counter are empty. And the only electronic device that seems to work is a shortwave radio. It fills the room with a commercial jingle: *For macho flavor, smoke Western cigarettes, the manly choice.*

Alfreda's husband, a short, deeply tanned fisherman named Orlando, reclines on a bamboo bench on the far side of the room. Their four-year-old son stands stock still by the bar and stares at me with a drop-dead gaze. That's when I figure out how Alfreda had a meal ready upon my arrival. Unless she prepared it for some unseen guests, it must've been their dinner.

As I sign the register, I notice that I'm their first guest in more than two months.

Before settling into my hut for the night, I ask Alfreda if she's heard the stories about witches eating people. She returns a puzzled look and asks, "You mean *manananggals*?"

"I guess. Are they different from the healers?"

She laughs. "Oh yes. The healers are mananambals. Manananggals are much different. They are terrible things. Like demons." She attempts to fill in the details with hand gestures, but all this tells me is how indescribably horrible they are. "They are witches and they have wings like a bat."

She's struggling for more detail, so I offer this: "And they eat people?"

She nods. "That is what they do."

"And they live on Siquijor?"

"Here? No. There is no such thing," she says in a reassuring tone. "They have all gone, long ago."

Rudy the tricycle driver arrives early the next morning before I have so much as stirred. Orlando has been up long enough to decide to take the day off and join us. We ride down the beach, up an access road and onto the main road, where we stop to gas the tricycle. The fuel is pink and comes in five one-liter glass bottles labeled Coca-Cola. Rudy drains them with quick, swirling motions that create whirlpools rather than splattering glugs. That's fortunate because Orlando and another man are standing right next to him, smoking cigarettes.

A rattling twenty-minute ride takes us through the town of Larena. The island strikes me as one that was heavily afflicted before it was abandoned by the outside world. All the road signs are in English, including a lengthy town ordinance forbidding graffiti and vandalism. Still, anarchy symbols, swastikas and other heavy metal icons are splattered around town. Preparations are underway for one of many holiday dance parties. A tower of disco lights stands in the middle of a schoolyard. Concert hall speakers flank a basketball court, blasting out the Violent Femmes. Two blocks away I can still hear the music, though now it's strictly ballroom. At the Larena Tennis Club, a trash fire smolders on one of two dirt courts.

Back out in the farmlands, a sign carries the subtle message: DRUGS WILL KILL YOU. The signboard of a country church reads: CHRISTOPHER LAMBERT IN THE HUNTED. A little further down is a new dollar-green Mercedes. It fits so snug in the carport that I imagine the driver had to crawl out through the trunk.

Ten minutes later, we arrive at the house of Isiero Bocol, known locally as Sidro the Bubble Man. His house is made of unfinished wooden planks nailed together under a rusty corrugated roof. Plants in tin cans hang from a steel pipe suspended from the eaves.

Sidro instructs us to leave our shoes on the porch. Inside, the hardwood floor is smooth, dark and cool. A Coleman lantern hangs from the ceiling. The walls are decorated with a 1996 Donald Duck Happy Home calendar, a picture of the

Taj Mahal, a cellophane-wrapped poster of the Crucifixion, and poster ads for orange drinks, corn chips and Rich Mami Noodles. In other posters, Filipino women are falling out of their clothes to promote Tanduay 65 liquor. Above them are a series of faded diplomas and yellowing family photos. Plank benches line the walls, but the centerpiece of the room is a Megabass stereo with dual cassette and three-foot surround-sound speakers. When we arrive, it's blaring out a country/western version of "Take It Easy".

Sidro is eighty-eight years old. Mostly, he's thin, but has ropy muscles and a rounded out belly. He has at least one gold tooth and a head of thick dark hair. Round tortoiseshell glasses obscure much of his weathered face.

He turns off the stereo, takes a seat in a corner and spits in my general direction. Three neighbors in their late teens or early twenties are lingering in the opposite corner. Sidro seems indifferent to their presence as well as mine. He doesn't even bother to make so much as eye contact with anyone. I ask what sort of powers he has.

Rudy starts to answer without consulting him: "He gets his powers from a god or some kind of devil."

At that, one of the neighbors begins to laugh. "It's not a god or a devil," she says. "It's *Diliparihas Nato*. The One Not Like Us."

"A kind of spirit?" I ask.

"You could say so," she says with confidence. Her name is Grace, and her English is far better than Rudy's. He, however, feels compelled to interrupt her explanation of Not Like Us, providing me instead with information that I later learn does not coincide with Sidro's version of the story. At certain points, Grace can barely contain her laughter. But even with my prompting, she refuses to undermine Rudy's authority.

Meanwhile, woodfire smoke drifts in from the back room, growing thicker. No one seems to mind. Sidro is busy working on Orlando's shoulder. He pokes and rubs at it for a good five minutes, then reaches for a glass and a smooth black stone the size of a pecan.

"Not Like Us gave him that stone," Rudy says. I glance at Grace, who nods to confirm that much.

Sidro drops the stone into the glass, then pours water over

it. He places the bottom of the glass against Orlando's shoulder, then, with a bamboo straw, blows bubbles over the stone.

"The stone is magic," Rudy continues. "It can withdraw the bad particles from the afflicted part of your body."

Sidro examines the water, but finds nothing. He blows and blows again, but still to no avail. Orlando will need an herbal remedy, Sidro says. And he leaves the room to consult Not Like Us.

He returns carrying a small corked bottle filled with something that looks like it was raked out of the bog. He asks if I want some too. I decline and ask him about his healing methods.

Rudy begins to repeat something he said earlier, when suddenly Sidro looks dead at me and answers in the local dialect and a smattering of Latin. Grace translates almost as fast as he can speak, but Rudy continually interrupts her. Between them, I understand the old man is telling me this much: "Forty-eight years ago, I met Not Like Us. I was sleeping, and he came to wake me. He told me some words in Latin—" He recites these words. "—and told me to memorize them. Before that, I never heard Latin. I never studied it anywhere else. But now I can speak it." More Latin. "There isn't a book in the world to teach you these phrases. Then I noticed that when I used the Latin together with the stone, I could heal people."

I ask how he learned to use the stone.

"Nobody can learn it," he says as a boast or a warning. I can't be sure which. "It is an ability. If you try to learn, but don't learn every step, you may kill someone, even end up in prison."

"But what gave you the idea to put it in water and blow bubbles?" I ask. Clearly something is getting lost in the translation. The best answer I can get is: "It is not easy to adapt. Maybe when I die, I can leave the ability with another."

I ask a number of other ways, but the old man seems to be losing interest again, patients are waiting on his front porch and the woodfire smoke is bringing tears to my eyes. I nod toward the patients and say, "Looks like you're going to have a busy day."

"No," says Grace. "His busy day is Friday. That is Not Like Ours delicate day. His powers are stronger. They're strongest during Holy Week."

"Why Holy Week?"

She answers as if I should already know: "Because of the days when Jesus is still dead. You should be here for that. It is an important time on Siquijor."

As Rudy, Orlando and I leave the house, the music cranks up again. I cross the street to find a manta ray that wasn't there before. It has a four-foot wingspan and it's lying in the dirt, belly up. Its leathery tail curls into the road. Nearby is a kiosk with posters similar to those in Sidro's house. I buy a round of Cokes, then notice a bag of Nips. It's just candy, like M&Ms; but twenty years ago, I ate them every day. Something kicks in like a wave of regret. It's enough to snap me back and recall a moment like it was last night.

My father sent me alone to the store to buy him a cup of ice cream. As I rummaged through the freezer, two young women grabbed my head and ran their fingers through my hair. "So light," one said. "Like a chick." "What's your name?" the other asked. "Frankenstein," I said, borrowing the reply from David Carradine's masked character in Death Race 2000. I was aware of how lame I sounded as soon as I said it, but the women just giggled and squeezed my head harder. I was still broiling with embarrassment as I returned home. Halfway there, under an empty parking deck, I felt a slight sensation of falling and rising. The lights flickered. The ground gently and quietly trembled. Then suddenly I was surrounded by total darkness and voices from the mental ward, maniacs screaming for Jesus.

I don't remember how I made it home.

Leaving Sidro's, the tricycle struggles to climb a mountain road. Halfway up, a tire blows. Rudy doesn't carry a spare. Instead, he and Orlando set about repairing it with the foil from a pack of cigarettes, some dirt and a fire in an oil can.

The roadside is heavily forested. I pace along the treeline until I notice, just a few feet above my head, a spider. Its body is about the size of my thumb, its legs longer than my fingers, and it appears to have two teeth larger than those of a full-grown cat. Another one is not more than three feet away. Then another. And another. In a two-minute stroll, I count fifteen. I point one out to Orlando and say, "Does it bite?"

"Yah."

"Bad bites?"

"Yah." His reply is punctuated by three stick-crunching footsteps. The source is too deep in the forest to be seen.

Tire repaired, we ride on. The forest thickens and the road dissolves into a track of mud. Two hours after leaving the Bubble Man, we arrive at a village defined by a kiosk, a water pump and not much else. From there it's a 300-yard hike into the jungle to the next healer's house. We meet his wife along the path. Rudy explains that I want to interview her husband. She sadly informs us that he's not at home. I ask if I can see the house anyway.

"But I think you have been there already," she says in English.

I tell her I haven't, so she leads me to her home. It's a crudely mortared, bare cinderblock structure with grilled windows. The view is all jungle, but the room smells strongly of pine. Several children spy in through open doors. The floor is wrinkled, though spotless linoleum. A few pieces of wicker furniture and a glass cabinet crowd one corner. In another is an altar with various saints, flowers and a bottle of herbs identical to Sidro's. Behind the bottle are a bullhorn (the kind police use) and a bowling trophy. Another larger altar fills the end of a darkened hall.

Oddly, I do get a sense of having been here already. The children seem especially familiar. They're terrified of me. Eye contact alone is enough to make one shriek and burst into tears.

The calico with a stub for a tail came back. With all the hazards for cats—the traffic around the hospital compound, the incinerator, the guards who kicked them—I'd worried she might not stay around. But there she was, playing in the patch of grass we generously called a back yard. My brother and I watched her as she stalked unseen prey. We tried to guess what it was: a mantis, a cockroach, a gecko. The cat froze, crouched, bobbed her head. Tail twitching, ears up, then flat. A lightning pounce and a faster retreat. Then we saw the head rising out of the grass until it was taller than the cat. She hissed, but the snake hissed back louder. She backed down, then pounced again, this time catching it under the jaw. Only after it was dead—long dead—did we confirm that it was a Philippine cobra almost as long as I was tall. Still, my father used an even longer stick to pick it up and drop it over the fence. And still, he wouldn't let us keep the cat. But he made damn sure she felt welcome in our backyard.

We rattle back down the mountain, cross the Poo River and get back on the main road near a town aptly named Lazi. The slouching shacks in this listless place are couched up next to a beach that looks like an endless stretch of pillows. One shop in town offers one-hour photos. Another, one-hour ID laminating. I wonder what the hurry could be.

The next healer's house is much more accessible than the last. The healer, however, is not. I follow Rudy inside, where he introduces me to the healer's son. He's about thirty-five or forty, has large, bulging eyes and sinewy limbs. "You have some questions about my father's powers," he says in English, "but I don't think he is interested in talking to you."

I take a step back toward the door and apologize for the intrusion. "I've traveled a long way to see him," is the best excuse I can offer.

"I understand that," he says without a hint of sympathy. "Perhaps you should come back for Holy Week. He sees many people then." He makes it sound so easy.

"I'm not sure if that will be possible," I say. I hesitate before asking the next question: "Do you think he could just take a moment for a photo?"

He steps closer. "No. It is against his religion."

I apologize again and leave. By then I'm ready to give up the hunt. Who am I to invite myself into these people's homes, antagonize their children, waste their time with so many questions, write down everything they say and photograph everything I see? What am I doing here?

"I'm sorry," Rudy says. "We're not having much luck now, but I know more we can see. Come."

My sister and I were sleeping on the beach when a girl about my age woke us and said she had gifts for us. They were the most beautiful shells I'd ever seen. She told us her father brought them from the bottom of the ocean just for us. My sister and I looked at each other for an explanation. We'd seen her father. He had no arms.

Rudy pulls the tricycle off the road, jumps off and starts digging tools and gear out from under the seat. "Another flat?" I ask. Orlando points up the road. Rain is screaming toward us like a tractor-trailer. It hits before Rudy can get the apron over the handlebars and soaks us further by blowing in from both sides. Minutes later, it's gone, but the right half of my body is wet. I ask Rudy to take me back to the Paradise. "I'm sorry," he says with a helpless smile. "It is Typhoon Rudy."

Rudy wasn't kidding about the typhoon bearing his name. Typhoon Rudy is moving in, and Typhoon Trining is on its heels with ninety mile an hour winds. Tidal wave warnings are in effect, and I'm sitting in a hut so close to the water it's making me seasick. The coast guard has ordered all boats to stay put. All holiday dance parties have been postponed, and discos and sing-along bars are closed for fear that lightning will damage the equipment.

That doesn't stop us from going out for a few beers. Rudy, his wife, a girlfriend, Orlando and I ride into Larena in search of anything that's open. We find a sing-along bar that will open for us, if only for drinks.

Rudy tells me about friends who were supposed to visit him. Some from Europe and Australia, and one from Taiwan. He pulls out his wallet to find their names. Actually, it's more of a scrapbook than a wallet. Inside are far more papers than pesos, and each scrap seems to hold a memory. The names and addresses begin to pile up in front of us, but he can't find the one from Taiwan. "He was coming this year," he insists as though I might not believe him. "But now the year is almost over." Tears well up in his eyes. "I don't think he is coming."

Among the scraps he finds two ID cards. One is his tricycle license, the other names him as President of the Fishermen's Association. "This is very important," he says, handing me the presidential card. "The fishermen here nearly destroyed everything in the sea when they fished with dynamite and poisons. In order to complete my task as president, I had to convince the people of my village to help me build the reefs again . . . . First we built 150 bamboo barriers. Then we had to place 150 cement barriers." He illustrates the reefs by crossing his index fingers, forming an X.

"I saw those near the Paradise," I say. "Only they were used as posts for barbwire."

"Yes," he says. "That president was lazy. He didn't finish his reef. Mine is finished. Now we have fish again." He turns to Orlando, who raises his glass in agreement.

Rudy raises his glass and his voice. "When I finished the reef, I was allowed to plant [hardwood] trees to replace the ones we lost. Now these trees, they are taller than me!" He takes back his card and examines it. "So, in twenty years, when they are big, I can renew."

I wait for him to say more, but that seems to be his final goal. Twenty years of watching trees grow—not counting the years of reef building—so that he can renew his presidential card. Of course, he'll help improve the ecology and long-term economy. But from the way he holds that card, these benefits seem, for the moment, of lesser importance.

The next day, the typhoons are still nearby, all coast guard warnings are still in effect, but the worst of the weather on the island is a stiff breeze. Rudy arrives while I'm eating breakfast and says, "I have a friend I want you to meet. He is the Bubble Man."

"I met the Bubble Man."

"No, you met Sidro the Bubble Man. You have not met Juan the Bubble Man."

"Another Bubble Man? I thought Sidro was the only one."

Rudy shrugs. "But there are many."

"How many?"

"Five. Or maybe four. One I think is dead. Anyway, we should go. He is waiting for us."

Juan's house is about fifteen minutes away. He lives on a small farm just off the main road. Rudy and Orlando greet him and others in his family with slapping handshakes, and we all take seats on his front porch. A portrait of Jesus hangs above the door. Beneath that is a full-size, laminated image of Santa Claus. The door is wide open, but all I can see is a pink Christmas tree. It's not more than six feet tall, doesn't have more than ten limbs, but it seems to be sprouting out of a mound of gifts.

"Why haven't you opened your Christmas presents?" I ask Juan.

He laughs and (according to Rudy's translation) says, "We don't do that until New Year's Eve."

"New Year's Eve? We open ours on *Christmas* Eve. American children cannot wait any longer than that."

Everyone finds this uproariously funny. Everyone but the children. Seven of them hover by the porch railing, watching cautiously and flinching every time I so much as scratch my head or shift my weight. Behind them, bleached sea shells shift and stagger around the yard. It takes me a moment to realize they're hermit crabs.

Juan is wearing a loose, white T-shirt and gray shorts. He has a close-cropped receding hairline, and pale blue eyes. His cheeks are deep and hollow—even when he's smiling, which is almost all the time. He doesn't give his age, but he's considerably younger than Sidro and relatively new to the bubble business, or *bolo-bolo*, as the craft is more commonly known. He's been practicing for only thirteen years.

Orlando points out an aching area in his hand. Juan examines it, then gathers up his equipment. It's basically the same as Sidro's, only the straw is fashioned out of a section from an umbrella stem rather than bamboo. And the stone, though identical to Sidro's, didn't come from Not Like Us.

Juan hands me the stone. "I found this stone while farming," he says. "I threw it away, but then I found it a few days later. I told my wife to throw it away, but it came back again." He takes the stone, drops it in a glass, then pours water over it. "Finally, one night while I was sleeping, Agta came to me." The children gasp at the mention of this name. Hearing that, the adults laugh.

"Who's Agta?" I ask.

"He is a giant," Rudy explains. I ask what he looks like. He discusses the question with Juan, then replies: "He is big."

"And?"

Rudy confers again, then says, "He is black with curly hair." He pinches and twists a lock of his own hair into a short, tight kink. "He lives in this forest." He points to a wooded area on a nearby hill.

Juan continues his story: "Agta told me that I must use the stone to heal. I said I don't want to. But he said I must." He presses the glass against the back of Orlando's hand and blows until veins bulge in his forehead. Then he raises the glass and stirs the rock around with the straw.

Nothing.

He changes the water and does it all over again. When he pulls the glass away this time, Orlando rubs his hand, then flexes it. "Okay," he says to no one in particular. Juan holds the glass up and points something out to Rudy, then to Orlando. I can see it from where I'm sitting. He pours it out into his hand and sets it on the table. Orlando touches it and says to Rudy, "Cemento." In fact, it does look like a piece of cement about the size of an uncooked grain of rice. Rudy agrees that it must have come from his reef. I figure it could have just as easily come from under Juan's fingernail or out of his lungs.

By then, Juan is preparing for his next patient, a woman in her late teens with a California T-shirt and a fresh bruise around her right eye.

"What happened to her?" I ask.

Rudy consults Juan, then replies, "She cannot see very good out of one eye." He pauses to watch Juan place the glass over her eye and blow. After the second attempt, Rudy says, "I don't think he can help this one."

The typhoon struck just before lunch. The classes flooded so fast we didn't have time to get out. We just stood on the tables, watching the water rise and flow into the cages of spiders and dragonflies we'd caught, and then into the cages of mice. A snake swam in, whipping its body and holding its head above the water as though fighting a current. Nobody made a sound until it submerged. Just as the water was even with the tabletops, the janitors waded in and carried us out in their arms. When we returned, the only class pet we had left was one small fish in a muddied aquarium.

Typhoon Rudy lingers in the area, keeping me stranded for days. Though the sky remains clear and the sea only mildly choppy, no boats are permitted to leave. A few sneak out at night anyway. They sink. Everyone on board drowns. The bodies are never recovered from the shark-infested waters.

To add to my sense of isolation, only five phones are on the island. Tracking them down takes the assistance of Rudy and about seven other volunteers I've never met before, but all we really find is that none are working. None of this would matter, really, except for the fact that I must return to my teaching job in Seoul. It's hard for me to understand how my new friends can sympathize with this dilemma when most have never even been off the island. Simply describing Seoul is difficult enough.

"It's the same size as this island," I tell them. "And it has mountains and rivers like this island. So just imagine Siquijor with twelve million people on it. Then throw in, say, five million TVs, eight million phones and a couple hundred thousand buses, cars, trucks and airplanes."

They seem to understand. "We have an airplane," one says.

I've heard rumors of an airstrip on Siquijor, one built by the Japanese during World War II. I even asked Philippine Airlines about it, but they assured me it didn't exist. The volunteers sound pretty sure it does. Three escort me to a seven-passenger Piper. I take the last available seat, the one next to the pilot. "I'm the copilot today?" I ask.

He smiles and nods. He's wearing a baggy T-shirt, blue jeans and sneakers. He can't be older than nineteen. The plane wheels around until sunlight refracts through the windshield, rendering the outside world invisible. And when we take off, the pilot uses a dirt road instead of the runway. No ticket is issued, no fare is requested. I feel I'm being smuggled off the island.

That night in Dumaguete, I hear on the radio that two small planes crashed in the area today.

During the flight back to Manila, I find the social pages take up a large part of newspapers, reporting who was doing what at which Christmas party. Each piece on the opinion pages quotes more Scripture than the average sermon. The reports of fireworks and gunshot revelry continue. And in the classifieds, there's a Christmas Promo from Saint Anthony's Plastic Surgery Clinic: "Thirty percent discount on Bust Augmentation, Virginity Restoration, etc."

By the time I reach Manila, I'm filled with its unique holiday spirit, so I splurge for a dinner at a downtown folk-rock club called Hobbit House, where all the employees are midgets, then check into a decent hotel room with a jacuzzi and excellent room service: Arabic cuisine, Danish beer and a Filipina masseuse. Nothing is like the Manila I remember.

I keep waiting for another memory to strike, but nothing has come to mind since I left the house of the second bubble man. It seems strange, but that afflicted and abandoned little island brought me closer to remembering Manila than the city itself. Perhaps it had something to do with the healers' magic. Or maybe that bag of Nips triggered the whole thing.

"Would you like some candy?" the taxi driver asks. My guidebook warns of drug-laced candy and unwitting tourists who accept it from strangers, only to wake up hours later robbed of everything but a pounding headache. But it's New Year's Eve and I'm on my way back to the airport, back to Seoul. Not nearly enough time for such a crisis, so I accept. What he gives me is in fact a drug, or at least tastes medicinal. I read on the wrapper that it has all the ingredients of cough drops, which are often sold here as candy.

I kick back and watch the last of Manila drift by. Slowly, it becomes more familiar: the cinema billboards, hand-painted in Easter egg colors; the vendors at every intersection, selling food, papers, toys and individual cigarettes; the bulldozers razing homes in an Islamic slum community.

I think of Imelda, who, for some incomprehensible reason, is now a congresswoman. "Human rights violations . . . never happened under Marcos," is her quote in today's paper. Explain that to the 9,070 confirmed victims of torture and other atrocities under his rule.

But that has little to do with what I remember. I wish now that I'd gone back to Saint Luke's and my school. I wish I could've found Irfan. Or even my teacher. I don't remember much about her, not even her name. I just remember one moment very clearly. She held me by the shoulders and shook me, sobbing over and over, "What am I supposed to do with you?" I don't think she had much experience with foreign children.

I've been thinking about her a lot over the past year, ever since I became a teacher in Seoul. If I saw her today, I'd tell her that many of my students are just as foreign to me, that I understand how she felt, and that I'm very, very sorry.

Still, I can't remember what I did to upset her so.

Facing the Enemy

IRAQ: 1997

The dead man in the road provoked mixed reactions. I saw him first, the body under the sheet, two blackened feet poking out. Another man risked the same fate as he swept up the windshield glass and pieces of chrome. Oddly, there was no blood on the road, and the sheet was spotless. Dr. Jim Jennings leaned forward and, as though pointing out another site on the tour said, "Oh look, a body."

This was Jim's fifth trip to Iraq to provide medical training and the last of two million dollars worth of medicine and supplies. As president of Conscience International, a private relief organization, Jim had assembled our international delegation and was leading our excursion, despite U.S. government warnings that such actions could lead to "criminal penalties . . . up to 12 years in prison and $1 million in fines."

At sixty, Jim was an inexhaustible man with a seemingly inexhaustible knowledge of archeology, world religion, and the entire history of the Middle East. For me, it added up to team meetings that would last well past meal times, past midnight, resuming just after dawn for tours of ancient sites with lectures that spanned a thousand years per hour. Before we'd even left Jordan, he was killing us with deprivation of food and sleep. I admired his conviction, but I already felt like the dead man in the road.

Simon Bloemendaal, the Dutch member on the team, reacted to the body as though he wished he hadn't seen it.

When Jim pointed it out, he turned away, albeit too late, and said he'd seen enough.

Simon, who had introduced himself only as a forty-four-year-old father of two daughters, was given to expressing childlike wonder with the world, as though it were one long cartoon. Later in the trip, he revealed that he was also a skydiver, a marathon runner, and a nurse who had worked in Doctors Without Borders rescue missions in such joyous locations as Bosnia, Somalia, and Rwanda—any of which could've accounted for his aversion to dead men.

Others on the team included David Buchanan, an American physician who worked in Mexico, Costa Rica, and Chicago's less privileged neighborhoods; Manuel Munoz, an Argentinean with Spanish citizenship who also made the rounds with Doctors Without Borders in Central Africa and Peru, and now worked as a hospital administrator in Holland; and me, with my limited health-training experience in a few African nations. By far the least qualified member of the team, I felt like an idiot in their presence. Simon tried to reassure me that it hardly mattered: No one was really prepared to deal with the crisis in Iraq.

The events prior to my departure were disturbing at best. The UN inspection team had been kicked out of Iraq. U.S. carriers moved into the Gulf, threatening military action. Foreign Minister Tariq Aziz had announced that Iraq was ready to fight, and ABC aired footage of the Iraqi government issuing weapons to women, while hooded suicide squads marched through the streets of Baghdad and commandos ripped apart and ate live dogs in a Saddam-staged demonstration.

Seeking advice for travel in Iraq, I called the Vinton's in Santa Fe. Bob Vinton had been one of the more outspoken hostages in Iraq in 1990, and survived the ordeal unscathed, according to Robert Wiener, then the Executive Producer of CNN Baghdad. However, when I asked Sue Vinton if I could speak with her husband, there was an awkward silence before she told me her husband died five weeks after returning home.

"Don't worry," she concluded by the end of our unsettling conversation. "The Iraqis are kind people. They'll take good care of you."

More than twenty-seven hours after leaving New Mexico, I arrived in Amman, Jordan. The final flight was packed, but I was assured to have the armrest the entire time because the girl sitting next to me had no arms. The drive from Amman to Baghdad was another ten hours in two Chevy Suburbans packed tight with luggage and medical supplies. In Jordan, the narrow, crowded, two-lane highway kept our speed down, and the border crossing was tedious. The Iraqi side looked worse: Members of an American news crew passed the time by rollerblading the perimeter of the security zone.

We waited an hour in the Iraqi Government Executives Rest House, watching a static-ridden Arabic soap opera on a twelve-inch black-and-white TV while Iraqi guards rifled through our cargo. Jim had the foresight to pack extra of the things they wanted most: cigarettes, aspirin and Zantac. (Seems that guarding Saddam's borders was enough to give the most hardened soldiers a nicotine habit, headaches and ulcers.) The guards expressed their gratitude for the relief by expediting our crossing in record time. We left the rollerblading news crew behind.

On the remaining six-lane stretch of white, empty highway, we reached speeds up to 110 miles per hour, slowed only by fog and thunderstorms that grew more intense as we approached Baghdad. I played a few cassettes along the way, but the Jordanian driver seemed to despise my taste in music; he frowned, turned down the volume, ejected tapes as I tried Los Lobos, Flat Duo Jets, Ry Cooder. He hated everything except for one band, Black Uhuru, which caused him to break into spontaneous offbeat clapping.

We arrived at the Al-Rasheed Hotel well after dark and found we'd be in good company: Russian Liberal Democratic Party leader Vladimir Zhernovsky and Nation of Islam leader Louis Farrakhan were among the honored guests.

The next day, a crowd of anxious parents waiting outside the Saddam Hussein Children's Hospital told us that there was no medicine. It sounded like a cordial warning, a helpful bit of information they passed along to any new arrivals, and they seemed surprised that we went in anyway.

They were right: The pharmacy shelves were bare, though

two people manned the counter. All other supply rooms were empty as well.

No towels or soap could be found in the wash areas, and the bathrooms apparently hadn't been cleaned in months. The entire hospital smelled like death. The ventilation system was inoperable, and every exterior door except for the main entrance had been chained or welded shut. At best, one in every ten light fixtures worked, and the halls and surgical suites had taken on a dim green flickering glow. The gift shop, however, had a good supply of chips, drinks and plastic toys, but business seemed slow. I considered buying some candy for the children in the wards, but remembered I'd brought along some Starburst fruit chews.

The hospital, built to care for 200 children at a time, was currently taking in 600. As with many other hospitals in the country, it was facing a shortage of doctors and nurses. All foreign workers left in 1990, along with any Iraqis who had the means and foresight to get out while they could. The nurses who stayed earned about 2000 dinars per month. That and change was enough to buy a can of Pepsi.

Parents assumed nursing duties they hardly understood. Often that meant waving a raw oxygen tube under a child's nose, hoping that she would breath in the right amount of oxygen. The one mask I did see was adult-size, nearly covering a baby's entire face. The parents tried to seal the gaps with their hands.

"Look, the mother is crying," Jim said. "Take a picture."

I reached in my camera bag and found the fruit chews. I scanned the ward, but couldn't find a child who looked able to stomach them. So I put them back and took the picture, as Jim had requested. The parents didn't seem to mind me. But within the hour, their daughter was dead.

Tired and irate, we returned to the Al-Rasheed Hotel, eating a whole bag of fruit chews along the way. Security in the hotel was anything but subtle. The same goons loitered in the lobby day after day, glaring at guests and eavesdropping on conversations. I didn't pity the dullness of their work until I tried eavesdropping on guests. I caught this exchange between a concierge and one of Farrakhan's young assistants:

Concierge: "I don't understand. He wants his own room?"

him as Psycho John. He was a pasty, lanky, excitable man with a far-away look in his eyes, and he latched onto our group for rides, meals and information about in-country travel.

We even suspected that our Iraqi drivers were government agents. Jalal, a robust man who recited from the Koran every time he started the engine, acted as though he didn't understand a word of English, but couldn't contain his laughter when Simon told jokes in English that I had trouble understanding. Jassim revealed an English vocabulary of about twenty words, but shook his head and tisked when Voice of America reported more friction between UN inspectors and Iraqi officials.

One thing was certain: They were more than drivers. Their blue license plates indicated government cars to which all other drivers would yield, regardless of who had the right-of-way. This blue-plate special allowed us to cut in front of gas lines two blocks long, pass through military and police check points, run traffic lights and drive on the wrong side of the road at a hundred miles per hour.

Their most difficult task, however, was keeping track of us—particularly Manuel, who had a propensity for wandering away whenever the car stopped and taking photographs near military installations. Still, at times, we were able to sneak away from Jalal and Jassim. And when we were caught, the reprimands sounded more like an issue of our safety than of national security.

I never really felt threatened while in Iraq, except perhaps by the Aircraft Carrier *Nimitz* in the Persian Gulf. In fact, I was blissfully at ease when we snuck off the hotel grounds and caught a cab to a run-down movie theater in downtown Baghdad, where Farrakhan gave his speech.

The theater, about twice the size of an average American theater, was packed. In the men's room, not less than forty Ulama, Islamic clerics, carefully washed their feet in the sinks. Nation of Islam security crowded the lobby and cameramen filled the isles. An Iraqi reporter sitting next to me had only one sheet of notebook paper, on which he managed to write the entire speech.

I had a whole notebook, yet all I wrote was: "Farrakhan calls for an end to terrorism and for peace among Muslims,

Christians and Jews. Wins rounds of applause. So where's the damn controversy?"

Upon returning to the hotel, Simon and I decided to have Arabic coffee in a Bedouin tent set up in the lobby. Simon asked if I would take his picture with the Bedouin boy. It should've been a simple shot, but I spilled the entire contents of my camera bag on the lobby floor while setting it up. Then, just after taking the photo, I heard a low rumbling like thunder coming up behind me. Farrakhan's entourage was heading for the tent, and they showed no sign of slowing down as I tried to repack my camera bag. In fact, Farrakhan himself nearly stepped on me.

As they departed for their rooms, I noticed Psycho John hugging a loaf of French bread and cozied up to the man in African regalia.

I asked John about it over breakfast the next day.

"I spoke with Farrakhan for more than an hour," he said. "I had a lot of advice for him." I shuddered at the thought of Farrakhan enduring this man's lunacy for a full hour. One of his more enlightening statements was this: "I told him there's a World Court in the Hague."

As we drove away from Baghdad, Simon told me, "Next time, if you want your meeting with Farrakhan, you know what you need: A loaf of bread and a far-away look in your eyes."

Mosul

We cruised up Highway One in Jalal's and Jassim's 1990 Cutlass Sierras. Jim and David rode with Jassim. Simon, Manuel and I went with Jalal. We liked Jalal better. He let us smoke, play loud music and handle his weapons, like the automatic rifle he kept in the trunk. We listened to an AM broadcast of American music called *Radio Monte Carlo*. Sinatra crooned out "My Way" as we rolled through the fog, past farms, herds of sheep, ten-foot portraits of Saddam, and fields of oil and anti-aircraft guns.

Stopping in Samarra to see the Great Mosque and its spiral minaret, a 170-foot structure once mistaken for the Tower of Babel, I met the Mohammed family as they enjoyed a Friday afternoon picnic. The father asked me where I was from, guessing Italy. Considering the strong military presence and anti-American graffiti in town, I wasn't sure I wanted him to know. So I told him New Mexico, hoping he'd think (like many Americans) it was a part of its namesake.

"Yes, I think it is next to Arizona?" he said, sounding unsure. "You are American. Welcome to Iraq." He introduced his wife and children, then insisted I join them for the family picnic. I would later learn, after meeting so many Iraqis, that his reaction was typical.

The presence of heavy artillery increased and darkness settled in as we drove into Mosul. The Ministry of Health had arranged for us to stay in the enormous Hotel Ninevah Oberoi, which once offered all the Western amenities: Disco, bowling alley, pinball, billiards, swimming pool and bomb shelter. Now its empty lobby and halls echoed with dreary pan flute muzak, its elevators didn't stop at every floor and its toilets leaked sewage on the bathroom floors. Most lamps lacked lightbulbs and the menus in the restaurant were for display purposes only. The current food shortage kept our choices limited to lamb burgers and kidneys. Worst of all, they lacked coffee.

We visited the Iraqi Red Crescent to check on food distribution. Their offices were without power, and so cold that we could see our breath when we spoke. They offered both tea and coffee, but seemed embarrassed when we asked for the latter. "No coffee," the administrator sadly informed us.

Still, he seemed happy to report that only about a third of the population in the region relied on the Red Crescent for food, and that they were receiving enough foreign rice, oil, sugar and powdered milk to provide each person with 1000 calories per day. Cutting down from 1500 calories in previous years had helped stretch supplies.

The results were apparent in Mosul's pediatric hospital. Some babies suffered forms of malnutrition so severe that the Iraqi doctors, who never saw a case of malnutrition before 1991, weren't able to make a correct diagnosis. Simon, having worked in Somalia, recognized it immediately, though later confessed he'd never seen it before among people with skin so fair. Other babies took on a pale shade of blue in incubators that functioned only as deathbeds. The hospital staff, with their Western education and training, was having trouble adapting to Third World conditions.

Simon and I paired up to give a presentation to the nurses in the hospital. However, the hospital administrator provided us with about twenty male nursing students. They filed into the conference room and stared at us as though we were levitating. I knew then that we had a problem.
"Who here speaks English?" I asked.
After an awkward silence, one student held up his notebook and said, "Michael Jackson!" The others displayed their notebooks as well, showing me that each had carefully decorated their binders with magazine cutouts of Michael Jackson, Madonna, and an assortment of Lebanese singers. The saddest part was that not one binder contained any paper.

Jim did his best to fill our afternoons with educational field trips to ancient sites around Mosul, but I had long since given up trying to follow his multi-millennial lectures. This ancient land between the lower Tigris and Euphrates rivers, known as Mesopotamia, was home to some of the earth's earliest known civilizations. Beginning with the Sumerians in the fortieth century BC, who invented the cuneiform alphabet, wheeled vehicles and the plow, the region was once home to several thriving city-states, including Ur and Babylon. Successive local conflicts and invasions by outside empires led to Mesopotamia's decline.

Saddam, a history buff since his early years, keeps his people well versed in history so they can understand his excuses for displaying his fierce annoyance with the world. Greeks, Assyrians, Persians, Mongols, Turks—each had trampled this land at least once. During Jim's lectures, I chose to record only his more curious statements. At an excavation site to the north of Mosul, I wrote: "One of the oldest schools in the world . . . 721 BC . . . the students would sit here and the teachers would hit them with a stick . . . . We are within ten miles of the Kurdish region, where last week 20,000 Turkish troops invaded."

At the Mosque of Nebi Yunus, I wrote: "In terms of warfare, Assyrians were the Nazis of the Mediterranean. They invented psychological warfare and stacked heads like grapefruits at the market . . . Jonah of whale fame is said to be buried here, but shrines in Lebanon and Palestine also hold this claim."

But for all that Jim knew about these sites, storehouses were waiting to be discovered. Iraq had succeeded in excavating an estimated five percent of its sites before the Ministry of Antiquities virtually shut down. The museums were closed, the digs ceased, sites fell into disrepair. Archeologists were reduced to tour guides for the rare occasions of visitors like us.

Baghdad

Back in Baghdad, I took a sauna, swam laps in an overheated Olympic-size pool, and wondered why they couldn't keep the babies warm in Mosul.

The next morning, I woke to gunshots and calisthenic shouting. A ragtag army troop was training in the parking lot next to the hotel, and they displayed all the enthusiasm of a junior high baseball team with a 0-7 record. Some jogged, others walked, most took frequent cigarette breaks. Only half were in uniform.

After breakfast, Jim, Simon and I met with ABC correspondent Mort Dean. His scalp was stained to camouflage his thinning hair. His teeth were stained and ground down. He looked exhausted. He'd been filing reports until three a.m. It was now eight a.m., and we'd dragged him out of bed to tell him about the dismal conditions in Iraqi hospitals. He listened politely, but concluded it wasn't newsworthy. After all, he said, the American people would only blame Saddam.

I asked him what was news in Iraq, since we hadn't heard any in the past few days. He told us that the Iraqis had executed four Jordanians who were caught smuggling car parts out of Iraq. Jordan was threatening to shut down the border if Iraq didn't release the fifth smuggler.

The prospect of being sealed in this country indefinitely distracted me so much that I didn't initially realize the absurdity of it all. There were no parts to be smuggled from Iraq; and if there were, Jordan had enough to make such an operation as ridiculous as smuggling pineapples from Siberia to Hawaii. More likely, the Jordanians had been smuggling weapons into Iraq to arm Saddam's opposition. Yet Mort conveyed his report with such newsman authority that, at the moment, it sounded believable.

Basra

Basra was to be the last venue for our traveling medicine show. But for some mysterious reason, the Ministry of Health failed to provide us with the authorization to travel. Jassim told us not to worry, that he and his blue plates would be our pass. The only problem was that we couldn't travel via Babylon and Ur, as Jim had requested. The government was losing control along the southern part of the Euphrates, Jassim suggested. Bandits and opposition groups were not likely to welcome our blue plates. Jalal emphasized this point by running his index finger across his throat.

Instead, we took a highway that followed the Tigris, and stopped for lunch in the piss-poor city of Kut (rhymes with "foot"), a name that caused Simon to burst out laughing.

"It's a slang word in Dutch," he explained. "It sounds to me as if we are having lunch in a vagina."

In fact, the lamb kabob they served us tasted as though it came from another orifice, so Manuel and I chose instead to wander the streets. When Jassim decided we had strayed too far, he called me back from a block away: "Mr. Stephen! Come! Now!"

Suddenly, it seemed everyone in Kut knew my name, and everyone I passed cheerfully greeted me. Shopkeepers, soldiers, children, old ladies—all smiled and said, "Hello, Mr. Stephen!" as I made my way back to the car.

Iraq turned from mudflats to marshes as we headed south, and numerous military bases took on the look of Camp Swampy. Some still showed scars from previous wars, some were just suffering from neglect, though it was hard to distinguish the difference.

The Basra Hospital for Children was in worse shape than its counterpart in Mosul, even though it wasn't stressed by overcrowding. Medical supplies were low. I watched in horror as a doctor divided a single dose of antibiotics among four children. When I suggested that might do more harm than good, he suggested that I tell their mothers which child should get the full dosage.

Another ward was full of mothers who had just given birth by Cesarean section and were now shuddering and groaning in pain. When I entered the room, one cried out in Arabic. The doctor replied to her, almost in a scolding tone. She closed her eyes and resumed groaning.

I pressed the doctor for a translation: "America, give me analgesia." He smiled with a nervous laugh, then added, "I told her it wasn't your decision."

The Basra Sheraton had all the charm of a rest home gone bankrupt. Pan flute muzak warbled on a continuous loop. After hearing "Chariots of Fire" for the eighty-millionth time, Simon asked, "How do you call this in English?"

"Lobotomy music," I said, wondering how the staff kept themselves from falling into drooling stupor. A sign in the lobby announced the reopening of the health club, with a Swedish sauna, Turkish bath and Scotch shower. I went just to find out what a Scotch shower was, but the doors were chained shut.

This had once been a spectacular hotel. "The third best Sheraton in the world," the manager wistfully recalled. He led me on a tour, describing how it once was: Vines had coiled down from the interior balconies, giving the lobby the feel of the jungle. Women from the Philippines and Thailand had danced in the cabaret and disco. Caravans of Kuwaitis crowded the casino every weekend. Some guests would jump from shanasheel balconies and land in the swimming pool.

"We'll serve drinks again someday," the manager promised, referring to a 1994 law that banned alcohol from hotels and restaurants. "After all, this is not a mosque."

A city where Sinbad began his legendary voyages, Basra now had the ghostly pallor of the luxury liner *Titanic* sitting at the bottom of the ocean. The streets were quiet by nine p.m., and the electricity failed frequently. A Jurassic-sized Donald Duck stood on the waterfront among the rusting remains of an amusement park. Here it was easy to imagine how the ancient cities in the cradle of civilization had slipped away unnoticed into sand and swamp. But the most amazing aspect of Basra, considering its close proximity to Iran and Kuwait, was that it had managed to survive this long.

From the moment I arrived in Iraq, I wanted to know more of its practitioners of traditional medicine, doctors who had no formal training. However, I found this to be a touchy subject among the medical doctors I met. They denied that such people existed in Iraq. "This is a modern country," was the typical response. "We have an excellent health care system, so there is no need for such people."

Still, I'd assumed as people realized the government hospitals and clinics were on the verge of collapse, they would seek alternative care. Private clinics would function as black markets for those who could afford it; those who couldn't would seek out anyone who claimed any knowledge of medicine.

My last day in Basra, Dr. Nahad from the Children's Hospital told me about the jidah, which translated to grandmother—or in this case, traditional birth attendant (TBA).

"Before 1988, a TBA practice was illegal in Iraq," Nahad explained. "But now we have a program to train them. Often, a mother will bring in her newborn for immunization. Staff will ask who delivered the baby, then go and provide the TBA with a two-week training course and necessary supplies.

"But if the delivery has gone horribly wrong," she continued, "the TBA fears trouble with the law, and will tell the mother to give the wrong address. So we are not sure how many there are."

She offered to introduce me to Zahrah Hammeed Nasir, the first jidah to complete the training program. Jassim fiercely opposed the idea, but agreed to take us after Jim confronted him with a few choice words in Arabic.

On the way to Zahrah's house, Nahad showed me the TBA textbook: a flipchart of about thirty pages, very few words, and drawings reminiscent of a children's picture book, only far more explicit.

One of Zahrah's daughters greeted us at the gate and showed us through a courtyard and into a modest single-room building. There was no furniture except for a table just big enough to hold a red rotary phone. Cushions lined the edge of the Persian rug, spanning the length of the half painted cement walls. Nahad paused at the doorway.

"What's wrong?" I asked.

"I'm afraid there are rats in here." She removed her shoes and entered anyway.

"Where's the TBA?"

"She is in her house, that building across the courtyard. The daughter says we cannot go into the house because her mother is too ashamed."

"Ashamed?"

"They are too poor."

Zahrah entered with a big smile of few teeth. I guessed she was approaching eighty, but Nahad said she was probably about sixty. More daughters and granddaughters followed, two carrying trays of dates and sliced oranges. After rounds of customary greetings, I asked Zahrah how she got into the delivery business.

"By accident," she said, according to Nahad's translation. "My daughter was going into labor and couldn't get to the hospital in time."

She introduced that granddaughter, now a twenty-seven-year-old elementary school teacher. "She wants to be a TBA, too," Nahad said, "And she's learned from her grandmother."

"Does she have any health training?"

"Of course. Since the war [with Iran], all working women received some training, how to give injections and so forth. But I told her she should go into the three-year midwife program."

"How about Zahrah? How much education does she have?"

Nahad consulted her, then said, "One year of elementary school. She cannot read or write."

We spoke for a while about other TBAs she knew, and how many babies each had delivered without any training or education. I asked her how many she delivered between the time of the first delivery in 1970 and her training in 1988. She said nine or ten.

"And how many since 1990?"

"I don't keep records," she said, straining to recall, "but I think about three hundred."

"You've been busy."

She laughed. "Yes, but not so much lately. Since August, only high-risk births have come to me, and I am not trained for that. I have to send them to the hospital."

"So you just call for an ambulance?"

This time Nahad laughed. "Ambulance? We haven't had an ambulance in Basra in, I don't know, five years? They're all broken."

Just then the midday call for prayer echoed from the mosques, and Jassim called us from the gate. Zahrah seemed surprised. She'd assumed we were staying for lunch.

"Can we stay for lunch?" I asked Nahad.

"I think not."

"But won't she be upset?"

"Yes, of course she's upset," she replied, as though it were a silly question. "But Jassim is furious."

Jassim, who had been so confident in taking us to Basra without the proper travel documents, was now panicking about getting us back to Baghdad in time. It seemed the blue plates might not work so well after dark. If we were stopped at a checkpoint, they would ask to see our papers. What would happen after that was anybody's guess.

We sped back to the hospital, Jassim cursing (I'm sure) the entire way. We dropped off Dr. Nahad and picked up the others without cutting the engine, then Jassim cursed some more. I'd never seen him drive so furiously; and after ten minutes, he pulled over at a restaurant and sat down for a leisurely lunch. So leisurely, in fact, that the rest of us had time for a three course meal, two Turkish coffees and a shoeshine.

Back on the road, speeding along a few miles north of Basra, Jassim pointed out a stretch of road where he'd spent several days in combat against Iranian troops. I later found this description of the Iranian offensive: "The Iraqis mowed down wave after wave of Iranians until the tide stalled two miles short of Basra. The slaughter was so stunning that it entered Iraqi lore as 'the Great Harvest.'"

We followed an endless stretch of high-tension wires and

towers that looked like steel pagodas. Past the thatched houses of Marsh Arabs, beyond the scrapyards of bombed out trucks and just before an unremarkable overpass, Jim slapped his thigh and announced: "It was here! It was right here!"

It was the site of what was believed to be the Garden of Eden.

Babylon

The next morning, I read the Book of Daniel to Simon as Jalal drove us to Babylon. We hoped it would provide us with some history on the city, but mostly we just laughed out loud at Nebuchadnezzer's casual use of extreme violence and Daniel's frequent fits of narcolepsy.

When I was done, Jalal asked to see the Bible. He admired the ragged copy, but held it upside down, just as Simon had done when leafing through Jalal's Koran. Then Jalal closed the Book, kissed its cover and delicately handed it back to me.

At Babylon, we met Ibrahim, another archeologist reduced to tour guide. He showed us through the palace of Nebuchadnezzer II and quoted room dimensions in the manner of a real estate agent. "And here is the throne room, fifty-two by nineteen meters, plenty of room for entertaining."

That was true, but as for entertaining, we were the only guests to visit this ancient wonder in the past two days. Ibrahim seemed lonely. And nervous. Just beyond the palace walls stood an artificial hill, upon which Saddam had built one of his many palaces.

"Please don't photograph the palace," Ibrahim said. "Or the soldiers will come down here and make a lot of trouble for me."

It was one that the UN inspectors so desperately wanted to tour. Ibrahim had shown them around Babylon two days earlier, and one inspector asked, "When you're done giving us the tour of this palace, how about taking us on a tour through that one on the hill?"

Ibrahim seemed to appreciate the UN's sense of humor, and laughed as he told us the story. But the UN's Iraqi escorts, he said, were not the least bit amused. "Some people are just so serious," he added with a sigh. "I just want it to be normal again."

Normal, he explained, was resuming with the excavation and restoration of Babylon, and being able to afford food and medicine for his children without having to sell off everything he owned. He pulled at his lapel and said, "This is my last jacket. But if my boy needs medicine tomorrow, it will go to the black market."

I asked Ibrahim if he ever wanted to leave Iraq, if only to visit Berlin, where museums housed Babylon's most precious artifacts. He said no, that he had too much work to do here, and was just looking forward to the day when he could start again.

Al-Amiriya

Jim told Jassim and Jalal to take the rest of us to the Al-Amiriya shelter; he'd already seen it. Jassim, as usual, protested before agreeing. We drove through downtown Baghdad, then pulled into a parking lot where a spray-painted sign on a chain-link fence read, "Down America."

Jalal introduced us to a somber woman dressed in black who called herself Mada Reda, or maybe Mother Reda. We didn't have a translator with us, so we just quietly followed her into a building that had once served as a bomb shelter. Now it was a memorial to the 473 people who died there on February 13, 1991.

A red carpet was the only slash of color in this room of blackened floors and walls. The first thing she showed us, though it hardly needed pointing out, was a gaping hole in the ceiling. Reinforcing steel rods dangled like a dead squid in a shaft of sunlight, and the exposed cross-section of concrete was as thick and rugged as a post-quake L.A. overpass.

A single laser-guided missile had created this hole. A second missile passed through it and detonated inside the shelter.

Among the dozens of pictures and paintings on the wall, Reda pointed out portraits of four young children and said, "Mine." She showed us charred handprints, child size, stuck to the ceiling; pronounced outlines of bodies pressed against the wall, one apparently shielding an infant; and photographs of the few who survived and the many who didn't.

She led us down to the lower level and noted how the lower half of the white walls were stained light brown. She said, "Water." I tried to guess what that meant, and concluded that a water main had been blown apart, filling the lower level five feet deep. She led us through the corridors, pointing out darker patches of brown and pinching the skin on the back of her hand. I couldn't figure out what that meant either, until I examined the patches closer.

It was skin. Some of it with hair. Some of it forming parts of faces. I can only guess that the blast heated the water to a temperature that boiled the skin off the people trapped down here.

At the conclusion of her two-word tour, Reda led us back to the parking lot and left us there. Jassim was working on his car. He handed me a brake pad. It was worn down, and metal flaked off when I touched it. He took it and put it back.

Hours later, as we cruised around Baghdad, I said, "Jassim? Are you angry with America?" He didn't understand, so I repeated "you" and pointed at him, then "angry," making an angry face, then "America," putting a hand to my chest.

He shrugged, "Why?"

I said, "Al-Amiriya."

He tisked and said in a long, deep tone, "No." Then, with the most effort I'd ever seen him use to communicate with me, he said, "Clinton, Saddam," and released an exasperated sigh. "But you and I are people. Same people. OK? No problem."

Our last night in Baghdad, Jalal and Jassim drove us though an upscale shopping district with broad sidewalks and elegant window displays. Expensive cars cruised the streets a little too fast, music blared out of cafes and the liquor store stayed open late. Behind a grove of date palms, the sky glowed orange from the fire of an oil refinery.

We stopped between two Italian restaurants and tried to guess which would serve better pizza. As was often the case when choosing between restaurants, we picked the one with the most UN vans parked in front.

Jim said he was letting the drivers go home early, so now would be the time to say goodbye. The announcement caught me off guard. They had delivered us safely through nearly

1500 miles of Iraq, all without running across another body in the road, and I wasn't sure how to thank them.

I extended a hand to Jassim. At first he just looked at it, as though insulted. Then he threw his arms around my shoulders and kissed me twice on each cheek. I returned the courtesy on the second pass.

"Jassim, you're the first man I've ever kissed," I told him.

I was sure Jalal would be the second, but he was already on his way back to his car. I tried to stop him, but he just pushed me away.

That's when I saw he was crying.

Habits of Flying

CHINA: 1989-1990

Flying Pigeon

Shortly after the Tiananmen massacre of June 4, 1989, I prepared for a teaching assignment in Siping, China. Though ready for a year of sacrifices, I could not have anticipated the list of items that I was forbidden to bring into their country: Weapons, Drugs, Pornography, Political and Religious Propaganda, Mountain Bikes.

The last item ripped my breath away. How was I to survive a year without my trusty Cannondale? This faithful bike, which I'd christened Betsy, had carried me safely across the greater part of North Carolina's mountains and beaches and everything in between. She had delivered me from potentially deadly encounters with mountain ledges and railroad trestles, vicious copperheads and packs of feral dogs, hillbilly deputies and the broad side of countless minivans.

This wasn't just a bike. She was a bold machine forged from American sweat and steel, a crimson chariot that knew her way around tor and vale.

But it was precisely this kind of flashy craftsmanship that the Chinese Party sought to hide from the People. Our new breed of bikes, mountain bikes in particular, threatened to disgrace the Chinese model, the design of which changed little since 1950, when Huo Baoji first unveiled his carefully crafted Fei Ge, a classic model based on the 1932 English Raleigh roadster. Alas, my trusty Betsy would have to stay behind and await my return.

I arrived at Siping Teachers College on a dusty dawn in early September. Strains of a familiar tune echoed throughout the dreary gray campus. It was the music from the movie *Born Free*, and it woke the students for their morning exercise drills.

My Foreign Assistant and the Dean of Foreign Affairs showed me to my apartment and told me they'd come back later to give me an orientation of the town and college. In the meantime, I was to rest up from my journey. Wait for us here, they said. They didn't tell me at the time, but they figured I'd need about five days.

I waited about five hours before setting out on my own. My first order of business was, of course, to secure a bicycle. I didn't waste time shopping around, as the only model available was the *Fei Ge*. Huo Baoji had Flying Dove in mind when naming his creation, but due to a glitch in translation, the bike became known as the Flying Pigeon.

Weighing in at nearly fifty pounds, the Flying Pigeon was a beast of a bike. It was also a work of art in its simplicity. Pedals, chain, wheels, frame, seat and handlebars—that's all you got. Handbrakes were included, but rarely functional. And like Henry Ford's Model-T, the Flying Pigeon came in any color you wanted, as long as you wanted black.

I snapped up a used Flying Pigeon at a roadside repair shack for a mere ninety-five Yuan, about twenty-five dollars. (New bikes cost up to Y230 and a ration coupon). I sped off toward downtown Siping, an industrial city of 400,000 weary souls. It seemed half the population was out plodding along on bicycles identical to mine.

The only difference was mine went faster. I rode at the breakneck speed I'd grown accustomed to while racing to classes over the past four years. I rattled down boulevards, weaving through the masses like a barbarian. I passed tractors and buses and army trucks. As the only white boy in town, I got stares. Imagine a Mongolian warrior in Des Moines running his fool head off everywhere he went. That's how ridiculous I looked.

I couldn't help it. That's what bikes did to me. They infused me with energy and a giddy sense of liberation, no doubt a remnant from those adolescent nights when I would sneak out and ride off to meet friends who had done the same.

I rode everyday in Siping. On my fifth day, my Foreign Assistant returned to my apartment and scolded me for going into town unescorted. I wondered, briefly, who had ratted me out, but it didn't matter. There was no way anyone was going to stop me from doing it again.

My enthusiasm for my students was all that matched my joy of biking. Throughout the autumn, they accompanied me on my rides into town. They taught me Chinese phrases useful for requesting bicycle repairs. I taught them how to race madly through traffic, and how to stop when the brakes failed.

We rode in sunshine and in the face of fierce yellow winds blasting in from the Gobi Desert. And we rode despite the cabbage.

The cabbage arrived on a warm October afternoon. Vehicles the size of dump trucks barged in from the countryside, leaving a wake of slick, sour leaves. They unloaded the cabbage in town, in front of the Number Two Department Store, in piles that reached above the second floor. So abundant was the cabbage harvest that the Party announced everyone had the "political duty" to buy lots of it.

My students told me that snow always followed the cabbage harvest. I didn't believe them, but the next day a snowstorm hit like sticky rice in a ceiling fan. We rode in spite of it.

Gradually, however, they stopped riding with me. Then they stopped visiting me. Only one of my better students, who went by the English name Lester, agreed to meet with me, but only off campus. He would borrow a roommate's bike and ride into town well ahead of me. Then we'd meet at the house of an artist we knew. By trade a painter of Party-line signboards, this artist spent every free moment creating what he believed was contemporary Western art. That included skulls arranged Warhol-style and crucifixes that doubled as clotheslines. He longed for the freedom to exhibit his underground avant-garde creations.

He once challenged me to draw a picture of freedom.

I sketched out the first object to come to mind, though with my talent for the abstract, it passed for neither a Cannondale nor a Flying Pigeon. It was just a bike.

Lester later confided that the Dean of Discipline discouraged my students from talking to me outside the classroom. He would further reveal that this guarded attitude toward me stemmed from the behavior of my two Western male predecessors. The first, a Canadian, developed an inappropriate relationship with a student. He was deported and she was expelled. The second devoted an inordinate amount of time to thumping Bibles and damning the godless communists. He died under mysterious circumstances.

The Dean of Discipline had good reasons for turning me into a pariah. I just wished he'd shared them with me first. I would've understood. Instead, I sank into unfathomable loneliness, with only my Flying Pigeon to keep me company.

Regrettably, mistrust between Chinese and Americans was often mutual, as I found out when I realized that I was the only person in Siping paranoid enough to lock up a bicycle.

I continued cycling deep into the bleak Manchurian winter. My riding outfit consisted of a long quilted coat, a fleece-lined leather jacket, a fleece-lined hat with earflaps, two shirts, jeans, sweat pants, wool socks, wool-lined boots and a scarf wrapped around my face. Still I kept up my usual pace just to stay warm.

The outfit allowed me to travel incognito. The quilted coat was standard issue for Chinese police, the hat Chinese army surplus. I occasionally slowed down to blend in and marvel at other cyclists. What they lacked in pace, they often made up for in payload. A family of three easily enjoyed a Sunday outing on a single bike. Dad pedaling, Mom on the rack over the rear wheel, kid on the handlebars. I never saw a bike helmet, but some children did ride encased in plexiglass boxes strapped to the rack, like little emperors in two-wheel Popemobiles.

Cyclists in Siping and elsewhere often cruised along carrying a couple of full-grown pigs or a flock of ducks or an armoire. The antics of the Shanghai Acrobatic Troupe, famed for carrying up to thirteen adults on a single bike, no longer seemed like such remarkable feats.

But no matter what they carried or where they went, the Chinese always rode at the same trudging pace. In the only bicycle race I saw in China, the winner was the one who came in last without falling over.

I rode the bus only during the most inclement weather, miserable days made worse by riding the bus. Boarding a bus or train in China, or even purchasing a ticket for one, is akin to attending a Western concert. More specifically, it's like that one frenzied moment when hundreds of fans collectively decide to rush the stage. As a result, one of the first lines of Chinese I learned was *Ni wei shen me tui wu.* Why are you pushing me? But in cultures and situations where the boundaries of personal space are as intimate as a rugby scrum, such a question went largely ignored.

Once, while riding the bus into town, we passed one woman crumpled on the side of the road. She writhed in dirt as a bloodstain spread around her and her Flying Pigeon rested in pieces at her side. An hour later, on my return trip, I saw her again, in the same place, only she wasn't moving.

On another ride, a man boarded the bus and began shouting at the passengers. Everyone ignored him until he raised a meat cleaver and repeated his message. That cleared the bus, but I never figured out what he wanted.

The mentally ill ran rampant in Siping. The city was home to one of China's biggest mental institutions, and their patients enjoyed wandering off into town and elsewhere. Siping had earned a reputation for this segment its population. When I introduced myself to people outside of Siping, telling them where I came from, they would often laugh and remark, *Ni cong Siping lai le*—You've come from Siping—which is a regional way of saying, You're crazy.

Siping was known for little else. It didn't appear in any guidebooks. Paul Theroux had passed through twice without stepping off the train. He only mentioned that a madman reached his destination here.

Unlike Theroux's madman, or the nutcase with the meat cleaver, most mental patients in China displayed a few distinguishing characteristics. They dressed in white and often had their faces powdered white. I can't guess why, except to venture that after years of dealing with foreigners the Chinese learned to associate white skin with insanity. They were also invariably bloated to a degree that resembled the side effects of certain antipsychotic medications no longer in use in America, which suggested that all patients received the same treatment, regardless to the specifics of their illnesses.

When I tired of the madness in Siping, I rode off in the other direction, into Liaoning Province. I rambled along dirt paths through fields of corn stubble, on to their provincial towns where government buildings did not display Mao's red star, but instead featured three red circles arranged into the unmistakable silhouette of Mickey Mouse, or *Mi Lao Shu* as he's known across China.

I traveled far and wide on the endlessly expansive plane. With a horizon always in view, I understood the absurdity in bringing a mountain bike here. There was no mountain. No hill, tor or vale either.

Trees also seemed absent from most parts of China, but in Liaoning I found what appeared to be a eucalyptus forest growing in perfectly lined rows. I wheeled through the symmetrical woods, following an empty, freshly paved road (another rarity) for miles until it dead-ended at a large iron gate. A lone soldier watched me approach, his eyes widening, his hand reaching for his rifle. I turned around and didn't look back.

That evening, I got another visit from my Foreign Assistant. He warned me to stay away from secret military bases. I promised I would. He also reminded me to stay out of "closed areas." I agreed to that as well, but wasn't sure where they were. So I asked him would he mind if I took off a weekend for a ride to Inner Mongolia. In return, he asked me why I was so determined to make him lose his job.

Dance Party

I grew increasingly lonely, but much of my isolation in Siping was my own fault. From the start, I felt myself withdrawing from social activities and shunning the local amusements. The first party I attended at Siping Teachers College was for teachers only. We gathered in a classroom and loaded up on greasy peanuts and warm soda. One teacher introduced himself as Dr. Gary. He said he had a lot of questions about America, and would I be so kind to answer them. I said I would try.

He placed a hand on my thigh and said, "The American women, they are very loose. It's true?"

"Excuse me?"

"No, I don't think you understand me. I mean this as a good thing." And he laughed in nervous grunts. I decided then to avoid him for the rest of the year. I would've left the party at that moment, but the Dean of Foreign Languages announced it was time to sing. One by one, we were ordered to the front of the class, handed a microphone, and instructed to sing.

I'd been warned about moments like this, duly advised to have a song prepared, but I'd recklessly ignored it, figuring I could wing my way through spontaneous demands for entertainment. I've been known to belt out a few notes in public, often without receiving complaints.

I did not, however, fully appreciate the awkwardness of the situation until now. This time, I didn't have musical accompaniment or a karaoke monitor. Of all the tunes that sprang to mind, I could remember sufficient lyrics for only three: The Dead Kennedy's "Too Drunk to Fuck" and Sugarhill's "Rapper's Delight." The third is almost too embarrassing to mention, but you don't grow up in the South without letting it worm into your brain.

I turned to all those cheerful faces anticipating my American musical stylings, slowly raised the mic to my mouth, gritted my teeth into a smile and sang: *Oh, I wish I was in the land of cotton . . . .*

The applause I received was warm and sincere, but not altogether enthusiastic. They wanted to hear familiar tunes, I gathered. When other teachers belted out songs like "Jingle Bells" and "Edelweiss," the crowd went wild, cheering and clapping madly after every stanza.

Still, I would repeat my performance at several banquets, and I thought I was getting pretty good at it, thought I had it down pat when the Mayor of Siping inexplicably invited the college's four foreign teachers to one of his banquets. In celebration of the fortieth birthday of The People's Republic of China, he'd also invited the district's highest ranking cadres, a news crew, and various musicians who repeatedly played a depressing, soulless rendition of "Rivers of Babylon."

I shouldn't criticize. My performance went over like a mime for the blind. I'd tried to gussy up my act for the TV cameras, but nobody, not even the Americans, seemed to appreciate my Sinatra rendition of "Dixie." I imagined viewers at home kicking in their TV screens, but remembered with relief that I knew but a few people in China who owned a TV, and all of them were here at the banquet.

I blame the *baijiu*. This toxic rice wine—along with the social obligation to guzzle it at banquets—is what turned me into a swaggering Vegas lounge singer. I had planned to temper my drinking and quit smoking upon my departure for China, but to refuse a cigarette or a toast of *gambei* (bottoms up) was an insult here, tantamount to belching out loud and spitting on the floor. (Conversely, belching out loud and spitting on the floor was the norm here.)

The other three foreign teachers, being women, were exempt from the drinking requirements. Jeanette, the Russian, insisted on keeping up with the gentlemen, but the two Americans passed their shot glasses on to me. I considered accidentally spilling them, but this was no ordinary baijiu. This was Mao Tai, the Dom Perignon of baijiu. The bottles alone carried such prestige that people often collected the empties to display in their homes. Some went as far as filling them with cheap baijiu to further the illusion. One entrepreneurial cadre made a small fortune in selling refilled bottles, I read in *The China Daily*. He plead guilty to the offense. The courts ordered his execution—gunshot to the head—and billed his family for the bullet.

Baijiu flowed with wild abandon at all banquets, which were otherwise formal occasions with elaborate dishes like roast sparrow, fried frogs, and endangered turtle soup. The multi-course meals could cost a month's wages or more and go on for hours, not to mention the time spent on preparations. Someone had to wire up the mics and the spinning disco lights, arrange the plastic flowers and neatly position cigarettes on the tables. And all that shiny paper bunting didn't just hang itself. Someone had to go all out to get the ambience just right.

As a guest at such occasions, I strived to conduct myself in a dignified manner, even if that meant performing like a circus chimp, but my biggest cultural challenge was doing so while flying high on baijiu.

On the other hand, a little baijiu might've helped at my student's parties. I attended one "dance party" on a Saturday afternoon. Students had taken over a classroom, shoved the wooden chairs and desks aside, while teachers brought in crates of warm soda. A plodding electronic rhythm on a worn cassette honked out of a portable stereo.

The guys dressed up for the dance, sporting ties and jackets and the kind of boot-heel shoes not worn in the West since the last days of disco. Some had permed their hair in the style of Larry, the swinging bachelor from *Three's Company*. But as soon as they arrived, they clustered in one corner and rolled torn strips of newspaper into cigarettes. The girls, meanwhile, waltzed over the concrete floor. When they finished, a guy might muster the courage to dance and select another guy as his partner. And the two would dance, arms length apart, a hand to shoulder or hand to hip, the other hands clasped. I wanted to ask if they could try to look more, what's the word, gay? But they danced with this far away stare, all too cool to smile, and frankly they looked too bored to be gay.

The event dragged on for hours, almost until sundown, and I swore to myself that I would never again attend a dance party.

Six weeks later I got a call from Lucy, an American teacher at Changchun University, or Chang Da. The connection was bad, but it held out just long enough for her to invite me to another dance party.

Chang Da, two hours away by train and a short bus ride down Stalin Boulevard, was a horrendous slum built according to Stalinist blueprints. As in the rest of northern China, buildings here had the charm of cinderblocks. Difference is these cinderblocks were overcrowded and falling apart.

Typically, eight students shared a single dorm room, and those who couldn't get assigned to one room slept in classrooms instead. Still, in some ways they fared better than Lucy. Her apartment was on the sixth floor. An elevator would've been useful, but only during the six or so hours per week when electricity flickered through the building. Heat and water reached her floor for about two hours each week. We shared her bed that night, in a room the size of a walk-in closet, both of us dressed in hats, coats, gloves, and boots.

Yet Chang Da hosted dance parties that put Siping to shame. They had beer. They had a huge stereo system. And they had guests from all over the world. Aki Fu was a teacher from Japan. Nearing his sixties, he knew only a few lines of English. "Dance party" was clearly one of his favorites, I gathered from the way his face lit up when he said it. For banquets, he'd memorized the first few verses of "You are My Sunshine," and for anyone who lit a cigarette near him: "No smoking, goddamn son of bitch cocksucker!"

Then there was the unlikely trio of Kim, Kestutis and Klaus. Krazy Kim the North Korean spoke no English, but pursued Lucy with an unambiguous passion. Kestutis sang Lithuanian dirges when he got drunk and homesick. And Klaus was a German who just kind of sat around and scowled a lot. There were Belgians and Brits and Aussies and Kiwis. And there were the African students from a crosstown college, the Jilin University of Technology, or JUT. In all, about thirty people showed up for that dance party in the Chang Da banquet hall. Three, maybe four, were Chinese.

Four hours into the party, at around midnight, a campus security officer barged in and tried to shut us down. Lucy immediately cozied up to him. A tall South Dakotan with big frizzy hair, she vastly outsized the officer, but gently coaxed him toward the beer table and later dragged him out on the dance floor.

When I expressed my astonishment to the Chinese students, telling them that mine would never throw raucous parties like this, they shrugged as if it were nothing. "Last year, before the crackdown, dance parties were much better," one student said. His English name was Hunter, and he described how their demonstrations for democracy culminated into campus-wide bashes that would spill into the street. "And in Beijing, even better."

Hunter had gone to Beijing for several demonstrations. He was about two blocks away from Tiananmen Square when the tanks rolled in. He said he didn't know any of the 3000 demonstrators who were killed, but many of his friends had since disappeared. Chinese authorities had since arrested more than 30,000 students, and the crackdown was far from over. Many feared they'd be next and strived to disassociate themselves from all foreign influences. This helped explain the low Chinese representation at dance parties.

Hunter longed for the return of that festive atmosphere in the Spring of '89. Classes were boycotted, dance parties erupted, and bonfires blazed almost every night. He seemed profoundly sad that it was over.

I was sorry I'd missed it, but I tried to offer an optimistic spin. "At least you can concentrate on your studies now."

He shook his head in doubt. "It is not so easy now. We burned so many desks."

I had noticed the shortage in the classrooms. Two, sometimes three students to a desk. But the problem gradually resolved itself as the crackdown continued and more students went missing. Considering his level of participation, Hunter should've been among them. He'd been questioned several times, but apparently responded with the answers the authorities wanted to hear.

And despite the crackdown, he continued to operate an illegal bar in a crawlspace on the ground level of an administrative building on campus. He called it Club Hawkeye, after his business partner, who got his English name from a character in *M*A*S*H*. Entrance into the club required stooping though an unmarked doorway, into a windowless tunnel with a pristine red carpet and chalky red walls. It lacked chairs and tables, the ceiling was too low for those, but candles and a battery-powered tape deck added to the beatnik ambience. He also sold beer and whisky, though lacking in capitalist incentives, did so with no discernable markup.

A Zambian named Moses told me that the dance parties at his school, JUT, were better than Chang Da's. I couldn't imagine how the Africans had time for any kind of social activities. They'd been sent to China to study computer engineering.

To complicate matters further, their classes and textbooks and exams were in Chinese. Yet every Saturday morning, as soon as classes ended, they'd kick off a party that would last until midnight on Sunday.

It would begin with music, strains of Milli Vanilli echoing throughout the African dorm, Third World thumping out "Reggae Ambassador" or Maxi Priest with his reggae version of "Wild World." There would be crates of beer in forty-ounce bottles and clouds of smoke from spiked cigarettes. The Chinese word for it is *dama*, but Moses called it happy smoke.

If selling fake Mao Tai is a capital offence, I wondered, then what is the penalty for possession of hash? Whatever it was, the Africans didn't seem worried. They had their own way of dealing with the authorities.

At midnight, with a dance party in full swing in the cafeteria, a tired old security officer shuffled in and tried to shut down the music. Manda, who was large and muscular and bristling with dreadlocks, stood in his way. Enraged now, the officer shouted and stammered and waved his arms wildly. I understood just one word: *Houzi*. Monkey.

Manda's eyes darkened and his jaws clenched. He hooked his index and middle fingers into the officer's nostrils and dragged his face down to crotch level, all the while growling out a string of what was surely a host of obscenities. I jotted down his last line: *Tsao ni ma*.

And the beat went on . . . .

When I returned to Siping, I asked my students what the phrase meant. They collectively gasped before one responded, "Teacher Stephen, you must never say this. It means—" He blushed as he searched for the words. "—to deflower your mother."

Foreign Invasions

Expats in China, regardless of nationality or occupation, could be neatly divided into two categories: Ducks and heathens. Ducks were covert missionaries, evangelists who'd come to proselytize where it was expressly forbidden. The rest of us, the heathens, simply wanted to experience China with a little gusto.

Siping Teachers College, inadvertently or not, had a history of recruiting ducks for foreign teachers. The American teachers who preceded me were ducks. The two American women there now were ducks who regularly held Bible study meetings in their bedrooms. That helped explain why the place was so dull, and why I jumped on a train every chance I got, which was about every other weekend.

In retrospect, I can't say exactly what drew me to Changchun, only that I felt more at home with a Zambian or a Lithuanian or a North Korean than with the Americans in Siping. And so the wacky, wondrous dance parties continued throughout the semester, each one bigger than the last. Oddly enough, they seemed to migrate north as the weather grew colder. Thanksgiving and Christmas parties were held in the city of Jilin. And the biggest blowout happened in Harbin on January 9, 1990.

Harbin is kind of like the Montreal of China. It's about as far north and looks like it belongs in another country. Perhaps the most beautiful city in China, Harbin managed to avoid Stalin's designs, thanks in large part to the Russians, who were able to decorate with onion domes, scalloped turrets, spires, and cupolas before handing their outpost over to the Kuomingtang in 1946. It still remained as a popular stop on the Trans-Siberian Railway, and its markets were stocked with Russian goodies like furs, caviar and vodka.

The city hosted a music festival every summer, but was best known for its Ice Lantern Festival in the winter. Every year, from January through March, ice sculptors created crystalline dragons and horses and towering pagodas, most lit from within using florescent lights in a multitude of colors. According to the Chinese tourist literature, they transformed the parks of Harbin into "a frozen fairyland."

Harbin also gained small notoriety in 1985, when an American businessman fell asleep with a lit cigarette in the Swan Hotel. At least ten guests perished from the resulting fire, and the American served eighteen months in a Chinese prison for his negligence.

Bedside ashtrays at the Swan Hotel now contained note cards that outlined the hazards of smoking in bed. And as an added precaution, armed soldiers patrolled the hallways.

Every foreign teacher in Jilin Province was invited to Harbin, courtesy of Mr. Yu, the provincial Director of Education. This high-ranking, though terminally cheerful cadre hoped to liven up the first days of our winter break with a tour of Harbin. More emphatically, he wanted to treat us to a dance party.

Immediately following the usual banquet, where he'd entertained us with an enthusiastic rendition of "Jingle Bells," Mr. Yu ushered us into the Swan Hotel Ballroom, where he once more sang the Christmas ditty, this time among a dizzy array of disco lights and a fog machine.

A band then took the stage and launched into a set of Chinese pop tunes and other dreary electronic noises. They effectively drove the foreigners from the ballroom, transforming our dance party into a kind of progressive drinking event. The thirty of us, with Mr. Yu tagging along, moved room by room, floor by floor, ever upward but in diminishing numbers. Sometime after midnight, with only ten or so remaining, we discovered a fire escape leading up through a narrow concrete shaft to the rooftop. From here, the lights of Harbin radiated throughout the quiet night, and from this altitude it did indeed resemble a frozen fairyland, one with Russian spires and onion domes punctuating the skyline.

Kestutis broke the silence with a mournful Lithuanian folk song. Mr. Yu followed this with a hearty chorus of "Jingle Bells." Anthony, a pasty Brit, lit a cigarette and passed it around. Mr. Yu took a long drag, but I don't think he realized it was packed with hash.

Some hours later, only Jessica and I remained standing. She was a recent Georgetown grad, tough in tomboyish way, but quick with an irresistible smile. We wandered the halls in search of our respective rooms. Along the way, we met two soldiers. One asked, I assume, what we were doing, prowling around the hotel at this late hour. We didn't know how to answer, and so, in a show of goodwill, Jessica offered up a drink from her bottle of vodka, which they gladly accepted.

I then offered to trade my camera for their handguns. They temporarily agreed to the deal. I didn't realize the sheer

stupidity of it all until after I got the film developed: Pictures of Jessica and I with Chinese eyes and mischievous grins, of us striking James Bond poses, of us aiming the guns at each other in a mock shootout, of us pointing the barrels directly at the camera.
A simple caveat about photographing armed soldiers in China went: You shoot them, they'll shoot you. However, nobody had warned against aiming a gun at a soldier who was photographing me.

Dali

Abandoning the heathens in Harbin, I rode southbound trains for five days and nights, followed by an overnight bus to Dali, where I found an entirely new flock of heathens. European backpackers mostly, they'd entrenched themselves in this mountain town hoping to establish the new Kathmandu, the original one having long exhausted its hipness as well as its capacity for backpackers.

The town seemed eager to accommodate them. Local outdoor markets, traditionally stocked with live pigs and fishing nets, now carried water bongs and tie-dye shirts. Somewhat ironically, antique souvenirs such as opium scales evoked reminders of an earlier drug culture that flourished for nearly a hundred years.

The British introduced opium to China in 1773. Lacking any resources the Chinese actually needed, they hoped drug trafficking would balance their trade deficit. The scales indeed tipped in Britain's favor, quickly and dramatically, and more than twenty-five years passed before the emperor realized the new trade was draining the nation's wealth. He declared a war on drugs, but it would take sixty years and four Opium Wars to eradicate the menace. By 1860, the Middle Kingdom was a husk of a nation, one largely exposed to an onslaught of foreign powers—French, British, Russian—all bent on seizing pieces of the failing empire.

As foreign invaders go, backpackers are among the least pestilent. At worst they foster a peculiar industry that caters to their exotic whims. It's not always pretty, but it is a far cry from the hideous garishness and carnival atmospheres that have developed around larger attractions like the Great Wall of China.

In Dali, cafés and hostels mushroomed from cobblestone roads, places with names like Jim's Peace Café and The Tibetan Café. Unlike anyplace in northern China, menus in Dali featured Eurotrash favorites like yogurt and muesli, as well as items like Salvador Dali Pizza and Dali Lama Pasta Salad. They'd assembled libraries of Western music, tenth-generation copies of the same bootleg cassettes heard in any backpacker destination. Bob Marley and The Grateful Dead usually lilted out of their stereos, with only a few aberrant tunes thrown into the mix. An old school rap by Kurtis Blow, for example. Or U2, with Bono singing in a breathy timbre: *Outside it's America, outside it's America . . .*, as if anyone wanted to believe that.

Outside was a war going on. Mingling with scent of hash and incense were choking clouds of gunpowder. With New Year celebrations going full blast, Dali, like the rest of China, was locked in battle against evil spirits, driving them back with a nonstop assault of pyrotechnics and dancing dragons and revelers with drums and whistles. Rockets screamed down the streets while firecrackers hopped and skipped to a machine-gun rhythm.

Street vendors sold every variation of charge and sparkler, including some that had been outlawed in all fifty states back home. My favorites were these little sticks of dynamite that could completely vaporize a toy tank or a stuffed panda, though I suppose now that the giddy fun in blowing stuff up could be partly attributed to the potency of the local dama.

The little missiles and bombs rained down on Dali day and night in a continuous barrage. As the week wore on, more and more townsfolk sported bandages on their eyes, ears and fingers until it appeared as though gauze were a fashion statement, a kind of holiday de rigeur.

I spent my twenty-third birthday hiking out of town, up the Cang Shan Mountains, past the snowline, on to a Buddhist monastery. The monks there greeted me with tea and a bowl of noodles. And when I told them, *Jintian shi wode shengri*—Today is my birthday—they sang me a song and gave me a Coke, the first I'd seen in many months.

More than the constant celebrations, or anything else in Dali, I enjoyed its bathhouse. In Siping, hot water arrived in my apartment once a week, two buckets of it, scarcely enough to soak my feet. In Dali, I could bathe in a stone tub with water up to my neck, steam curling around my head, for hours a day. It washed away months of Manchurian soot and warmed me to my core.

I set out alone from Dali and spent the next three weeks wending my way on planes, trains, buses, and boats, with stops in Kunming, Beijing, Nanjing, Shanghai, and Dalian before returning to Siping. During the semester that followed, my attendance at dance parties elsewhere dropped sharply. For the entire month of April, I was inexplicably placed under restriction, forbidden to leave Siping.

At the same time, Spring apparently thawed the heart of the Dean of Discipline, and soon students found their way back to my apartment. Again we rode around on our Flying Pigeons, our bicycle gang reunited, but this time I wanted to show them the natural beauty of Liaoning. What I wanted to show off more was the stunts I could pull on its rutted paths. I raced up a dirt mound to jump a small ditch. It would have been a simple maneuver on a mountain bike.

My landing was clean, but then so was the resulting break in my fork. It split like a wishbone, sending me over the handlebars. Once my students recovered from the shock of witnessing their teacher fail a stunt not even the Shanghai Acrobatic Troupe would attempt, they all laughed, which was all I'd wanted in response anyway. And repairs set me back only a few yuan, less than two bucks.

During one of these rides to Liaoning, sometime around midsummer, I pointed out the marijuana plants that flourished along the edges of the corn and cabbage fields and asked my students why the farmers were growing dama. They adamantly denied the accusation and insisted that the Party had successfully eliminated all drugs from China.

I asked how they explained the hedge of six-foot stalks right in front of them. Their answers varied from "It is just a weed," to "We only eat the seeds as a kind of snack," along with several sincere assertions that there was no dama in

China. I thought I might try it out, just to prove them wrong, if only to myself, but I lacked the inclination, and more so, the knowledge to harvest it.

Letters from China

My foreign assistant often neglected to share information that would've proved useful to me. If he'd warned me about Party plans to devaluate the Yuan, as he'd warned the other Americans, I would not have lost a quarter of my savings overnight. And if he had told me I could call the United States from Siping, I may not have gone to Changchun quite as often. But when he finally got around to telling me that I had a car and driver at my disposal, it hardly made a difference. I still relied on my bicycle.

Sometime in early July, as I was returning from errands in town, three of my students stood in the middle of the road and blocked my way. I figured they were playing a game, kind of like chicken, so I aimed my bike for Nancy, the one in the middle.

Nancy stood her ground. I squeezed my brakes, but they failed. I hopped off the pedals and dug in my heels. It was too late. She caught the handlebars as my bike drove her back several feet.

"Teacher Stephen, you must stop!" she gasped, her face contorted with fear. "There are some bad men! Please help us!"

I followed her eyes as she glanced over her shoulder. A man in an army jacket was yelling at a younger woman, one of my seniors. I froze up for a moment, not knowing how to respond as the man backed her toward the curb.

"What's he saying?" I asked.

"He is saying that college girls think they are too good for factory workers," she answered. "He is calling her some very bad names."

As I got off my bike, I could see what was about to happen. The senior, Angela, continued to back away from the man, unaware of an uncovered storm drain directly behind her. What's worse is I knew that because of my initial hesitation, I would not be able to stop her in time. Sure there were plenty of other people near her, most close enough to reach her or warn her. But this was China, where people won't bother to assist a hit-and-run victim as she bleeds to death on the side of the road. Nobody wanted to get involved.

Angela was lucky. She stepped at the edge, lost her balance and tumbled to the sidewalk instead of falling directly into the drain. I ran over to stop the man before he reached her. Enraged, he shouted at me, his nose nearly touching mine. His breath, reeking of baijiu, almost brought tears to my eyes.

Everything around me became perfectly confusing. A crowd was gathering. Some of the other men sported the same army jacket and drunken disposition as the adversary in my face. I wondered if they would help him in a fight, but figured that they, like everybody else, didn't want to get involved.

As the man shouted at me, Nancy translated as much as she could: "He is saying foreigners always meddle in the affairs of others. He is telling you to go back to where you came from." And just in case I didn't fully understand, she added: "He is criticizing you."

I told her to take Angela back to the college. The gate was only fifty or so yards away, close enough for the security guard on duty to get a good view of the show. Nancy tugged on my arm. "You must come with us."

I wanted to go, but I didn't want to leave my bike behind and I couldn't turn my back on the man. He was still trying to get to Angela and I kept up a steady waltz to block his way. I turned to check on her. She limped around behind me, trying to walk off a twisted ankle. I shouted at Nancy, "Get her out of here! Now!" Before I could turn back to face the man, I felt his hands on my shoulders. I responded with a quick, hard shove. He seemed fairly solid on his feet, didn't topple over like the reeling drunk I'd hoped he'd be, but he did back down, muttering something about the *waiguoren*—foreigners, barbarians—as he slunk away.

Word of the incident quickly traveled throughout the campus, and students and teachers greeted me as "Teacher Stephen, the hero" and "Teacher Stephen, the good example" for days thereafter. Angela came to my apartment to thank me. She'd dressed up for the visit, in a formal gown all pink and taffeta. I told her I was sorry I didn't help her sooner. She didn't seem to understand why I would apologize. I didn't try to explain.

I didn't tell anyone what I really felt about that day, that I behaved like a coward. If I'd been a braver man, I would've hooked my fingers into that man's nostrils and told him to go deflower his mother. But it didn't happen that way and I wouldn't get a second chance. That was the last time I rode my bike into town.

As my time to leave China neared, I sensed a change in my students. They seemed unhappy. A few actually burst into tears as they said goodbye. It surprised me. The only one I felt I would miss was Lester. He seemed sad, but more so, envious of my freedom to escape. There was nothing I could say about that, nothing I could do but leave him to care for my Flying Pigeon.

The last party I attended in Siping was a banquet held in my honor. The host was the old lecher, Dr. Gary. I'd declined his invitations throughout the year, but accepted his final one on my last night in Siping.

He also invited about ten of his closest friends, boisterous men who spoke no English but welcomed me with songs, cigarettes, and baijiu. The one woman in attendance sat close to my side and kept my glass full.

Dr. Gary asked me if I thought she was beautiful. I told him yes, she was one of the prettiest girls I'd seen all year. He said I could have her. I asked exactly what he meant by that. He flicked a cigarette in the direction of his bedroom and said I could have her.

I politely declined, mostly out of my suspicions over his generosity. I was already uncertain why he'd spent so much money on a lavish banquet for me. His motives didn't become apparent until weeks after my return to the States. He sent a letter explaining how much he wanted to come to America. He'd completed all the necessary paperwork to do so, he assured me. All he needed was a sponsor.

I wrote him back, explaining regretfully that I did not have the money required of a sponsor. The way I understood it, if he should he fail to find work in America, then I would be legally bound to provide for his well being or his passage back home. I was just getting myself on my feet again, working at a video store until I could find more suitable employment.

The tone of his next letter took on equal measures of anger and desperation, none of it very subtle in reminding me of the bonds of our friendship, which he had forged at great expense on my last night in Siping.

I issued him one last apology and never heard from him again.

For that matter, I never heard from the Africans again, or any of the foreign teachers in Jilin and Changchun. Only a handful of my students kept me posted on their lives, sending me Christmas cards and wedding photos and, later, baby pictures. Most of it seemed like correspondence from strangers, and I often found it difficult, if not impossible, to reply.

I've since recovered most of my correspondence from China to friends and family back home, inane letters that ramble upward of twenty pages each, all cheerful observations that boasted of the profound friendships I was cultivating here and my keen ability to comprehend this mysterious nation.

My journals, by contrast, amount to a 300-page tome of self-indulgent soul searching, a quest for the truth about China and my place in it. I often tempted myself into a full-blown conversion, convinced by the notion that I'd be better off as a duck.

It is also heavy on disjointed incidents expanded into unfinished short stories that read like feeble imitations of Camus and Sartre. And there are pages and pages of truly bad poetry. But the bulk of my journals is excessive pining and melodramatic expressions of soul crushing misery. Forlorn over two girlfriends I'd left behind, I spent countless nights translating my lovesickness into a dreadful masterpiece of gothic melancholy.

Now, thirteen years later, I compare my letters and notes for a sense of what really happened and what went wrong. Ultimately, I suppose I came away from the whole experience with a sense of disappointment. I'd gone into the Middle Kingdom fresh out of college and full of naive optimism. I'd gone to change lives and enlighten minds with liberal ideologies. But the foreigners who went before me, particularly those in the spring of 1989, had already done so, and with disastrous results. It seems now everybody in China got it all wrong, and so the walls of communism would crumble elsewhere that year.

Bearing Witness at the DMZ

KOREA: 1995

At 7:45 a.m., in the parking lot of the USO in Seoul, an American woman braces herself against the Siberian winds and complains bitterly in a Midwestern accent. She can't believe that the Hardee's down the road is closed at this hour. She was counting on downing a few biscuits before bearing witness to the world's most oppressive regime.

By 8:05, the bus, filled to capacity, is rolling. By 8:15, that woman (or one that sounds just like her) is well into the process of cataloging her travel experiences. Disney World seems to hold a special place in her heart, though her husband (who's not present to defend himself) suffered an anxiety attack on the *20,000 Leagues Under the Sea* ride.

I can't help but overhear her droning in an accent that can grate hardened cheese. Her voice drowns out our tour guide on the PA system. This distraction only adds to the guide's frustration with the English language. Her job becomes more difficult when the windows on the bus ice over—both inside and out—making it impossible to for most to see the sights she's trying to point out along the way. And despite copious notes, she says little that can be deciphered by most on board. Her voice falters, she confesses her nervousness, and her English worsens to the point where many tourists laugh openly at her. It's her first day on the job, perhaps her last as well.

From my vantage point in the front seat, I can see endless miles of barbed wire, sentry posts and heavily armed guards separating the Freedom Road from the Han River. This scene remains very much the same over the next hour and a half, until we reach Freedom Bridge. Soldiers of the 1st Battalion 9th Infantry guard the southern end of this single lane stretch of icy wooden planks over the Imjin River, and they will deny access to any Korean without a special permit. That's what makes this place so attractive: I get to tour a part of Korea that's off limits to most Koreans.

A soldier boards the bus to ensure that everyone is complying with the dress code: "No sleeveless shirts, mini-skirts, halter tops, form-fitting clothing." And, most importantly, "No outer clothing of the sheer variety." Terrorists from a non-allied nation need not worry. No one checks for weapons or passports at any point.

Photography is strictly banned from this point to the entrance of Camp Bonifas, but there isn't much to photograph anyway, except for rice paddies and utility poles bejeweled with yellow smiley faces.

Once inside the camp, we are free to wander, take in deep breaths of diesel fumes and explore the sandbagged bomb shelters that are strategically positioned along the roadside and next to the swimming pool. However, most tourists choose to wait in the Monastery, which serves as a bar, a souvenir shop and a duty-free shop. Here they purchase official DMZ shot glasses, pens and key chains adorned with the motto "In Front of Them All." Most, however, avoid the dubious bargains on liquor, cameras, binoculars and sunglasses.

Soon, an American soldier rounds up our group and herds us into a briefing room, where we're exposed to a full hour of slides, history and propaganda. The American tourists listen politely, saving their questions until the end of the presentation; questions like, "When was the Korean War?" and "Did any of the fighting take place outside of the DMZ?" The soldier fields these questions with the remarkable patience that is characteristic of a man who has already survived years in this high-tension wasteland.

He then rehashes a few of the rules for visitors, such as: "Don't fraternize with or gesticulate in the presence of the Chinese or North Koreans." And, "Refrain from disseminating any information that could be used for their propaganda purposes." And to avoid any confusion, he makes it clear that the good guys are wearing blue, the bad guys, brown. Finally, he issues laminated guest badges, but not before instructing us to sign away our right to sue in the event of injury or death as a result of enemy action.

Now we're all ready to witness one of the last bastions of the Cold War. A special bus shuttles us over to the Joint Security Area (JSA), where North and South Korean soldiers stand as if posing for DONT WALK signs. But despite their color-coded uniforms, many tourists regard with suspicion any armed soldier of Asian descent. One cowers behind the American soldier, asking tactfully, "Are they friendly?" To which the American soldier patiently replies, "Yes, ma'am. They're here to protect you." And she sighs in relief, much in the way her husband did upon learning that the Captain Nemo's submarine ride at Disney World never really went underwater.

But truly one of the biggest thrills in the DMZ is the microphone cord that bisects the JSA conference room. Step over this cord and you've stepped across the Military Demarcation Line. In essence, that means you can go home and tell your friends that you stood on hostile North Korean soil (or carpet, anyway). Jump back and forth and you can tell them you visited the enemy territory six or seven times. Just beware of the other tourists as they launch a frenzied stampede six inches to the North.

In case you can't fathom the purpose of a dividing line in a negotiation room, think back to those hot summer days you and your brother spent in the back seat of the station wagon on the way back from the beach. The vinyl seat is hot and sticky, you're tired and hungry, and you've got sand in your drawers. To make matters worse, your brother has decided to sprawl all over the seat. Naturally, you have to smack him back to his side. He, of course, smacks you back. To resolve this issue without making your father stop the car, your mother reaches back and draws an imaginary line down the middle of the seat, adding that whoever crosses this line is going to be in some serious trouble. But that plan will never work because you're both hot and bored, and the imaginary line has just turned the seat into a playing field. So you and your brother end up seeing who can smack the other the most times before your mother turns around again and smacks the both of you.

That's pretty much the deal in the conference room, only nobody's mother is there to smack some sense into those boys. So instead they end up playing games, like seeing who can bring in the bigger flag.

These games aren't limited to the conference room either. Two villages in the DMZ, the North's Kijong-dong or Propaganda Village and the South's Taesong-dong or Freedom Village, are still playing the flag game. At last reckoning, the North is ahead with a flag that's a hundred feet long. It's so large that only a stiff wind can unfurl it. The rest of the time, it hangs limp and blends in with the tower, rendering itself virtually invisible. If left out in the rain, it would become so heavy that it would tear itself in half. In effect, it has become a metaphor of the nation for which it stands.

Heavily armed vehicles escort us to a hilltop near The Bridge of No Return. Here, in the comfort of a set of wooden bleachers, we spy upon both villages. Noting the Korean soldiers in our caravan, a tourist asks, "Are they . . .?" To which our American soldier/tour guide responds, "Yes, ma'am. They're on our side and they're here to protect you." He then translates all the HOLLYWOOD-style signs placed by the North, facing the South. Most are geared at slandering the South with the usual anti-American clichés. Meanwhile, patriotic music blares out of Propaganda Village, rolling over the hills with the intention of luring folks out of Freedom Village. It's an obnoxious ensemble of horns and drums, interspersed with patriotic slogans voiced by North Korea's version of Tokyo Rose. And it will play late, late into the night.

One final attraction, almost as exciting as the microphone cord, is a tree stump. Its story begins on an August morn in 1973, when four UNC guards and six Korean Service Corps workers (i.e.: good guys) set out to accomplish the routine task of trimming a poplar tree that stood near the Bridge of No Return. A KPA guard (i.e.: bad guy) told them to leave the tree alone, claiming it was a special tree that was planted and nurtured by the North Koreans. Naturally, a riot ensued. In the end, an American Lieutenant, an American Captain and the whole damn tree got axed down. Each side claimed victory: A section of the felled tree is on display at the Monastery, while the ax allegedly received a place of prominence in the North Korean War Museum.

And so the tour ends. The bus windows have thawed for the scenic drive back to the USO, only the guide is too humiliated to point out the sights a second time. Instead, she distributes vouchers redeemable for a scoop of ice cream at the USO, just in case the DMZ left a bad taste in our mouth. But even that might not be enough, as one tourist remarks: "Oh, I don't like this cappuccino ice cream. It tastes like coffee."

Sometimes it's hard to believe that a two and a half mile strip of land makes any difference between living in a world where people are free to be as ignorant as they choose, or under a government that, by shutting out the rest of the world, enforces ignorance.

I've got fifteen months in Korea to ponder this dilemma. Though I spend most of my time teaching English, learning Tae Kwon Do and drinking soju, not a day passes without mention of what the North Koreans might be up to now.

The military presence is a constant reminder. Every morning I see soldiers training on the cement banks of the Han; and though I'm aware they're preparing to clash with South Korean students, I'm certain that their gas masks and baton-swinging techniques could have military applications as well.

And occasionally, I must confront the U.S. Army. This happens anytime I need goods that aren't available in Korean markets, namely cheese and deodorant. These items are often pilfered from the commissary and sold on the black market in Itaewon, a Seoul 'hood that's positively crawling with drunken G.I.s out for a brawl.

But despite my aversion to soldiers of any breed, I never fail to sign up for USO tours to the DMZ. They're offered only a few times a year, and are often canceled when North-South tantrums flare.

So once again, I find myself on a bus poised at the southern end of Freedom Bridge. An American soldier bounds onboard and announces, "I just want to remind you, no pictures until you reach the camp. That cool?" Assuming silence is consent, (as if we had a choice,) he salutes the passengers and turns to leave, not even bothering to check if anyone is in violation of the dress code.

His Korean counterpart, however, is not satisfied. He pushes the American soldier back on board and insists they take the customary walk down the isle. The American lets out a nervous laugh and says, "I'm not sure what we're doing here. What's up, Corporal Kim?"

Corporal Kim doesn't reply. He just presses on until they reach the end of the isle and every seat has been checked. Content, they both saunter off the bus and wave it through. That's when it dawns on me: This tour is perfect for anyone who wishes to experience life in a military state—the check points and road blocks, the anti-tank walls and conspicuous display of weaponry—like *The Year of Living Dangerously* in only four hours.

It's all that and more, with a mini-safari thrown in for good measure. Many endangered species, such as the Manchurian Crane, are now beginning to flourish in the DMZ for the simple reason that birds cannot trigger land mines and people can. Lately, however, many visitors to the DMZ come in search of another dying species. They're most likely to spot it from the Unification Observatory, where eight high-powered binoculars are stationed and trained on a desolate stretch of hills just north of the Military Demarcation Line.

The binoculars are so powerful that a viewer can see shimmering heat rising off a road that is invisible to the naked eye; and what at first appears to be a discarded oil drum turns out to be a bombed out locomotive. But the visitors don't seem interested in any of this. They're growing impatient, tempted to scan the horizon, even though an armed South Korean sergeant has warned them—implored them—not to move the binoculars.

Suddenly, someone spots movement in front of the ghost town called Propaganda Village. "I see one!" he gasps.

The sergeant begins to issue another warning, "Please don't move—" But it's too late. The other seven binoculars swing in unison, tracking the figure as it heads for the rice paddies.

Another tourist confirms the sighting. "It is!" And he selflessly surrenders the binoculars to his wife, saying, "Look, hon, it's a communist!"

I must confess here that I was not above the intrigue to

take a peek through the lenses and spy on the communist as well.

Outside the observatory, a young Korean soldier approaches me. He's just a kid, really, but with his gun, fatigues and helmet, he's an intimidating sight, particularly because I have just been aiming my camera at things that aren't supposed to be photographed. He has a strained look on his face, and with considerable effort, he manages to say, "How do you feel—" He clenches his jaw, then continues, "—about Korea?"

"Love it," I say.

He nods, then says, "How do you feel about—" With a slight, jerky motion, he gestures toward the tower.

"Informative," I reply. "Why do you ask?"

He bows his head and says, "My senior." He pauses for a furtive glance over his shoulder. "He is very angry."

"Angry? Why?"

In tortured English, he says something that I understand as, "Because I don't talk to the visitors as much as I should." He glances over his shoulder again. A sergeant is approaching. The young soldier flinches and says, "That is my senior."

I suddenly charade an amiable conversation, smiling, nodding, gesturing grandly and saying very little that makes any sense. The sergeant stops and takes note, then walks away. And in the helmet's shadow on the young soldier's face, ever so slightly, a smile alights.

Back on the bus, I hear a giddy confession whispered in the seat behind me: "I've never been on an adventure before." Now, reflecting on all the inaction and lengthy propaganda speeches heaped on us in the past hour, I'm inclined to think that this man wouldn't know adventure from a hole in the ground, which turns out to be an oddly coincidental thought, because the next attraction on the tour turns out to be just that: A hole in the ground. And the man's voice just gets giddier: "This is going to be great!"

The hole in the ground is a passage to The Third Tunnel of Aggression. Throughout the tour, the different guides gave us various estimations on how many tunnels the North Koreans dug under the DMZ. One said ten or more, another reported twenty-seven, while yet another seemed pretty sure that there were more than a hundred. So far, only four have been discovered, with the third being the most shocking because of its size and proximity to Seoul. With this tunnel, 30,000 North Korean soldiers could cross the DMZ undetected, then pop up from the ground like the living dead from their graves, less than twenty-eight miles from Seoul.

It's a disconcerting thought, at the least. But the South Koreans took tender care to hide all sense of the potential horror by cleverly disguising the entrance under yellow, green and pink pastel camouflage. It's safe to say that this hole—South Korea's pinnacle of anti-tunneling counter-intelligence—would be virtually invisible in an Easter parade.

Now exactly why hordes of tourists want to descend 240 feet into the soggy bowels of the DMZ and see the third tunnel remains a mystery. Nothing is down there but water, rock and a couple of armed guards. And the ascent to exit can be a serious challenge to the average tourist; occasionally tour guides have to call in the guards to carry someone out.

My reason for this spelunking expedition involves messages on the tunnel walls. I descend hoping to see these communiques that the North Korean workers left behind, these black smudges that read, "speedy accomplishment" and "secret." It's difficult to imagine the mentality of a worker burrowing through solid rock, suddenly struck by the urge to write memos to himself and his comrades. Did he feel that the work was going too slow? Did he think the others might forget that it was a secret? We can only gaze and ponder upon the inscriptions much in the way we would upon the cave drawings of a lost tribe of subterranean gnomes.

That is, we could, but the writing is in the fourth tunnel, not the third. Sorely disappointed, I return to the earth's surface and emerge, thankfully, into the relatively free world.

And so another tour ends. Once again, I have done all that I could to witness a part of history and the remains of a society that, for better or worse, may not be with us much longer. It's sad news for the endangered species that depend on a no-man's land for survival. Yet I can't shake the feeling that this hostile environment in the DMZ also creates an ideal climate for some political species that ought to be extinct.

Wishing Away the War

VIETNAM: 1995

I never intended to write anything about the Vietnam War. It just didn't feel like territory I should cover. No one I knew fought there or protested against it. What was I doing when Saigon fell? Probably fighting my own war with bottle rockets and pinecones. I was eight and oblivious. My impression of Vietnam came from an elementary school classmate, Trung Banh. It was simple then: Trung was cool, so his country must be cool, too. We should have been ambassadors.

For years, the idea of Vietnam as an era rather than a country was alien to me, and I often felt that those involved would have preferred to keep it that way, as though they didn't want my generation tampering with their nostalgia. But all the war movies and years of hearing the words Nam and war used interchangeably stole my initial impression.

Now I just wish I could go there and take it back.

My chance to do just that comes with an invitation from another Vietnamese friend and classmate. An Pham and I met at an seminar on international journalism at the University of North Carolina. We discovered a common interest in finding humor in everything, even the most boring of lectures. I soon learned of his other amazing talents. He could make a gourmet meal out of leftover hotdogs and coleslaw. He could throw a smashing soiree at a moment's notice. And he could play the accordion in a way that actually sounded pretty good.

Now working for the Ministry of Foreign Affairs in Saigon, An arranges and translates meetings between foreign journalists and local figures. He calls to tell me that he has ideas for interviews that have nothing to do with the war, and he's very enthusiastic about them. "I will introduce you to some models," he says. "I know all the top models and dancers in Ho Chi Minh City." I tell him that's not exactly what I have in mind for a story on Saigon. He says not to worry, that he has many ideas.

I arrive in Ho Chi Minh City on a cool June night, sometime after midnight. By nine a.m., An and I are on our way to meet Diep Minh Chau, an artist of whom I know nothing except that he once used his own blood to paint a large picture of Ho Chi Minh and three pioneers. We arrive at his gate, where five hairless dogs greet us. Chau walks up behind us.

He's seventy-six, but looks older. His thinning, shoulder-length hair is gray and white and yellowing with nicotine, and white strands curl out like antennae from his eyebrows. His eyes are brown encircled in pale blue and his fingernails look like yellow claws. He's a wiry, shuffling, moon-faced man with a gaping smile, delighted almost to the point of laughter to receive guests. Nearly fifty years have passed since he painted that picture in blood, and the first thing he does is show us the scars on his arm.

He opens the white metal gate, being careful not to turn the dogs loose. They escape anyway, all five hairless ones and three others, and run amuck in the traffic; then, noticing the gate is about to close them out, they bolt back in.

Inside, the yard is dense with palms and jackfruit trees. A fountain near the fence seems as if it hasn't worked for years. It's surrounded by marble figures, including a smooth, milky bust of Ho Chi Minh. Chau says it's his favorite. Dozens more rain-stained statues stand around the yard and on the front porch—dwarf-size heroes on wooden crates and twelve-foot statesmen bound in blue tarp. And there are at least fifty more on the first floor of his home.

Chau leads us around the side of the house, but finds the door locked. He rings the doorbell impatiently, then reaches through a broken pane of glass and fumbles with the lock inside. At that moment, I notice something red falling out of a window on the second floor. A water balloon. It lands with a slap at the far end of the driveway, where the dogs are busy sniffing. It doesn't break, only rolls around, and the dogs go mad trying to figure out what it is. I look up at the window, see no one, then to An and Chau, who seem not to notice.

I follow them up a dark, cobwebbed staircase, through a bedroom and into the kitchen. From the outside, the house looked like a mansion, but from within, despite the tall ceilings, it feels crowded, stuffed with ragged books, amber-tone photos and overflowing wastebaskets. All of the wooden shutters remain latched, but a steady breeze and the noise of the traffic push through the slats.

We sit around the kitchen table. A servant brings us lotus tea and cashew cookies. Chau distributes cigarettes, 555, a brand made in Singapore, and insists we smoke and eat cookies.

An explains to him that though he's brought journalists here before, this is the first time he's brought a friend. It strikes me as the sort of ceremonial line that he's so fond of saying. Chau responds graciously and offers me another cookie. He then shows me a photo of Ho Chi Minh posing next to his portrait in blood.

"He was the only one I believed could lead the country," Chau says, according to An's translation. "I have good instincts. I knew I would meet him one day." He also shows us an English translation of the letter he sent with the picture. It's addressed to "My Old Father Ho Chi Minh." In it he wrote, "The Autumn Revolution under your leadership set free my art . . . After listening to your 'Proclamation of Independence' . . . I felt extremely moved and busting [sic] into sobs, I cut myself to draw blood from my youthful arm in order to paint your picture . . . All my body, my life belonged to you." He signed it, "Yours respectfully, Zone 8, on September 2, 1947."

This fan letter and painting, I gather, seemed to appeal greatly to Ho Chi Minh's ego. He immediately called for Chau to join him in his jungle hideaway in North Vietnam, where the fighting was the heaviest, but failed to provide any transportation. Consequently, Chau walked for eight months, carrying the supplies required for both an artist and a soldier.

According to Chau, artists on the battleground were common. "We would bring all the paints and canvases to the front line," he says. "But almost half of us were killed." He lights a cigarette, though one is still burning in the ashtray, and adds a word that doesn't need translating: "Bombs."

The idea of artists and their canvases out there getting blown away would strike me as absurdly humorous if it didn't really happen. I ask if he ever expected that being an artist would be so rigorous. He straightens up in his chair and replies: "Independence is greater than any art. You should use your art for that cause instead of using that cause for your art."

He slips into this sort of rhetoric suddenly, often and at great length throughout our conversation. It seems to strike him like a fleeting mood or a flashback, often making it difficult, sometimes impossible, to get a straight answer from him.

I follow one such response with a moment of silence, then a tactful change of subject: "So, um, what was it like living with Uncle Ho?"

His face brightens. "We lived as father and son. Living in the jungle, we were like one big family." As if on cue, his wife appears from the bedroom with a stack of photos. She shows me one of Uncle Ho with his dog, though the front half of the dog is cropped out of the picture. "He loved that dog," Chau says, tapping the photo. "Its mother would stay outside Uncle Ho's cave to protect him, but one night it was eaten by a tiger."

He takes the stack of photos and, while his wife retreats for more, pulls out one of Uncle Ho eating lunch. His voice grows louder, more excited. He talks at me as though he can't wait for An to translate. "Look! You can see his sandals!" And he handles the photos as though they are playing cards, dealing one after another. "Here is a house we built for him." He points out a thatched hut that's slightly larger that a two-car garage. Then he clears a space on the table to map out the jungle, using a fruit bowl for a valley and packs of cigarettes for the hut and cave.

"Were you comfortable living in the jungle?" I ask.

"Uncle Ho always had his own way of making you feel comfortable, without stress and at ease." He sips his tea and smiles. "When the planes were bombing, he just walked out of the cave to see what they were doing."

Chau's wife, whose name is never mentioned, rejoins us, placing four warm cans of 333 beer and four glasses of ice on the table. She sits next to Chau and begins pulling off the fliptops. It isn't yet eleven a.m. I ask her, "Where were you while your husband was running around in the jungle?"

Chau answers for her. "We were married in the jungle. Originally, she was high society, a relation with the royal family, French educated. But for the cause of the revolution, she went to the jungle. She had her first baby in the jungle. The mosquitoes were so thick there I could catch a handful in one swipe." He grabs the air in front of him. "And we could not find a doctor or a nurse, so the baby had to wait from seven p.m. until four a.m. to cut the cord. And then at six a.m., I just kissed my wife and the child because I had to leave for Hanoi. I just looked at my daughter and saw she had a high nose like her mother. I said, 'Well, I feel satisfied I will not have to pay.'"

"In those days," An explains to me, "the father had to pay some money to the groom's family if his daughter was not attractive. A high nose, like hers and yours, is attractive. A flat nose, like his and mine, is not."

The conversation revolves around marriage until the beer runs out. At one point, Chau says, "One day I asked Uncle Ho why he didn't get married. He said to me, 'You know, I also have a need to get married. But with the revolution, you never know when you will be put in jail. You volunteered for the revolution, but why make a woman suffer with you?'"

"Didn't he have a girlfriend or anything?" I ask.

His hesitancy to recollect makes me doubt the answer that follows: "No. No girlfriends. He just devoted himself to the cause of independence." He stuffs a cookie in his mouth and follows it with a cigarette.

I press on about Uncle Ho. "Was he always so serious? Didn't he have any sense of humor?"

With that, Chau breaks into shaking laughter and proclaims: "He's the king of jokes! Once when we were crossing a river, some people asked him, 'Now that you are in your sixties, how do you feel?' Uncle Ho answered, 'The part over the water feels sixty.'" Chau indicates the depth of the water by running the edge of his hand along his beltline. "'But the part below the water is just twenty.'"

Gradually, as he shuffles though the stack of photos, his laughter subsides. He stops at a photo that shows himself crying while carving out an image of Ho Chi Minh just after the Old Father passed away. He tucks the photo back in the stack and returns to the one of the portrait in blood. "My only regret is burning down the huts we built. They were historic structures, but we could not leave a trace of where we were. Ho Chi Minh always told us to plant a mandarin tree in their place. He said, 'In case others pass by here, they may need something to eat.'"

"But it seems the only ones to pass by would've been the enemies who were looking for him," I say. He laughs softly, enigmatically.

A cat saunters into the kitchen and leans against Chau's leg. We've been talking for four hours when he says, "I have so many stories to tell you. You must stay with me for at least three days."

I decline, reminding him that he's too busy with his work for the twentieth anniversary celebrations. He recently completed an eight-meter, 180-ton granite bust of Ho Chi Minh, but has plenty more to accomplish. Still, he extends his invitation.

An finally insists that we must leave him to his work, and his wife seems to agree. I have just one last question. "How do you feel about art in Vietnam today?" His reply sounds as if he memorized it long ago: "Formal training for artists in Vietnam is only seventy years old. Before that was only folk art. During the thirty years of war, we artists were also soldiers. Only during the last twenty years have we had time to learn our own art. As chairman of the Ho Chi Minh City Art Association, I try to help artists in their search for something good . . . . Right now, artists are free to follow any trend in the world. I just wish that they would create something of their own."

I ask him for the names of any artists who he thinks show promise. He can't (or won't) name one. He simply suggests that I check out the galleries for myself.

I do. And I find forgeries, mostly, of Dali, da Vinci, Picasso and van Gogh. There are walls full of 1970s-ish nudes and political caricatures, and piles of black-ink village scenes on silk that sell for a dollar each—American currency accepted, if not preferred.

It makes me wonder who won the war.

I believe An senses my disappointment with Saigon's art scene, but I'm not sure if he understands it. I'd always assumed he had great taste in fine art if only because we always found ourselves in agreement when we visited galleries in North Carolina. But then, we visited only the galleries that featured my work. I suppose now it was presumptuous of me to credit him with such exquisite taste in art.

He suggests we visit a different sort of museum: The War Remnants Museum, formally known as the Museum of American War Crimes. The title has been changed so as not to offend Western tourists. Its contents, however, have not. On display are an assortment of bombs, instruments of torture, a guillotine, and, in the Agent Orange room, pickled babies that are deformed beyond comprehension.

It also houses a collection of photos and illustrations depicting the grisliest forms of torture, carnage, mutilation and degradation that the human mind is capable of generating. But the worst of it is not so much the photos of severed heads and shredded corpses, but the GIs who were holding these things with such glee that they just as well could've been holding up rainbow trout.

I pass through room after room, holding my head low. I notice many other foreigners slinking though in the same way, speaking in hushed voices, if at all. The few people who speak at normal levels seem obscenely loud. They're the only ones who laugh, play with the torture devices execution and actually seem to be enjoying themselves. They're Vietnamese tourists.

With two rooms left to explore, I leave the main building and duck into a souvenir shop. The merchandise there is also somewhat unsettling: American GI dogtags, GI watches, compasses and toys made from spent ammunition. An explains that the Americans left warehouses of this junk behind. I wonder who would want to own a piece of such history.

Stranger yet, the most impressive feature in this museum of modern horror is a puppet show. Known as *roi nuoc*, the uniquely Vietnamese art performance traditionally takes place in a pool of green water. An points out the small blue theater between an American tank and the prison cages, and says, "Let's go. You'll feel better." I suggest we postpone it, but he insists.

After the show, and still shaken by the museum, I ride on the back of his motorcycle to a courtyard restaurant. Despite my lack of appetite, I eat just about everything put in front of me. "This is incredible," I say of a particular dish I've been hogging. "What is it?"

"Bo Tai Chanh," he says, smiling. "It means 'raw beef and lemon.'" He explains how it's prepared: "You must squeeze it," and he looks as if he's trying to wring out an invisible towel.

"Hate to change the subject like this," I say, "but who am I going to meet next?"

"You want to meet the models?" he asks hopefully.

"Actually, I was hoping to talk with some political prisoners." The smile drops from his face. "Oh no. I cannot do that."

"Gangsters, then. You have any gangs in Ho Chi Minh City?"

"Of course, but I cannot. Think of my reputation!"

"Well, as long as I've started writing about the war, how about taking me to a veterans hospital?"

Now his expression has gone beyond disappointment. In fact, it's the closest I've ever seen him to being angry. "You must remember, I work for the government now." He lowers his voice. "Talking about such things will put me at risk."

"No one here will know. It's not like I'm writing for *Newsweek*."

"Doesn't matter. They will find out. They will read it."

"I won't use your name."

"They will know."

I suspect he's being just a little paranoid, but decide not to push the issue. Instead I settle for a fortune teller whom he trusts well. She lives in China Town, down a dark, narrow alley, in a street-level apartment that's almost entirely caged in chain-link fencing. The government doesn't yet approve of her business, An explains as he hurries me inside.

The fortune teller spends hours telling me about my past, present and future, but the only remarkable thing she tells me is that I must leave Asia before November or else I will be in a serious accident. I tell her I can't leave earlier than December. She stares dead at me and tells me to go back to Africa. I'm reminded of a witch doctor in Tanzania who predicted that I would see him again within two years. That was fifteen months ago. In time, both predictions would turn out wrong, but I still wonder how she knew I'd been to Africa in the first place.

Later that day, we cover half of Saigon on his motorcycle. He takes me to temples and massage parlors, noodle shops and chicken markets. Another market offers baskets full of chicken feet, dried lizards, CD players, bowls of eels, U.S. Government issue flak jackets, computer software, cobra wine (with the cobra still in the bottle), and a wider assortment of personal hygiene products than I've seen anywhere in Asia. He takes me to his favorite hang-outs, his high school and the hospital where he was born.

However, he doesn't seem interested in talking about his childhood during the war, or the countries he lived in after the liberation of Saigon. Instead, he always talks about the future. He's got plans. Big plans. A new, wealthy generation is growing here, and they're looking for new ways to spend their money. An has it all figured out.

"Chippendales!" he declares. "Real cheesecakes!"

"You mean beefcakes."

"Yes! Male strippers! Only we do it like a fashion show so I can get a license. We'll put on a big show, a traveling water show. On a boat."

"A showboat?" I offer.

"Yes! And we will take it down the Saigon River to all the new developments. They have nothing to do down there. They will love us! We'll have pachinko parlors and a big fountain with girls dancing in it."

"What about the talk show?" I ask. He told me this idea years ago when he lived in the States and got hooked on Donahue, but now he seems to forget. "Remember? Where you're the host and nobody gets to see your face?"

"Oh, that," he says, waving the idea away with the back of his hand. "No, that comes later. Vietnam is not ready for that now."

I never took his ideas seriously back in the States. I'm not sure if I do now. But his friends—all highly educated, well traveled professors and government workers—they seem to share similar ideas. Sure, they laugh at An's fantastical elaboration, but their objections are only half-hearted.

Five of us talk it over for hours one night in the Paloma, an upscale bar in a trendy district. The conversation is mainly in English, but a good deal of French, Russian and Vietnamese gets worked in. An has always had a knack for surrounding himself with an international coterie. Hindi, German and Japanese were primary languages at his parties back in Chapel Hill. Sometimes it made me wonder why he always invited me. I'm reminded of that feeling in the Paloma.

He loves this place and is friends with all the employees. "The singers here are fantastic," he assures me. "One was educated in the best music conservatory in Bucharest." He names it, but it quickly slips my mind as the band begins to play. They sound exactly like the BeeGees. It's *Saturday Night Fever* in Saigon.

"I will have them play on my showboat," he promises. His ideas seem more plausible as his friends list new industries that make other Asians so wealthy. Five-story video game arcades that cater to Japanese executives. Wedding halls in Korea that churn out newlyweds every fifteen minutes, and dog hotels with rates that exceed those for humans. I think of all the theme parks in Seoul alone: Adventure World, Funny World, Seoul Land, Farm Land, Fantasy Land, Dream Land, not to mention the Vegas-style casinos and nightclubs based on ancient Egypt and other enticing locations. An is beginning to make perfect sense, and it depresses the hell out of me. If he and his friends had a choice, I imagine they'd turn Saigon into a tawdry Broadway musical. Sure, to them it's new life rising from nations that wars left for dead. To me, selfish as it sounds, it's the death of cultures, of travel, of my best reasons to live.

"Look around you," An says with a sweeping gesture. The place is packed, upstairs and down. Expensive drinks and bowls of ice cream cover every table. "These people have money. They want to have fun. They are too young to remember the war, and they live like foreigners." One woman, not older than twenty, cradles a life-size baby doll with curly blonde hair. Everyone at her table is groping for it. An smiles deliberately and says, "We call them 'domestic expatriates.'"

I force myself to smile back, while desperately thinking of a polite way to tell him that this is the last thing I want to see. And that's odd, because if anything in Vietnam has nothing to do with the war, the domestic expatriates are it. But the way they put the war behind them reminds me of the galleries: A crass display of imitation Westernism. Then again, what was I expecting? Besides those idyllic memories of an elementary school classmate named Trung Banh, I'm really not sure what I'm looking for.

I just know it's not here.

My search north of Saigon proves to be equally fruitless. Fifteen minutes in Nha Trang and already I can see it's overrun by European and Australian tourists. On the beach, they're greeted by locals offering fresh fruit, massages and a special leg-flossing treatment for the ladies. Pieces of styrofoam and blue china wash up on the shore. I pick up a piece of china and show it to a fisherman. He laughs, regarding it no differently than styrofoam.

Small restaurants and hotels clutter the main strip, and high-rise hotels are underway. In the bars and cafés, the music of choice is Air Supply, BeeGees, Nirvana and, to a lesser extent, an assortment of Vietnam-era rock 'n' roll. A beachfront amusement park offers three rides: two sets of kiddy jet-fighters and a rickety Ferris wheel. Ten cents is enough to get me a dozen shots from a cork gun at the shooting gallery. The prize is any pack of cigarettes I can knock off the shelf. It's not easy because every time the Ferris wheel turns, the lights dim. The kiddy planes slow down, too.

I take a cyclo (bicycle rickshaw) through town to visit the local taxidermy shop. Exotic mammals I've never seen before crowd the walls, their faces frozen in ferocious expressions. A dozen or so live sea turtles flap about, belly up on the floor. Monkeys hunch in chicken-wire cages that look like crab pots.

One is chewing its ankle to the bone. I pull a camera out of my bag and immediately two shopkeepers shove me out the door. Behind them, three women are kicking the turtles under a dead-mammal display.

I take the cyclo to a Buddhist temple to decide where to go next. My compulsion to keep moving is getting stronger. It's a frustrating feeling, like insomnia, or like that panicked feeling you get when the library is about to close and you don't even know what kind of book you're looking for.

I climb aboard the first bus leaving from The Short-Haul Bus Station. It's about half the size of a school bus and its wooden benches are packed beyond capacity. Still, they have room for me to sit on the engine case between the driver and a few other passengers. It rattles out of town and over the mountains. Sparks and gas fumes punch through the cracks in the casing. Then it roars along the coastline, through villages and finally over miles of flat, fresh tarmac surrounded by rice paddies. Just as I'm certain I've reached the middle of nowhere, the bus stops and the driver tells me to get off.

According to my guidebook, Ba Ho—"three waterfalls in a forest"—is just a half mile away. I wonder how that could be possible, considering there isn't a tree in sight. I begin walking down a buffalo track. The first people I encounter are three children and their mother squatting at the edge of a cemetery. The children throw berries and seeds at me. And when they run out of those, they throw small rocks. I wonder how long it's been since the last American was here.

I pick up my pace and overtake a buffalo cart at the edge of Phu Huu village. I've already covered two miles by then, I'm sure. The sun's glare presses on me, dragging me down. A casuarina grove in the village provides some relief, but I feel certain that I won't make it back to the road unless I spend a few minutes standing under the waterfall.

I slow down to see how the folks in Phu Huu spend their Thursday afternoons. Music pours out of one building. It looks like a country church with open walls and wooden planks for pews. It's packed full of men, but only one is singing. He holds a microphone and stares up at a monitor, bleating out some karaoke tune that I don't recognize. I cross a wooden bridge and peer through dark open doorways. In one house, I see a pack of boys squatting on the floor and playing what looks like a Nintendo game on a 28-inch color television. In another, the exact same scene. More Nintendo. In a third, a teenage girl sits behind a large black Singer sewing machine that must pre-date the war.

I doubt there are more than twenty homes in Phu Huu, and within five minutes of entering it I'm on my way out. At the far edge, a man on a motorbike pulls up beside me and, through with gestures, offers a ride. After a moment's consideration—of the sun, of how steep the path is becoming—I hop on his bike and hold on tight. We speed past angry dogs and a deserted checkpoint. The path becomes not only steeper, but more narrow, and rugged as if forged by rain rather than men.

Finally, the path is too narrow to take the bike any further. We dismount and I follow him up a footpath. Skinks in shades of phosphorescent green scatter as he hacks back the branches. The footpath ends at the bottom of a stony ravine, where a trickle of black water seeps down through massive boulders.

I wonder if this is the place or if a drought has stolen the falls. The latter hardly seems possible since the monsoons have been fairly regular throughout the past week. But judging by the surrounding refuse, this has been a popular destination with Vietnamese tourists. They've left behind sardine tins, 333 beer cans, 555 cigarette packs, lighters, plastic bags and a black leather business shoe. I wonder who could possibly walk this far in a pair of business shoes, and then back in only one.

Back in Saigon, An invites me and four other friends to his home for lunch. The house is surrounded by lush gardens. Cages of exotic birds hang over the patio. Their songs drift through the wrought-iron windows and into the living room. Inside, an alter for his recently-departed grandmother dominates one wall. Overstuffed bookcases cover every other wall, floor to ceiling. The books in the bottom left corners are ragged and yellowing, while the top right corners hold recent, glossy hardcover editions, and in between are books of at least four different languages. His father sits by a window, casually reading a book the size of a toaster. He pauses long enough to say, "It's about the civil war."

"What civil war?" I ask.

He laughs. "Yours, of course."

I start to ask him about working for *Time* magazine's Saigon bureau during the Vietnam War, but he's too deep into the book.

An can see I'm worn out from my trip. The room isn't hot, but my sunburn makes me sweat. He tells me to take a shower and rest in his room, where the air-con is on full blast. Later, as I'm stretched out on his bed and watching satellite television, he brings me a bottle of mineral water and apologizes for not inviting me to stay longer.

"As you can see," he explains, choosing his words carefully, "it is not very accommodating."

"To the contrary," I say, "it's a lovely home."

"Yes, well, anyway . . ." He lowers his voice. "It is not allowed. A foreigner. Staying here. The government won't—"

Someone calls from downstairs. Lunch is being served.

Years later I would learn that An's father was more than a *Time* correspondent. He was also a lieutenant and a spy for the Viet Cong. Despite his years of flawless service, the Vietnamese government figured his fraternization with Western journalists must have resulted in ideological contamination. And though he'd since served his time in reeducation camps, they still regarded him with certain suspicion.

An has one last surprise for my final hours in Saigon: Tickets to the Independence Day celebration.

"But I thought you celebrated that on April thirtieth," I say. He shows me a ticket. It's for our Independence Day, the Fourth of July. Curiously enough, it was scheduled to take place in Reunification Palace, where we officially lost the war. An says that the government made last-minute changes and barred the celebration from the palace. Now it's set for the Binh Quoi Tourist Village Number Two.

I suspect that he paid a good bit of money for the tickets, and that maybe they weren't easy to get. After all, it is the first American Independence celebration in Saigon in more than twenty years. However, I just can't seem to match his enthusiasm for the event. "I'm sorry," I tell him. "I just can't. I didn't come all this way to—"

He nods, understanding. His lunch guests seem to agree.

That evening the six of us take a three-hour cruise up and down the Saigon River. The boat is about twice the size of a canoe, and it's powered by what looks like a weed-eater. A woman steers from the stern. Several times throughout our tour, she must cut the engine to untangle plastic bags from the propeller. Considering the volume of the engine, I wonder if she and her toddler son are suffering from tinnitus. An assures me that they're going quite deaf.

We rattle down to the developments where An so desperately wants to entertain. On our way back, darkness settles in. Bats dart overhead and skim over the water. To keep other boats from crashing into us, our driver lights a kerosene lantern made from a tin can. From the bow, I can barely see its flame.

One of An's guests, a Ph.D. candidate with an annoying American accent, points out a restaurant boat in the shape of a whale. It's lit like Christmas and has large, jagged teeth. She's says that's where she caught the boat when Saigon fell. She was fourteen then, and without a clue as to where she was going. "No one knew," she says.

I ask her how big the boat was. "Oh, about the size of a yacht." She says *yacht* so it rhymes with *cat*. "It got us to Guam."

"Were you scared?"

She gives me this *Are you serious?* look, then answers, "Scared as hell."

The other Vietnamese revive the discussion of showboats. I turn away to gaze at the reflections in the river. On the far bank, electric billboards advertise foreign computers, cameras and fax machines. Bamboo and scrapwood houses on stilts crowd each other in the perpetual glow. I wonder if the people there even know what's written in the lights just above their heads. Or if they look up at them as giant stars to wish upon.

In memory of Diep Minh Chau, 1919-2002

In the Eyes of a Stranger

INDIA: 1992

Delhi

She said I had the most amazing eyes she had ever seen. In a slinky black dress, she threaded the party crowd and stopped me at the top of the spiral staircase in a marble mansion on Prithviraj Road to tell me about my eyes. She had to tell me twice because Prince was blaring on the stereo. I had just arrived in this country and was not yet familiar with the local customs. I'd been told that lying flat on the floor and offering a 'severe apology' (*kamaghani*) is a formal greeting elsewhere in India, so I accepted her comment about my eyes as a sort of general greeting—the Delhi version of 'have a nice day.'

But then she kissed me. A dizzying kiss. I thought I felt the spiral staircase turning like a corkscrew and wondered if I should have taken the elevator instead. I stepped back and bumped into a servant. He turned and offered what looked and smelled like chicken McNuggets. We both refused and the servant disappeared. That was when I wanted to ask her, "Am I in the right country?"

It didn't seem like the same country that I had arrived in the day before where, at three a.m., I found a driver waiting for me at the Indira Gandhi Airport. He spoke no English, so he resorted to jerky charades that failed to give me the slightest clue as to where he was taking me. He drove for over an hour, past slums and people sleeping on sidewalks. The streets narrowed down to a maze of lanes and the buildings were looking shabbier as morning crept closer.

Just as I began to fear that this was where I would be spending the next two months, the car stopped. I was shown to a yellow, dusty cell with scarlet curtains, unfinished furniture, and nothing on the walls but a few lizards and a poster of a blue-eyed blonde little girl with hands pressed together in prayer, Christian style. Air conditioning, TV, screens, locks and toilet paper—I noticed the absence of these things in the first thirty seconds.

Not that I was expecting them. I didn't really know what to expect from India. In school, my studies of India were limited to exactly one chapter in a social studies textbook. That was back 1978, when I was eleven. It was also about the time my father went to India. He came back full of horror stories about how people just dropped dead in the streets, killed by heat, starvation, disease or any combination thereof; about how trucks—like garbage trucks—would come around every morning before dawn to collect the corpses; and about how stupid American hippies would walk around barefoot until their intestines turned into sacks of worms.

I knew India had pulled itself out of drop-dead poverty, but wasn't really expecting the dazzling display of wealth and affection that I found in the marble mansion. It didn't seem real, and for a while I felt out of place. Not because I was the only white boy there, but because everyone else was trying so hard to mimic the West and failing spectacularly.

They told me about their piano bars, places where an Indian pianist sings stale American songs in his best American accent; and about the jazz bar, saying 'jazz bar' so it rhymed with 'casbah'. They used American slang excessively and incorrectly, combined with Hindi verbs that ended in '-ing'. And they wore expensive clothes that exaggerated recently fashionable Western styles to the point of silliness. Not that I looked any better in my kurta pajamas. Wearing traditional Indian garb to the party was Ankur's idea. I took his advice because I was his guest; but judging by the looks I got, I could've just as well been wearing lederhosen.

Ankur was hefty, over-privileged, college-bound brat, but I depended on his guidance during my initiation to India. He was particularly helpful in things like grabbing the steering wheel when I drove on the wrong side of the road. What's more, he was my boss's son.

My boss, Dr. Jain, though rotund like his son, was infinitely more intelligent. He was once one of India's most respected surgeons, but had since switched to national politics and was now a Member of Parliament—an accomplishment best appreciated in light of the fact that India, as the home to the world's largest democracy, hosts the world's most competitive elections.

A tireless champion of the Bharatiya Janata Party, Dr. Jain fueled a brand of Hindu nationalism that frequently operated in opposition to other religious groups, and his voice was growing louder as he worked toward becoming India's premier media mogul.

He'd recently founded Jain Studios, a state-of-the art production outfit that created health-training videos, TV programs, and not least of all, campaign messages. He also owned one of India's few twenty-four hour entertainment channels, Jain TV, and had plans to launch the Jain Satellite to beam out more programming.

However, one of his most innovative media projects was Video On Wheels: a fleet of fifty trucks, each equipped with rear-projection equipment and a hundred-inch screen. Stationed in eight major cities throughout India, the trucks ran regular route cycles to deliver programming to rural villages. And because these villages often lacked TV and cinema, he essentially monopolized visual media for an estimated 800 million viewers.

He referred to his trucks as video *raths*, a term otherwise reserved for portable temples and ornate vehicles used in religious festivals. And his ominous slogan to entice sponsorship was: "Make your presence felt at every doorstep of the nation."

Fascinated with this mobile cinema, I sought a summer job with Video On Wheels. Doubtful of my truck-driving skills, Dr. Jain instead hired me on at his magazine, *Surya*, where I quickly pitched this idea to the editor: Put me on the next outbound truck, and I'll bring back a story.

My editor liked the idea, especially since the next outbound truck was heading into Uttar Pradesh, India's poorest and most populated state, and one abounding in historical significance. Over 2000 years ago, it held the center of Ashoka's Buddhist Empire. In the sixteenth and seventeenth centuries, it contained the capital of the Mogul Empire. More recently, it hosted some of the most violent uprisings against the British Empire. And following India's independence in 1947, Uttar Pradesh produced its fair share of politicians, including five out of six of the last Prime Ministers, as well as Dr. Jain himself.

Uttar Pradesh, with its many sacred sites for both Hindus and Muslims, is also India's own Holy Land. This religious mix, combined with the aforementioned poverty, overpopulation and political ambition, amounted to a volatile environment. Or as my editor put it, U.P. offered endless opportunities for interesting stories.

I immediately geared up to leave on a thirteen-day route cycle, but there were the typical Indian delays, waiting for paint to dry and so on—the kind of stalling that makes Westerners marvel at the elasticity of Indian patience. It stretches further than Indian rubber. As I waited for the day of departure and word got around that I was planning to travel Uttar Pradesh by truck, my coworkers grew concerned. They said that I wouldn't last three days out there, that I would just drop dead in the street, killed by the heat and/or disease. I asked them how the crew manages to survive. The answer was always the same: "They're Indian."

On the road, my first and most persistent challenge was the *dhaba*, a kind of multipurpose truck stop. The first one seemed welcoming enough, even quaint with its thatched roof and brightly tiled countertops. And the food smelled delicious. I just couldn't identify anything in it. It looked like a mix of mustard and syrup, or just plain mud. It attracted a lot of flies.

On one bench the flies were thick as fur, giving the illusion of one long, shivering, headless quadruped. Feral dogs and a water buffalo roamed about, scavenging for scraps. Rats darted across the dirt floor of the open-air kitchen. The waiter was a polio victim, and he served us water from a can that previously held engine coolant. He didn't understand why I refused to drink it; I didn't want to tell him that his water was unclean, that it wasn't even fit for washing my hands. I felt that by telling him this, I would be treating him like an untouchable. It was a feeling of guilt I was forced to endure any time someone offered me anything that seemed unclean—cut fruit, uncooked vegetables and sweets that had been exposed to flies for the greater part of the day.

The dhaba challenge wasn't limited to food. I couldn't bring myself to bathe at any of them because something about six men crowding under a roadside water pump didn't strike me as particularly cleansing. I declined on a chance to bathe in the Ganges for the same reason. The water may be holy, but it smelled like hell. I had been looking forward to the experience, but I changed my mind when I saw something floating down the river. It was fleshy and swollen, like the belly of a pig or the bloated back of a drowned woman. I saw two of these things.

The irony of refusing to bathe in order to stay clean ceased to amuse the crew after two days. I was more than dirty. I was becoming one with the relentless grime of India—the smog, dust and dirt that hangs in the air all day and all night, creeping over and inside everything. The stench that comes from five men crammed for days in a cab built to seat three, with temperatures in the low hundreds, with *bidis* and incense burning constantly, and with unchecked exhaust and diesel fumes—this stench was sinking into my skin. I could feel it.

My senses were being bombarded by the dirtiness surrounding me: Garbage blowing into the fields; animals defecating in the middle of the road, people by the roadside; mounds of rubbish that would never be collected, leaving me to wonder why anyone had bothered to sweep it together in the first place; pools of stagnant water and open sewers that were clogged; and the eternal flame of burning trash. Earth, wind, fire and water—the Elements of the Universe were entirely polluted. I wanted the monsoons to come and wash it all away, but I knew the rain would just carry it all into larger bodies of water—water used for washing and drinking.

Lucknow

With speeds averaging twenty miles per hour, we rambled on toward Lucknow, about 350 miles southeast of Delhi. On the road, I spoke to only one crew member: Rajinder. I called him Raj. He told me that he was the only crew member who could speak English. He said he wanted to show me around Lucknow because he knew the city well. I was glad he said so because there was a lot I wanted to see, like the labyrinth in the Great Imambara, an Islamic architectural wonder said to rival the Taj Mahal, and the Martiniere School, where Kim (Kipling's young hero) studied. I especially wanted to see a Muharram celebration, where Shi'ite Muslims flog themselves in repentant jubilation.

But when we got to Lucknow, Raj said it was too hot to go sightseeing. I told him that it wasn't so hot, that hot is when you park your bike on the road and either the kickstand sinks into the asphalt or the tires explode. He wasn't convinced. And he and the crew wanted to sleep, which is what they did all day, while I watched bored vultures hanging out in a dead tree.

It amazed me how easily Indians can sleep. I've seen them sleeping on bicycles with their feet propped up on the handle bars, on the backs of water buffaloes, on pineapple carts, on the roofs of buses and moving trains. They sleep en masse, like team sleeping, littered along the roadside as if they just drop dead in their tracks. (I wondered if this is what my father had seen.)

I am floored by the idea that anyone can find comfort on a *khatia*, a common contraption that evolved elsewhere into the cot. The kahtia, however, is more like a hammock strung up by sadists, a string bed of abrasive twine stretched taught between wooden planks. What's worse is sleeping on one at a dhaba, where all through the night Tata trucks would roar by blowing their horns—some warbling like air-raid sirens, others just a long steady blast loud enough to blow down the walls of Jericho. There would always be a driver who spent the night repairing his truck, his only tool being a hammer. And in the morning I would wake up under a blanket of flies, with ten Indians and a sacred cow just staring at me as though I'd escaped from a zoo. Then I would wonder if I had slept at all.

So it was strange that I couldn't sleep during the day like the others did. And after a few hours of staring at vultures, while the others were still asleep, I decided to roam around Lucknow on my own. While here we were fortunate enough to have a place to stay, though it was more like camping. We were in an unfurnished house with no water in an otherwise affluent suburb, a few miles from the center of town. The other houses were boxy and freshly painted in bright blocks of Caribbean colors like pink, aqua-green, lemon, and lavender—sometimes all at once. Many had two cars in the driveway. Families of hogs trotted by, scurrying from puddle to puddle. Down the road, in front of a row of stores, a sinewy man with a hollow face seemed to be wrestling a motor scooter. He was actually trying to pick it up and place it in a bicycle-rickshaw, while three perfectly healthy police officers watched. A store owner explained to me that the scooter was in a no-parking zone, and was being taking to the police station. Not much later I crossed into the slums, where the sight of skeletal old men and a boy bloated with malnutrition made me want to return to the suburbs.

Once Raj decided he'd slept enough, he took me to a main road, where we caught a bicycle-rickshaw to the Residency. Three thousand British and Indian loyalists took refuge here when the 1857 Mutiny began. Two thousand perished in the ensuing three-month siege, and all that remains now is a park full of bombed-out buildings, some gardens, and various memorials proclaiming the bravado of those who tried but failed to hold down the fort—all very sentimental in the militaristic sense.

Raj said it was the only place in Lucknow worth seeing. He apparently had strong sentiments for these battle-scarred structures. I asked him what made this place better than the others, if he was saddened by the tragic massacre of the British and Indian inhabitants, or if he was moved by the besiegers' determination in their fight for independence. He said, "It is a good place to make a date. In fact, I brought my girlfriend here on our first date." And he sighed longingly, staring vacantly at the graves of 2000 men, women and children.

That night, shortly after showing me the Residency, Raj decided to return to Delhi—with most of the crew's travel expense money—where he had already decided to take up a job offer with a different company. Of course, he didn't tell anyone about this before he left; it was something I learned when I finally got back to Delhi. By then, rumor had it that Dr. Jain's assistants had hunted down his brother, who volunteered Raj's new address. (Another version of the rumor maintained that the assistants held a revolver to the brother's head when he volunteered this information.) Raj was found the next day, and he promptly returned the money. No charges were filed, thanks to the benevolence of Dr. Jain. (The other rumor maintained that the assistants beat Raj senseless, though it's not clear if they did so before or after he returned the money.)

Meanwhile in Uttar Pradesh, oblivious to the forays of Raj, I continued to tour the villages with the crew in the truck. The roads were getting worse. Earlier in the trip I had been concerned with only the number of dead animals in the road, and the vultures that were killed while picking over them. The vultures got flattened on the pavement. Their wings never stuck, but flapped in the breeze, as if still trying to fly away. I had been counting the dead animals and lost track at twenty-two when, just ten miles outside of Delhi, a car in front of us clipped a hound and sent it spinning and howling like a warped record on the wrong speed. The crew found this very amusing, reenacting the dog's trajectory with quick, circular hand gestures and laughing like mad.

But deeper into Uttar Pradesh, the number of accidents began to overwhelm me. Many resulted from high speeds on the wrong side of the road, drivers who ignored the yellow signs that clearly stated: NO AGGRESSIVE OVERTAKING. Other accidents involved buses and tractors. We came across a solitary tractor that had flipped over in the middle of the road. Nothing else was near it. I still can't figure out how someone had managed to flip a tractor on perfectly flat pavement.

Most accidents, however, involved the Tata trucks—those bright orange beasts that are decorated like temples and driven like hell. So many overturned because they had been overstuffed, and their contents spilled across the road, causing other vehicles to crash. The cabs of the trucks were almost always torn open, the axles split, and windows shattered. A crew member, Bijenda, who decided he actually could speak some English after Raj left, told me that the drivers were always killed because of the position of the steering wheel. Since his English was limited, he relied on gestures to explain how the wheel crushed everything inside the chest cavity without actually breaking the skin.

Ronahi

Roadside scenery changed little in Uttar Pradesh. Miles and miles of flat, dry fields with identical villages at the end of each stretch. I thought it strange that they were called villages; they seemed more like urban pockets—too compact to be called a town, too small to be called a city, even though they possessed all the grime, smoke, noise and traffic congestion of a large city. They were like slices of middle-class Delhi, but in the middle of nowhere.

Through these places our truck passed virtually unnoticed, even though it was painted like a circus wagon. In fact, the most prominent word on the truck was CIRCUS, in red and blue letters on a yellow background, with a couple of clown faces for good measure. It was an advertisement for Circus Biscuits, and I was embarrassed to the point of mortification to be seen emerging from this truck.

I liked the smaller, more rustic villages better. Not because they were any cleaner, though many were. I just had better experiences in these places. Not that the people were so different either. People behaved the same in both places—or at least they reacted in the same way to a white boy like me. Everywhere I walked, life around me stopped—and stared. Some people laughed at me; others glared as if to say, "Don't even think about moving into our neighborhood." Old folks looked confused, as if wondering, "Didn't we kick the British out years ago?" Children often threw things at me, usually onions, but sometimes small pieces of brick. Crowds would form around me, and the questions (always in Hindi) were always the same: "Where are you from?" "Why are you here?"

and "How much did your watch cost?" The crew grew tired of answering these questions, and I was beginning to feel like the center ring of a circus—or at least the freak show.

It was in one of the smaller places where a boy approached me and introduced himself by his English name, Jackie. He was the first person I had spoken to in several days who spoke good English, and he took me by surprise. I was sitting on the front steps of a school (which had been built by the British as a post office) with the usual entourage of children surrounding me, gawking and giggling. I was ignoring them for the most part, writing in my journal about what a nice village I was in, how all the children looked healthy, and how the people here didn't throw garbage on the rooftops nor pile it in their yards, when I heard someone behind me say, "This is not a village."

I turned toward the voice to see a very serious looking boy who had been reading over my shoulder. He said, "This is a part of Ronahi. It is a town, not a village."

I thought Ronahi was one of those urban pockets we left miles back. I said, "Do the people who live here also work here and purchase their goods here.

He answered, without hesitation, "Mostly, yes."

"Then it is, for all practical purposes, a village."

"You could say so," he replied. "But I prefer not to call it one."

I was amazed. After days of such strained dialogue about the most basic things, I suddenly found myself engaged in a conversation about the economic definition and negative connotation of the word *village*—and with a child.

"This is not a *backward region* either," he added, referring to the government term for places of slower development. However, almost any village in Uttar Pradesh certainly qualified.

He invited me to his house for a cola. He understood that I could not drink the water here. Along the way he explained that his father died ten years ago, when he was five, and that ever since he had been living with his brother, a ticket collector for the railway, in Calcutta, more than 400 miles away. He attended school there. That was where he learned English. He was in Ronahi for the summer to visit his mother. I met her when we arrived at his house. It was the only one in the area that had been painted—the same Caribbean colors I had seen in Lucknow. It was a low, box-like structure with the greater part of the front wall opened, revealing a color TV, a refrigerator, and a bed that took up most of the room. His mother was sitting on the bed with her back to the TV.

I put my hands together, nodded, and offered the standard Hindu greeting: "*Namaste.*" She reluctantly put her hands together and didn't reply.

Jackie grimaced and said, "That is not the proper greeting. Do this." He saluted me. "And say '*Salamwalekum.*'"—the standard Muslim salutation. I did as he said, and his mother smiled broadly, perhaps amused by my foreign pronunciation. I wrote this word in large black letters on the back cover of my journal. Jackie had to help me with the spelling.

We sat on a bench just outside the house. Jackie noticed a member of the crew watching us from about fifty feet away. It was the driver. Night was falling and he lurked in the shadows. Jackie said, "Your friend is worried about you."

"Should he be worried?" I asked.

Jackie laughed. "Nobody will harm you here. He just thinks he must be extra careful with you because you are a foreigner." And he invited the driver over for a cold drink, which the driver immediately accepted.

What Jackie had said was true: The crew was being extremely watchful over me, even to the point of not allowing me to stray from the truck. It was annoying. I had to rely on them to get anything, even food. And often they refused, claiming they were too busy, which usually meant they wanted to sleep. At one point in the trip I subsisted for thirty-five hours on nothing but the damn Circus Biscuits that were kept in crates in the back of the truck. Even then I could stand only one pack.

Darkness settled in. The driver insisted that we return to the truck. It was showtime.

A crowd had been congregating around the back of the truck for well over an hour. They found their seats in the dirt and grass, and stared at our colorful truck. More gathered round as the crew fired up the diesel generator and swung open the rear doors to reveal the screen.

Tonight's feature, the same as every other night, consisted of cinematic excerpts from the prolific Bombay studios known as Bollywood, which churn out more movies per year than the rest of the world's studios combined. Most are either formulaic adventure/romances based on Hindu scripture or remakes of popular American adventure/romances. The Patrick Swayze flick, *Ghost*, for example, was treated to at least seventeen Indian remakes.

What sets Indian cinema apart from the rest of the world is its unwavering devotion to musicals. Regardless of the level of adventure or romance, directors here almost always find occasion for numerous song and dance routines.

These musical numbers accounted for our entire program. Rather than bore the audience with story and plot, we screened what amounted to a series of Hindi music videos for a good hour or so, with only minimal interruptions for messages from our sponsor, Circus Biscuits.

Jackie hardly seemed impressed. He watched the first number, then said it was time for his bath and left. He returned halfway through the show, hair wet, but wearing the same clothes. I asked him what he thought of the program. He didn't answer at first. He looked a bit confused. Then he replied, "It is not a program. It is a picture."

I told him it that could be called either a program or a picture, that it didn't really matter. He became angry and insisted that it was not a program. After a confusing argument over semantics, Jackie said, "A program is what we do in there," and he pointed at an area of darkness.

I tried to remember what was over there. It took a moment, but I did recall seeing a mosque in the distance. I said, "You mean *prayer*?" He nodded softly, apparently embarrassed by the limits of his English, or maybe even the irony of confusing the words *prayer* and *program*.

We quietly watched frenetic dancers, all turbaned and glittery, all whirling and bouncing to jangly sitars and heavy percussion. Jackie said, "We don't like Michael Jackson here." I wasn't surprised. In fact, I was glad. A few years before, I taught English in a teachers college in a small town in the People's Republic of China. Though the Mickey Mouse motif was ubiquitous, appearing more often than the Red Star, not one of my students had even heard of Michael Jackson. This fact still excites me.

Then Jackie said, "I like Rambo." I was crushed. It got worse: he also liked Chuck Norris and Steven Segal. I wasn't sure who Steven Segal was, but it sounded like bad company. Jackie asked me if I had seen any Hindi movies. I had seen one: *Salaam Bombay*. He said it wasn't a real Hindi movie. (He was right. *Salaam Bombay*, a heartbreaking film about—and starring—Bombay's gutter children, did not contain a single musical number.)

All the while we were talking, an old man stood nearby, quietly watching us. Suddenly, he began to jabber and point to the book bag that I was carrying. I asked Jackie what the man was saying. Jackie said, "Nothing." After a great deal of labored persuasion, I finally convinced Jackie to tell me. He said: "The old man is a bad man. He is using slang. Bad slang. Calling you names."

"What did he call me?"

"He is saying that you Americans walk around with bags full of money. He thinks your bag is full of money so he is calling you some bad names."

"But why?"

Jackie said: "He is just having fun. He is a bad man. Just ignore him." Then he became a little emotional: "People here are stupid. They all want to go to the cities and make lots of money. They don't care about this place. It was once a good place, but everybody has gone to the cities. Now there is nothing. The people here are greedy. They are thieves. They fight for money."

I asked, "What do you mean *fight*?"

He said, "Fight—" He made stabbing gestures at my abdomen. "—with knives. My uncle is like that. He lives next door to us. He is a jealous man, so God has punished him. That's why he lives in such a poor house. We never see him anymore."

The show was almost over and the driver was signaling for me to get inside the truck. It was very important for me to be inside before the program ended, though I'm not sure why. Jackie said, "Promise you will write to me." I told him to write his address in my journal. He did, but it was his address in Calcutta. Then as I was climbing into the truck, he again made me promise to write. And just as I was closing the door, he yelled, "Wait! You are forgetting something!"

I checked my bag, looked around, but couldn't figure out what he was talking about. He seemed slightly irritated and said, "What did I teach you?"

I couldn't remember how to say it, so I peeked at the back of my journal. Then I turned to him, saluted, and said, "Salamwalekum."

I did write Jackie, as promised. And he wrote back. A postcard, depicting what looked like a Polynesian crew team, was glued to the cover of a blank greeting card. Jackie had filled the inside and back in his usual formal manner:

"I got your letter. I thank you from the core of my heart for your letter. I express my profound gratitude for your having cared to remember me . . . ." It goes on like that. He then offered the history of Calcutta, beginning with the arrival of Vasco da Gama and ending with the construction of the city's trains, zoos and various memorials.

He added: "Our father told us that Mahatma Gandhi said that a people without a history is like a man without a memory. India is the happiest country and powerful."

The second letter also came in a greeting card. Again, he filled every blank space, then continued on a page torn from a calendar. He included postcards of Indian mosques and scripture from the Koran, as well as a studio portrait of himself sitting in front of a painted seascape, complete with regatta and palm trees. He'd aged several years in the months since I'd seen him, and he looked worried.

Both his penmanship and his English had worsened: "You have asked me in your letter about my religion. I am Muslim. You know that king of India in ancient time Akbar the Great. He was also a Muslim."

His accounts from there are difficult to read, but he seemed to say that in ancient times there were two groups: Hindus, "unliterate man [who] have not a single knowledge," and Muslims, "brave and strong." He began to describe an ensuing conflict before abruptly turning to the subject of his family. "We are the medium class of man, but my father had died when I was five years." The rest of the letter offered his blessings to me and his family's blessing to me. Finally, he asked about my family so he could bless them too.

The writing in Jackie's third card, one depicting a golden sunset over an anonymous bay, is nearly illegible. He mentioned that I'd asked about recent floods near Ronahi. He wrote, "There is no canal to store the water. The government is not care . . . The villagers have no way to protect themselves . . . all the children had die and men and women can't do something they all die. The government is careless of the village. Looking only after the city all the richest people because all the rich people handle the economic of India . . . " Considering our initial debate in Ronahi, I thought it odd that he now referred to it as a village.

Having finished his description of the flood, he started on "a heavy mortal earthquake." He wrote, "All the people had die, there is no solid place to stand, all the houses are finished." His school requested donations from all students, and Jackie said he was able to give only 2000 rupees. I'm not sure what it works out to in dollars, but 2000 rupees was about enough to buy two train tickets from Calcutta to New Delhi, round-trip and first class.

"The country is doom," he concluded, "and all the India will remain this way." He ended his letter pledging his blessings to me, my brother, and my sisters.

That was the last I heard from him.

Ayodhya

What I saw as absolute weirdness was often overlooked everyday by Indians. And when weirdness happened without attracting the attention of anyone but myself, I felt as if I'd entered a state of surrealism not far from the Twilight Zone.

Cows, for example, are one of the most common sights in Indian cities—that in itself is strange. When anything bigger than a dog gets loose in an American city, people get crazy and the police end up spending half the day chasing the beast all over town. More often than not they'll corner it behind a burger joint and shoot it between the eyes. At least that seems to be the protocol when deer stray into my hometown.

But cows are worse. I don't trust cows or anything that looks like a cow. In Basti, I saw a cow trying to board a train. How it got into the station and past the ticket gate, I don't know. But it was there on the platform, negotiating the step across the gap, and no one in the station was giving it a second glance. I couldn't help but wonder: Where did the cow want to go? The point is Indians may see cows as holy; I saw them as traffic hazards and street thugs who took advantage of their divine status.

Chander could not understand the difference between my perception and his. He joined our crew in Faizabad, and he was to be my interpreter for the next few days. He wouldn't have lasted any longer than that, for he quickly grew tired of my questions. Our first day together, we saw a man lying on the ground, under a blanket. Another man stood over him, yelling and chanting. A crowd circled around them. The yelling man reached into the crowd and touched a child. The child fainted. The man picked him up, and the child began to puke blood. The man under the blanket started kicking his legs as if he were trying to ride a bicycle. I turned to Chander and asked, "What is it?" to which he replied: "It is nothing."

He gave the same answer every time: When I asked about a woman who carried a haystack-size basket on her head, about a man who draped snakes on children, about bearded men dressed in saffron with painted foreheads and golden buckets, about women who circled one tree 108 times—to these questions he simply replied: "It is nothing."

Later, a typical conversation went as follows:

Me: Chander, see that man over there? The one standing in the field?

Chander: (blandly) It is nothing.

Me: But he's completely naked.

Chander: (irately) It is nothing.

Finally, when he gave me this answer—after I had asked about a man with a caged bird and Tarot cards—I thought I just might kill him. I said: "No. It is something. Otherwise I would not be asking. It is something that I have never seen before. Now tell me what it is."

But he was more irritated than I, and he snapped, "Fine. I will tell you. This man is a disgrace to India. He is a lazy fool who does not want to work, so he sits out here all day with his stupid bird. If you want to waste your money, the bird will hop out of the cage and pick up a card. Then the man will tell you about your future, if you are stupid enough to believe it." He said this in front of the man, though it wasn't clear if the man understood any of it.

After that exchange, Chander and I argued about everything. Not surprisingly, our biggest dispute was over a certain shrine in Ayodhya: The Babri Masjid-Ram Janma Bhoomi. When Chander and I arrived at the shrine at seven o'clock one morning, I knew only the general background of its massive dispute, that the problem began in the 1500s when Babur, the first of the six great Moguls, flattened a temple built for Lord Rama, the Big Kahuna of Hindu deities. What's worse is the site was the alleged birthplace of Lord Rama, and on this site, Babur ordered the construction of a grand masjid, or mosque. And though the Mogul power dissipated in the early 1700s, the mosque remained as a sacrilege in the eyes of Hindus.

Petitions to destroy the mosque and erect a temple in its place entered regional courts in 1885, but remained unresolved. Deemed a disputed place, the shrine fell under government protection, keeping it off limits to all worshipers. During the communal riots of 1934, Hindu extremists smashed parts of its domes and outer walls, but the British government insisted on repairing the damage. To complicate matters further, stealthy Hindus reportedly snuck into the mosque on a December night in 1949 and installed an idol of Lord Rama. Authorities ordered its immediate removal. However, as many Hindus believed that the idol's mysterious appearance was the work of Rama Himself, no one dared disturb it.

And so the court battles continued, as did the rioting and civic unrest. I hadn't yet figured out who to blame for the perpetual chaos, but Chander would make a good case against Hindu extremists. He refused to let me photograph the structure, claiming that the police would shoot me. I told him to ask for permission. He refused. I insisted.

He crossed the road and found two officers sleeping in the shade. He asked them about photographing the shrine, making it clear that it was me with the camera. One officer shrugged indifferently. I began firing away, aiming the lens through the barricades and barbed wire, and above the sentry posts and sandbag walls. There were several monkeys climbing on the barricades, and they became skittish at the sight of my camera.

Afterwards we ascended a road to the shrine's entrance, where we found about fifteen policemen, all of the Central Reserve Police, sitting against a brick wall. I asked if I could photograph them. They refused. Two policemen then approached us and volunteered to be photographed, but it would have to be done away from the others, back down the road where we had just been. We had nearly an hour to kill before they would let us in the shrine, so back we went.

Along the way I asked the policemen how they felt about the dispute. One said, according to Chander's translation, that it was his duty to protect the place. I asked for his personal feelings. He smiled and looked at the other policeman, who then nodded back. The first policeman then said, according to Chander: "I think the mosque should be destroyed."

Surprised, I asked him, "You are defending a structure that you would rather have destroyed?" He said yes. I asked how many others who were defending this place would prefer see it destroyed.

Chander answered without consulting the policeman: "All of them." I told him to ask the policeman. He did, and the policeman gave a short reply that Chander translated as "All of them."

But then the policeman added this: "We don't think the mosque should be destroyed. We just want to change the interior and to remodel the exterior so that it looks like a temple." I asked him what was wrong with the way it looked now. Chander seemed disgusted with this question, but the policeman answered patiently: "It looks like a mosque."

"What's wrong with that?" I asked.

Now Chander was clearly disgusted. He began to explain to me the history of the temple—about it being the birthplace of the Lord Rama and how Babur tore it down to build the mosque. I told him that I already knew these things, but he continued right up to 1949, when the idol appeared. He said, "It was a miracle."

"Praise the Lord," I said.

He detected a hint of sarcasm in my voice. He asked me if I was Catholic or Protestant. I found the question about as trivial as, say, Do you subscribe to *Time* or *Newsweek*? However, I told him Protestant.

He said, "If you were Catholic, then you would believe that such miracles do occur, such as the appearances Mary. But since you are Protestant, you do not believe such things. Your prophet is Darwin, and that—" he pointed to a monkey "—is your god. Am I right?"

"No, that is your god. That is the Lord Hanuman," I said, referring to his simian deity. "Am I right?"

He became silent, so I began photographing the policemen. They puffed their chests out and tried hard to look stern. I asked if there had been any trouble here recently. They said there hadn't been any trouble, only a few riots. I pointed at his rifle, which looked like an elephant gun, and asked if he'd ever used it.

He said: "No guns. Just sticks. We are not that kind of people." He added something that Chander wouldn't translate. It had something to do with the U.S. military, and both the policemen and Chander found it hilarious.

Chander's mood darkened as we sized up the rest of the security. Nowhere had I seen a show of force quite like the one displayed by the Central Reserve Police. The barricades, barbed wire, sandbag walls, sentry posts and armed guards on the outside were just the beginning. A yard-thick brick wall had also been constructed to form a fifty-foot lane that led into the shrine area. A dozen or so policemen guarded the entrance to the lane, and it was here that I had to leave my book bag, camera and shoes.

At the other end of the lane, the queue was divided by sex: Male guards frisked male visitors, female guards delicately, though thoroughly, searched the saris of female visitors. All were then scanned by two metal detectors—one hand-held, the other walk-through. From there we descended an uneven staircase into a 300-foot-wide chasm. The ground was stony and dry, except in the middle where there was a water pump and a pool of mud. It would have been nice to have shoes.

Having reached the far side of the chasm, we ascended another set of stairs and found another security check point— more frisking, more metal detectors, the whole bit. Inside the shrine itself, where it was clearly decorated as a Hindu temple, the guards outnumbered worshippers by about twenty to one. And they were all armed. Their presence—and their guns—seemed like the ultimate desecration of a place of worship.

The guards hurried us from room to room, giving only enough time to glance at the idols. I don't even remember seeing the miraculous idol of Rama. It didn't seem important at that point. In the middle of it all a group of Hindus who, corralled like cows, were handing out pamphlets. I started to ask Chander who they were, but before I could say a word, he said: "It is nothing."

I stopped to ask them myself. One answered in excited Hindi, while another searched fervently though a stack of pamphlets. He extracted a pamphlet that was written in something that resembled English. It explained the plight of the *Kar Sevaks*, the devotees to the temple who intended to stay there and pray until the temple was liberated. It also stated: "It is the sacred duty of the entire Hindu-Community to finance this hole casue and thus donars will earn immence PUNYA" [sic]. Punya, I later learned, can be used to improve your station in the next life.

We moved onward, past more guards and more guns. An entire section of the shrine was reserved guards alone. I turned to Chander and said, "This is sick."

He didn't see it that way. In his eyes, the security was a necessity and the Muslims were to blame. He was convinced that the good and right thing to do was to tear down the mosque and rebuild a temple. And this was his argument: "The temple was built for Rama. The mosque was built by Babur. Babur was just a man, but Rama is a god. Therefore we should destroy the mosque and rebuild the temple. We should honor God instead of a man."

The logic was twisted so I didn't bother to reply. However, he knew I hadn't seen the light, so he tried again: "Rama is a god. Babur was just a man. Rama was here first. He was born here. The temple was here long before Babur was even born. Don't you see?"

"The temple was here first. Why is that so important?"

"Because Babur could have built the mosque anywhere. Why did he want to knock down the temple and build it here?"

I replied, though it sounded more like a question, "For the same reason you want to knock down the mosque and build the temple here?"

Chander turned away and said that I just didn't understand. "But that's exactly why I'm here. To understand," I told him. He modified his last statement: "You *cannot* understand."

He was probably right—for once. I couldn't really get a grasp on either end of the argument because I saw both sides as wrong. I wanted to tell him this, but I could see that he wasn't going to listen anymore. We silently agreed it would be best if we just dropped the subject and left town.

Before we went, however, I would need to pick up some souvenirs. Dozens of souvenir stands flanked the street that led to the Hanuman Ghara Temple, but I didn't see anything specifically relating to the disputed shrine. After an hour's search, I found what looked like a booklet of postcards. By then we were in a hurry, so I bought it without bothering to see what it really was. Inside, I later discovered, were photographs of the 1990 Ayodhya massacre. More specifically, it focused on the Hindu victims, men full of bullet holes, heads split open and brains on the street, the kind of images that almost certainly inspire further rioting.

When I returned to Delhi, however, I found something worse. Dr. Jain allowed me to review his Ayodhya video before airing it on national TV in time for the elections. It was an exploitative piece of shameless propaganda. It was both slick and grotesque—a new, state of the art version in a long line of the same old political manipulation that created the Ayodhya fiasco. From this I came to realize that in Indian politics, religion is not the opiate, but the amphetamine of the masses. And the pushers are just as guilty as the addicts.

Five months later, in December of 1992, radical Hindu groups razed the shrine, sparking a two-month wave of sectarian violence that left 1600 Indians dead.

Mahson

Simply leaving Ayodhya didn't settle anything between Chander and me. Maybe it was my fault. I was getting punchy from a lack of sleep, food and intelligent conversation, and from the fact that mosquitoes had chewed my wrists and ankles down to the bone. I feared my coworkers were right, that I might just drop dead out here. I took solace in the fact that I survived twice as long as they'd predicted, then abandoned the truck for a better life in the promised land of Mahson.

Mahson didn't appear on any maps or in my guidebook, but I knew it was only few miles beyond Basti. More importantly, I had friends there, or at least the parents of a friend. I had not met them, but my friend—Amit, a fellow journalism student at the University of North Carolina—said if I ever happened to be near Basti, I should drop by. When I looked it up in the atlas, I had to laugh. I told Amit that there was no way in hell that I would just happen to be out in those badlands, in some dinky village well past the halfway point on the road from Delhi to Kathmandu. But that was when we were in Chapel Hill, my hometown. Three weeks later, I just happened to find myself within spitting distance of his hometown.

His parents lived in a palace. Everything about it suggested extravagance: A front entrance wide enough for elephants to enter; above it, the double fish design of the royal family of Oudh. On each corner of the house were turrets capped with red, blue and gold onion domes; and in the center, a courtyard large enough to play full-court basketball. Throughout the house, the walls were covered with portraits that appeared to be from an era when photography was new, along with animal skins—leopards and tigers with fierce expressions fixed on their faces and crocodilian creatures with gaping smiles—from an era when hunting was considered heroic.

The library was packed with Western books. It was here I collapsed in an oversized chair and introduced myself to Amit's father, Mr. Pal. The discomfort I felt from grime and sweat was only slightly worse than my hunger and thirst. Mr. Pal, by contrast, looked cool, relaxed, and, above all, well fed. He seemed to know how to enjoy his years as a retired engineer. He was tall and nearly bald, with wide gray sideburns connected to a thick mustache. He kept his chin clean shaved. He had a commanding appearance, and a voice to match; but despite this, he made me feel like I would be welcome to stay in his home for the next five years.

He ordered the servants to bring me food—trays of it—and told me I could shower after eating. Then he asked the standard question, "How do you find India?" and not giving me a chance to respond, answered his own question, as Indians tend to do: "You must hate it. The heat, the blackouts, the poverty. And it's so dirty."

There aren't many variations to this one-sided discourse. I'd heard the refrain several times since coming to India, yet I can't figure out how, as a guest in this country, I am expected to reply. Yes, the standard of living here is, for the most part, lower than it is in the States. That doesn't mean I hate it. I wouldn't be here if I hated it. And while Indians may feel like they are behind in that respect, I have to wonder how long Americans will be able to continue consuming the obscene amounts of energy and resources it takes to maintain our standard of living. I doubt it will last throughout my lifetime.

The impending doom of an environmental catastrophe and a multi-trillion dollar deficit hang over our heads. Increasingly in America the water supplies are becoming tainted, the air quality is worsening, the cities are turning into slums, the police are getting jumpy, and the politicians are getting paranoid. By the time India comes close to what America is now, America will be what India was fifteen years ago. In short, the world is a bitch chasing its tail. This little nugget of cynical Taoism is half of what keeps me infatuated with the Third World.

I shared this theory with an Indian friend of mine in the States, and asked him how he thought Americans would cope if suddenly forced to live at Indian standards. He said, "The same way Indians are coping with their situation now." I thought he was referring to the amazing elasticity of Indian patience, but then he added: "They will riot everyday."

However, I did not enter this discussion with Mr. Pal. Instead, I simply picked up a mango from a silver platter, glanced around the library, and said, "I'm finding India just fine."

• • •

Delhi [redux]

Sometime shortly after I returned to Delhi, I noticed that my perception of my neighborhood had changed. It wasn't like an epiphany or any sort of jolt in perspective. It was just a change in the way I described the place, and I can't say for sure when it began. That which I initially described as "shabby" later became "quaint" and then "posh". I stopped referring to my neighborhood as "the ghetto" and started calling it "home".

Now I'm used to hearing the security patrol banging their bamboo poles and blowing their whistles all through the night. And they no longer hassle me when I'm walking back to my apartment at three a.m. In fact, they now amuse me—the way the older ones walk about with their pants pulled down halfway to their knees. The once arduous task of hauling buckets of water out to the cooler has become an unconscious ritual. And I don't mind the fact that my clothes come back from the *dhobi* as stiff as cardboard.

True, some things still freak me out. One deceptively calm Sunday morning, I took the bus to Connaught Place and ambled north. I had no idea where I was going, and I really didn't care. Then, just after passing the railway station, I realized that something was wrong. One man in the Delhi masses was moving toward me; and without initially knowing why, I began to stare at him. He walked with a sense of defiance, almost belligerence, though no one else around him seemed to mind. His eyes, though wide, betrayed an onset of exhaustion. His shirt was white with large crimson stains, and it was badly torn. The crimson was blood, and there was so much of it that I though at first it couldn't be real. He came closer and I saw more blood on his dark skin. Then I saw the knife in his arm. It was like a carving knife and somebody had plunged it deep into his forearm. He walked past me and I saw the blade sticking at least five inches out of the other side of his arm.

I thought: *This man has a knife stuck through his arm and he's walking around as if he's only worried about catching a train*. I started the follow him. I don't know why. It was like I wanted to tell him about this knife in his arm, but I didn't know what to say. I looked around and saw again that nobody else was paying much attention to him. I figured it was best to let him go and forget about it. But soon I saw more men with that belligerent gait, that distance in their eyes, and that blood. So much blood I wanted to scream: "Would somebody please tell me what the hell is going on?"

Instead, I pushed onward, following distant drums and the clamor of men shouting, through the thickening crowds and past clusters of policemen armed with bamboo poles. I figured if there was any real danger, they would have stopped me at that point. But they didn't. So I rounded the corner to see frenzied masses beating themselves senseless, flogging their own bare backs, tearing their own skin, and beating their own chests and skulls. Here I found that I wasn't the only one staring. In fact, the audience was at least four times the size of the procession. And in the middle of it all was what looked like a parade float, with a crescent moon towering above the crowd.

I thought: *Muharram* —the festival to commemorate the martyrdom of Imam Hussain, grandson of the prophet Muhammad. Self-mutilation is the Shi'ite way of apologizing to Hussain for failing to protect him at the battle of Karbala in 680 AD.

I had hoped to catch Muharram in Lucknow, where it takes on Mardi Gras proportions, but now I felt I'd seen too much. I retreated to a quiet corner of old Delhi. There I found an elderly man with a moustache like Hitler's. Resting on the sidewalk in the shade, he looked ready for a photograph. As I approached, however, I realized that he had no moustache. Instead, flies swarmed in and out of his nostrils. He wasn't breathing. That was the thing that nearly freaked me out.

So I haven't gone completely Indian. The nuances of its rich cultures are impossible for me to master. This fact became abundantly clear when I inadvertently left a bag of potato chips in front of a statue of Ganesh, the elephant-headed god of prosperity. Witnessing my gaffe more than once, the old colonel who let my apartment finally issued a stern warning: "Stop offering bloody potato chips to our god, he only likes sweet things."

I still find myself staring at the families who camp out in the shanties just beyond the gates of my enclave. I can't pretend I don't see the children begging at the street corners, especially since they're so attracted to Westerners. I can't get over the fact that election ballots here are bigger than newspapers. I can't get over the sight of a family of five traveling together on a single motor scooter. I still would rather walk in the street than share the sidewalk with a cow. And I still find myself slightly out of place at parties like the one I attended on Prithviraj Road.

Actually, I haven't yet returned to Prithviraj Road, but I did see that girl again—the one who told me about my eyes. I saw her at another party, but she didn't really notice me. The little tramp was busy staring into the eyes of another man. Worse yet, he was an American.

Tanzania Trilogy

Interview with the Witch Doctor

TANZANIA: 1994

"I would seriously advise staying away from the witch doctors," the Bavarian missionary tells me. He has a strong German accent and a lisp; as a result, I can't take anything he says seriously. "They are dangerous people."

"How dangerous could they be?" I ask.

"A woman here was about to deliver. She was only seven months pregnant," he explains, suddenly affecting a grim tone. "So she was ordered to the hospital. However, the women escorting her decided it would be better to take her to the witch doctor instead. The next day, there was a funeral."

"For whom?"

"Both the mother and the baby," he replies solemnly.

"Well, I'm not having any babies. I just want to talk."

The missionary purses his lips and shakes his head. "I would advise against it." Then he marches away.

Once he is out of earshot, one of his students approaches me from behind and says in a low voice: "Tomorrow I will take you to a real witch doctor."

It's Hans. He's tall with a smooth, dark complexion and a chipped front tooth. He has a fair grasp of English and a normally serious countenance, though at times he is prone to break into choking fits of laughter.

Hans knows I'm not here to meet witch doctors. I came to Tanzania to assist an American health organization with a training workshop for Tanzanian doctors and nurses.

The Christian Health Association of Tanzania recommended the Lutheran compound in Masoka primarily for its remote location. Nestled in a thousand acres of banana trees on foothills of Mount Kilimanjaro, the village offers nothing that resembles entertainment and other distractions. The nearest town, Moshi, is only six miles away, but it's an hour-long ride on a twisted, bone-jarring road.

The Lutheran compound, a haven of modern conveniences, is the perfect outpost for a productive workshop. The Bavarian missionary runs the business here with such order and economy that it's hard to imagine how the German colonialists ever lost control of this nation. The grounds are as tidy as a putting green. Meals are served punctually. And while I anticipated a computer lab, I didn't expect to find it fully functional. All of this adds up to a level of support and efficiency that I haven't encountered in any other conference facility in Africa. In short, I'm stuck in the middle of nowhere with not much to do. Hunting for witch doctors seems more productive than interrupting the workshop with motivational speeches and bonding activities.

I'm grateful for Hans as my guide. He's a local—his parents' house is a short stroll from the compound—and he's fairly enthusiastic about this unusual quest, as though he's possessed with my sense of restlessness. He doesn't seem to belong in Masoka. He's too bright and energetic for this sleepy hamlet. And his appearance is far more cosmopolitan than his fellow villagers. Though his sense of fashion is rooted in the early eighties, with a fondness for pinstripe button downs with standup collars and immaculately pressed pleated trousers, he wears it well, and young women tend to swoon when he is near.

As one nurse put it: "He doesn't know it yet, but he is too handsome for his own good."

Hans and I meet our first self-proclaimed witch doctor near the clock tower in Moshi. He is in the middle of a passionate speech, which he delivers in Swahili from atop what appears to be a shoeshine box. A crowd of about fifty watches curiously. According to Hans' translation of the speech, the witch doctor is selling "magic stones, good for extracting the poison from a snake bite."

"Do you think they work?" I ask.

Hans stifles a laugh and says, "No."

"What about everybody else here? Will they buy any?"

Hans shakes his head. "Nobody will buy his stones. They only gather around to see the snake."

"What snake?"

"In the box he is standing on. He has a snake in there to prove his stones."

"He's going to let the snake bite him?" I ask hopefully, reaching for my camera.

The witch doctor sees my camera and starts screaming at me. Hans jumps to my defense with a retort that makes the crowd laugh and the doctor fume.

"Care to tell me what's happening?"

"He said you cannot take his picture because you do not believe in his magic."

"And what did you say?"

"Neither does anyone else." He giggles.

The man, perhaps realizing that he is going to have a slow day in the sales department, then offers to pose with the snake for 500 shillings (about one U.S. dollar).

"That's too expensive," Hans protests.

The man replies: "He will sell my picture in Europe for a lot of money, and I want some of it." Hearing that, Hans nearly falls over laughing. The man, growing more furious, raises the price to 1000 shillings.

"You're not helping," I tell Hans after he translates all of this.

"Do you really want his picture?"

"Of course!"

"But he is a fake."

"If he lets that snake bite him, I'll buy his whole supply of snake rocks whether they work or not."

Hans just shrugs and begins negotiating with the man. Once they settle on the price—500 shillings—the man opens his box.

The crowd gasps and backs away. I wedge in closer, drop to one knee and steady the camera. The man spins toward me, six-foot snake in hand. "You will get rich in Europe," he says. But I lower the camera. Seeing this, he says something to Hans.

"He wants to know why you aren't taking his picture," Hans says.

"It's a python," I reply.

Hans returns a blank stare.

"His snake won't bite anyone," I explain. "It isn't even venomous. Look at it. It couldn't hurt a beached squid. Poor thing's nearly dead from the heat."

Hans leans in closer to inspect the snake wilting in the man's hands, then says, "Yes, but I told you—he is not a real witch doctor, so it would not be good for him to use a real poisonous snake. Anyway, you should take his picture. I have already paid."

I raise the camera and try to focus on the miserable snake as the man, a menacing grin spreading over his face, thrusts the snake closer to the lens, withdraws it, then thrusts it close again.

As we leave the man and his dwindling crowd, Hans, sensing my disappointment, promises to find me a real witch doctor. He leads me to a dusty clearing near the bus station, where about a dozen practitioners have set up tables to sell their potions.

We approach two teenage witch doctors slouching near a table covered with oils in corked bottles, herbs wrapped in newspapers, and powders in crucibles. After an amiable conversation with them, Hans says, "This one—" he points at the older of the two "—is named Msagate."

Msagate, frowning, interjects something.

"*Doctor* Msagate," Hans says, forcing back a smile.

Doctor Msagate beams.

"He is from Tanga region, which is famous for its witch doctors," Hans continues. "He was trained for three years by his father, who is also a witch doctor. The most popular remedies he sells are for stomach ailments and sexually transmitted diseases. He doesn't do curses. He can only advise on what course of action you should take to change your predicament."

"How much does he earn?"

"He says about ten thousand shillings a week."

"Ten thousand a *week*?" It's only twenty dollars, but the average Tanzanian earns slightly more than that a month.

"I don't think he is telling the truth," Hans replies, lowering his voice.

"Maybe we should find another witch doctor."

Hans nods thoughtfully. "I will find."

Two days later, on a chilly Wednesday morning, Hans leads me down a muddy path through banana fields to the witch doctor's house. I know we're close when I see a wooden sign nailed to a tree. In hand-painted letters, it reads: Prof DR BINTMARIAM MGANGA WA TIBA YA ASLI YA JADI.

"Witch doctor," Hans says, gazing up at the sign.

"It says more than that," I tell him. "What is *Mganga*?"

"Witch doctor."

"Then what does the rest of it say?"

"Doctor who treats in the traditional way," he says.

After hopping over a ditch, pressing through a grove of banana trees and edging around a thatched fence of dried banana leaves, we find ourselves in Dr. Bintmariam's front yard. It's a grassless patch of hard-packed dirt littered with batteries, dead rats, razor blades and two soda bottles buried up to their necks. Newspaper articles are posted on the outer walls of the house, reporting, among other things, the victories of Tanzania's Simba soccer club, the life and times of Bob Marley, and recent European trends in men's fashion. The cement walls, though apparently sturdy, are shedding paint and breeding moss. Around the windows, messages are scrawled in paint, one of which reads (in Swahili): *If you are serious, it will take only thirty days.*

An iron-grid door and bars in the windows keep the house secure, but the backbone of the home-security system is the bottles buried in the yard. Packed with magic roots and herbs, they act as a kind of security camera, providing the doctor with a clear mental picture of any "bad people" who approach the house.

The front door is open. Hans steps upon the front porch, leans through the threshold and calls out, "Hodi!"

No reply.

I peer around him. On the cement floor of the front room is a straw mat under a pile of blankets. Around it are bananas and mangoes in various states of decay. Corn husks and more batteries are scattered about. I see nothing in the house that requires electricity, not even lights. The house is dark, cool and damp, smelling of mildew, urine and animal musk. A message painted on the far wall reads: *Do not enter with shoes.*

Suddenly a screeching mass of fur leaps toward us. Hans jumps back, nearly knocking me off the porch.

I regain my balance and look for the attacker, but it's nowhere in sight. "What was *that*?" I ask.

Hans wipes his forehead and laughs. "Monkey," he says, short of breath.

As if on cue, the monkey—roped at the waist and tethered to the doorknob—saunters into the doorway. Hans laughs nervously. The monkey retreats into the shadows, chattering and picking its way though the rotten fruit.

Hans and I wait on the front porch. I ask him if I should take off my shoes when the doctor arrives. He surveys the floor inside, where, at that moment, the monkey has decided to defecate. "It is not necessary," he replies.

After twenty minutes, a man comes strutting into the front yard. He's wearing a black derby, a powder blue Members Only jacket, a sulfur-colored shirt and matching pants which bare the logo, CAT DIESEL POWER. He keeps his USA-brand basketball shoes stylishly unlaced. He has bloodshot eyes, stained teeth, sideburns, a mustache and a scraggly goatee. He can't be much older than thirty.

"He is the witch doctor," Hans whispers.

"Remember," I say, "no laughing."

Hans grins, baring his chipped tooth and many others.

The doctor greets us with a broad smile and a complicated handshake. He apologizes for his lateness—he was having lunch in Moshi. As Hans translates for me, the doctor's smile stiffens. Suddenly looking very concerned, almost sad, he says something in a dreadful tone.

"What's wrong?" I ask Hans.

"He wants to know what is wrong with you," Hans says. "He wants to know why you are not able to speak Swahili."

It is a common concern among most people I meet in Tanzania. Nearly everyone seems to suspect that I suffer profound mental retardation because of my limited knowledge of Swahili.

"Tell him that my university never offered courses in Swahili," I say.

Hans relays the message to the doctor, who appears understanding and invites us into his office, the second of two rooms in his house. Hans and I follow him, edging our way around the watchful monkey. We find his office in an advanced state of disarray. Fresh-cut tree limbs, Japanese newspapers, a wide assortment of roots and herbs, plastic film cases, a buffalo horn, gourds, bongo drums, glass vials, soda bottles, soiled rags, paper lunch bags, plastic shopping bags, paint cans, match boxes, empty packs of S/M cigarettes, a spear and other things I can't identify are arranged on the floor in no discernible order.

The doctor finds a clearing in the middle of it all and takes a seat. His nurse, a teenage boy wearing an Islamic hat, brings in two stools and offers them to Hans and me, then quietly reclines in a patch of sunshine against a wall the color of dried blood. After another round of customary introductions, greetings and handshakes, the doctor asks where I'm staying.

"The Lutheran compound," I say.

"With the Christians," the doctor says (according to Hans' translation). He points at my chest and asks, "Is that Christian?"

For a moment I think he's asking about me, but then I remember what I'm wearing around my neck. "It's a Saint Christopher," I tell him. "It protects me when I travel."

He smiles and nods knowingly, but I get the feeling he's amused by my superstitions.

"Christians give me a lot of trouble," he says. "They don't approve of witchcraft, so they try to keep my patients away."

Hans is having a difficult time translating, mainly because he can't stop fidgeting with his keys and convulsing with silent laughter. I reach over to still Hans' keys, then ask, "What about the Muslims?"

"Muslims don't give me any trouble because I am a Muslim," the doctor replies with obvious pride.

Not a very devout Muslim, I think. It's the month of Ramadan—a time of intense fasting for Muslims—and he's just returned from lunch.

"Hans, how do we know he's a real witch doctor?"

"He has a certificate," Hans answers, and he asks the doctor to show me his certificate. The doctor searches through notebooks and mounds of newspapers before producing two documents.

"These are his official licenses which he got from the district council health officials," Hans explains. (The Tanzanian Government, I later learn, does license doctors who practice traditional medicine, but only to keep a lid on flagrant quackery. It does not endorse other aspects of witchcraft, such as curses, charms and fortune telling.)

The doctor hands me his certificates and nods as if to reassure me of their authenticity. I examine the flimsy, yellowing paper, but can't decipher more than three words. I try to look impressed, then ask why he chose this profession.

"I got these dreams in the night," he replies. "And I went crazy for some time."

Hans starts choking on his laughter again. I elbow his ribs, but it only makes him laugh more. The doctor smiles patiently and continues: "Then, afterwards, I dreamt I would be a witch doctor. So my grandfather trained me, and by 1986 I had my own practice."

I ask him what a witch doctor does. At first he seems confused by the question, as if he doesn't know where to begin. He glances over his bags and jars of herbs, grabs a handful of leaves and shuffles some papers around. He shows me a notebook that contains a list of clients, the times they arrive, the diseases they have and the prices they pay for treatment.

Gradually, the room darkens and rain begins to rattle down on the corrugated metal roof. Then for the next forty-five minutes, the doctor cheerfully explains his favorite powers and medicines, while Hans, maintaining his solemnity for a change, translates. In short, this is what he tells me:

"He can treat many different diseases. For example, when a woman cannot get pregnant, she can use this drug so that she can conceive. Another thing, it helps for someone who is crazy. If another witch doctor has made you crazy, this drug makes your mind fit again.

"If you have a genie or a devil in your brain, he can rub medicine on you to make it get out.

"If somebody puts something in your stomach, like a large stone or some hair, he has a medicine that will get it out.

"If you leave your parents and you don't want to go home, he can give your parents some medicine that will force you to return home whether you want to or not.

"He has a medicine that can cure HIV; it makes you healthy for two days, but after two days, you must die. He tested it on a monkey, but he won't use it on people.

"Also, he has a drug that you can use when you are suffering from the serious stage of AIDS. It can give you health again, but it can't kill HIV. You can live for not more than one and a half years; then you'll die. Also he can tell you exactly at what time you will die, so you can alert your relatives. He has treated six patients with HIV. Two are still alive.

"He has a medicine that, if you bathe with it, it will make a loved one give you many gifts.

"If someone has done something bad to you, it's one of his tasks to know who it is. Then, if you want to kill that person, he can give you a medicine that will kill him. He has many different ways to kill people. He can command something—something you can't see by the naked eye—to kill you."

By the time the doctor has exhausted his inventory, the rain has slowed and sunlight filters back into the room. A growing number of voices drift in from the porch: villagers greeting each other in murmurs. They all have appointments with Dr. Bintmariam. I expect they will be angry that I kept them waiting, but I have one last question for the witch doctor: "Will you play your drum for me sometime?"

The doctor says he will play his drum for me now.

"But you have patients outside," I remind him.

"They will wait," he says with a shrug. He pulls his drum close and pats out a rhythm. It's smooth and melodic, not unlike a drummer backing up a singer in hotel lounge. His song, however, is a haunting chant.

"What's he singing?" I ask.

"I do not know," Hans replies. "We are not from the same tribe, so I do not understand his language."

When the song is over, I ask what it was about.

Hans relays this answer to me: "It's just a song to chase away the sultans."

"Sultans? What sultans?"

"The devils."

"You mean Satan?"

"Ah, yes," Hans says, realizing his mistake, "the satans."

The next day, immediately after blessing the lunch (in Swahili), the Bavarian missionary turns to me and asks (in English): "Will you be meeting with the witch doctor again?"

Again? I hesitate to answer, wondering who told him about our meeting yesterday. "Yes, I plan to see him right after lunch."

He raises both eyebrows and his eyes widen, but his tone of voice remains level. "You are learning much from him?"

"Yes, I think so."

"That is good. I think you can learn much more from him than I could." He chews thoughtfully on a gristly chunk of beef, and adds, "I don't think he would be so interested to talk to me."

"Sure he would," I say. "He's really friendly."

"Don't get too friendly with him," the missionary tells me. "Remember, we are Christians."

After lunch, Hans and I head back to the witch doctor's house. When we arrive, eight patients are already waiting silently on the front porch, blocking the doorway. Hans walks to the window and calls, "Hodi!"

"Hans, maybe we should wait our turn," I say.

He ignores my hesitation. Soon after, the nurse appears, then leads Hans and me through the crowd, back into the doctor's office. Two patients are sitting on the floor, facing the doctor.

As we enter the room, the doctor stands and greets me with a complicated handshake.

"Hans, is it all right if I just watch while he sees his patients?"

"Of course," Hans says without consulting the doctor.

"Ask him," I say.

Hans relays my request to the doctor, who answers, according to Hans, "Of course."

"Shouldn't we ask the patients if they mind?"

"It is not necessary," Hans replies.

I decide to take his word for it. The patients don't seem to mind my presence, much less acknowledge it.

The doctor sees fifty to sixty patients in an average day. Their visits last no longer than five minutes and they usually visit in pairs. Most arrive barefoot, though some have sandals, which they remove before entering the house. Their feet are hard and cracked like ancient pottery. The men's shirts are beyond threadbare; their dark, bony shoulders glisten through tatters and gaping holes. The women are usually wrapped in bright, lightweight fabrics (*kitenge*), though some wear

T-shirts and long, wraparound skirts (*kanga*) with unraveling hems. Most of them seem to be middle-aged, but I suspect that they're not as old as they look.

The first two patients are husband and wife. Their problem, Hans whispers to me, is a family dispute.

The doctor tells the husband to hand him a leaf from one of the branches on the floor. The husband obeys, and waits while the doctor lights a cigarette and studies the leaf. He tears a small chunk out of the leaf and examines his patients through the hole. He asks the husband five question, all of which the husband answers, "*Ndiyo.*" (Yes.)

Finally, the doctor prescribes a cure: The husband must sacrifice a goat on his grandfather's grave, spill the blood on the gravestone and pray. Two days later, he must pray again.

"Then what?" I ask.

"Then everything will be okay," Hans says.

The couple pays the doctor fifty shillings (ten cents) and thanks him profusely.

The only patient who arrives alone is wearing an old business suit, no tie, and dusty black-leather shoes.

"His business is failing," Hans says. "He once made lots of money, but now he doesn't get it. People, they don't come to buy his things. They go other places."

The doctor responds to the complaint by smearing oil and black powder on the businessman's face.

"This medicine," Hans explains, "will bring customers from far away."

Another patient, a small, bent woman, is lead in by a schoolgirl with a beauty-pageant posture. Hans points to the bent woman and says, "She has brought in some clay where she usually walks." She hands the doctor a sample of dirt wrapped in a leaf. The doctor examines it, then hands it back. "It was not enough," Hans says. "She must collect more and come back tomorrow." The bent woman now looks pained and dejected, but she insists on walking out without the schoolgirl's assistance.

The next two are farmers. One is covered head to ankle in a blue kitenge with a golden ax-head print. Her hands and feet are a bas-relief of veins and bones. Her face is smooth, but her eyes are sunken. The other woman is wearing a baby blue bandanna on her head and a fuchsia T-shirt. The print on her kanga is a pattern of electric guitars, crossed trumpets and red violins. She is plump, her skin tight, as if barely able to contain her body.

The first woman laments her predicament, while the second nods sympathetically. Hans translates the complaint: "Once she was getting milk from her cows, lots of maize, coffee, bananas from her farms. Then, all of the sudden, her livestock and crops died."

The doctor frowns and stokes his chin, then reaches for an instrument called a *jinikashkash*. It looks like an ordinary stethoscope, except on one end, where the cold metal disk should be, there's a gourd dressed in white beads and a piece of goatskin.

"It's magic," Hans explains. "He can listen to it and he can tell you what's your problem and what is needed for you to be okay."

The doctor fits the earpieces into his ears and shakes the gourd. A small bell, the kind a cat might wear, rings from within. He looks confused. He rattles the gourd again, but it doesn't seem to be telling him anything. So he reaches for another instrument. This one resembles a fly whisk made out of a cow's tail—except one end is fastened to an ink bottle filled with a dark red liquid.

"That thing is very powerful," Hans says. "He can use it to make you crazy for a moment."

The doctor whacks the bottle against the floor, examines the liquid, then whacks it again. A look of recognition emerges on his face. He tells his nurse to prepare some medicine. The nurse responds by taking one long drag off his cigarette before butting it out on the floor. He then collects some herbs from paper lunch sacks and mashes them together in a mortar, all the while chomping fiercely on his gum.

The doctor then places the mixture in an antelope horn, where it ignites and pops like a champagne cork. Thin smoke rises out of the horn, filling the room with the smell of wooden matches.

The doctor offers his diagnosis: Someone used witchcraft to kill the crops and livestock. He gives the contents of the antelope horn to the patient, instructing her to sprinkle it around her farm. Then he adds a few words that make both women clap their hands and squeal with joy. Hans and the witch doctor laugh, too.

"What's so funny?" I ask.

Struggling to keep a straight face, Hans replies, "Now, if anyone tries to harm them with magic, he will get sick and fall down dead."

"You think that's funny?"

"No, *she* is funny. Look at her!"

The first woman is on her feet, dancing an ecstatic jig, while her friend claps and whoops all the way out the door.

Friday, the witch doctor shows up unannounced at my apartment on the Lutheran compound. He greets me with the same handshake, but it no longer seems complicated.

Hans is not around. Neither is anyone else who can translate. So the doctor and I engage in a fruitless game of charades. We finally give up. For an awkward moment, we just smile politely at one another. At last, the doctor says (in the only English I've ever heard him use), "I'll be back."

A week passes without any word from the witch doctor, so I tell Hans that we must visit his home just one last time before I leave the village. "This time," I add, "I'll be the patient."

We find the witch doctor alone in his house. Immediately, I sense that something is different. The smell of urine is gone. The floors are clean. His blanket is folded neatly on the straw mat. And in his office, the bags of medicine arranged in neat rows, the newspapers bundled and stacked against the back wall, the branches in a tidy pile against another wall, and all of his paperwork and equipment laid out for easy, efficient access.

There's something different about him, too. Instead of a black derby, he's covered his head with a white cloth. "It is traditional for Muslims to wear this on Fridays," Hans explains.

Otherwise, the doctor's clothes are the same as every other time I've seen him.

Hans tells the doctor that I want a check-up. He says he is very happy, then asks me to write my name in his notebook and hand him a leaf.

He examines my name and tries to pronounce it, but he just can't seem to get it right. Then he looks at the leaf for a total of ten seconds and, through Hans, gives me his diagnosis: "You don't have a problem in your body, but sometimes you suddenly feel that your heart is beating so fast, and then it is normal again."

"That's it? Aren't you going to burn something in the antelope horn or shake your jinikashkash or something?"

With a sigh he slips the jinikashkash in his ears, rattles the gourd and listens. Then he thumps the bottle end of the cow tail on the ground and examines the red liquid as if reading a thermometer. He tears a piece out of the leaf and holds it up, but I get the feeling that he's just going through the motions.

A minute later, however, he announces another diagnosis: "Your business is well, but you have to do something for your family. You need to say a prayer for your grandfather—the one who died a long time ago. Then you need to do something traditional for him."

"Like what?"

"Like a sacrifice."

"What? Slaughter a goat on his grave?"

"Perhaps. Or you can just give the church some money in honor of your grandfather."

"And then what?"

"Then everything will be okay."

"Is something wrong *now*?" I ask.

The doctor shuts his eyes. I can see his eyeballs rolling under their lids. He says, "In America, many people are remembering you just now."

I check my watch. It's nearly noon. That's four a.m. back home. I wonder who would be thinking about me at that hour. "Is there anything else you can tell me? Don't you have any medicine I can take?"

He offers to sell me some herbs that will protect me while I travel in Tanzania, but he says I don't really need them. "There is no danger in your future," he says.

At that, the monkey screeches and claws at the walls. The doctor ignores it, but I'm certain it's a bad omen.

"Are you sure?" I ask.

Hans discusses the question with the doctor, then tells me, "He can give you a charm, something like your Saint Christopher. It will protect you when you travel and it will live for twenty-five years. But he has to go back to Moshi to collect some special herbs. He says you should come back at three o'clock to collect the charm. At that time he will beat his drums for you."

"Again?"

Hans nods. "He wants to beat his drums for you."

"Is there anything I can give him in return?"

"Containers," Hans replies after consulting the doctor. "He needs containers to keep his medicine in. Like this— " He picks up a plastic film case. "—only bigger."

"He wants Tupperware?"

"Yes, I think so."

"I'm afraid I didn't bring any."

Hans relays this bad news to the witch doctor, who is visibly disappointed.

"Isn't there anything else he needs?" I ask.

Hans confers with the doctor again, then says, "No. All he needs is the Tupperware."

After lunch, Hans is nowhere to be found. So at 2:55, I set off alone to collect my charm from the witch doctor. It's only minutes past three when I meet him along the road. He's with his nurse and another friend who doesn't speak English. The doctor hands me a pouch made of black cloth and bound in army-green string. I slip it over my neck and admire it as it dangles just below Saint Christopher.

"*Asante sana* (thank you)," I say.

"*Asante*," he answers.

Since there's nothing left to say—nothing that we are able to say, anyway—he shakes my hand one last time and leaves me standing on the dirt track in the middle of the banana fields.

• • •

That night, the Bavarian missionary and I dine by candlelight, because, once again, the power has failed. The power supply, which comes from Moshi, can't always reach remote villages like ours, though it's not unlikely that someone has stolen the power lines. (In fact, some unfortunate thief tried recently and was electrocuted.)

The water has stopped, too. Usually, the compound manager trucks in enough water from Mount Kilimanjaro to supply the nearby villages. But because of the severe drought, people have been coming from other villages late at night to steal water from the communal taps. So the compound manager had no choice but to shut off the water for a few days. Now he's facing a new problem: with the water shut off, the pipes are much easier to steal.

Tonight, however, the missionary has a different explanation for the lack of power and water.

"It's the Catholics," he says. "They know we are expecting dignitaries, so they halt our electricity and our water."

His theory seems a little shaky. He doesn't have much to back it up, and it's further complicated by the fact that the dignitaries never showed up.

Eventually, the conversation turns toward the subject of the witch doctor, and I tell him about the doctor's diagnosis of me.

"Is it true?" he asks.

"What he said about my heart is true. Occasionally, I feel my heart race. Just for a second or two. It's like a rush in my chest; it seems to happen for no reason at all."

The missionary doesn't look impressed.

"Also, his second diagnosis implied that both my grandfathers are dead. That's true. One died just last year, and I don't remember exactly when the other one died because, as the witch doctor said, it was a long time ago."

He still looks skeptical, so I show him the charm around my neck. "It protects me while I travel, like my Saint Christopher." I show him the saint, too.

He gazes blankly at my chest and says, "I would advise you not to wear that." But I can't tell which one he means.

The End of the Earth

TANZANIA: 1994

My Tanzanian friend, Dr. Mahimbo, wouldn't tell me how he managed to book me on a flight that, two hours previous, did not exist. But I feared he'd made a grave mistake when the twin-engine plane touched down among U.N. helicopters and C1-30s in Mombasa, Kenya.

"This is part of the normal route," a British passenger assured me. "The detour comes later." She leaned closer to my seat and added in a confidential tone: "Apparently, we have a VIP on board who wants to go to Zanzibar."

Zanzibar. Just hearing made me dream up a speck of green in the Indian Ocean, just off the far side of Africa. This is the place that puts the "zan" in Tanzania. When Tanganyika and Zanzibar merged in 1964, they chose a simple equation to create their new name. It's the same equation that gave us words like *Calexico* and *spork*, but the formula works much better for Tanzania because it incorporates the exoticism that is Zanzibar.

This is the legendary Isle of Spice, where the lines between history and fable become blurred. For centuries, its allure has attracted pirates, sultans, traders, pilgrims, romantics and plunderers. And now, apparently, it's attracted a VIP as well.

The Brit and I scanned the faces of the other passengers, trying to guess who it might be. Since I knew very little about the island, I hoped to quickly befriend this VIP. The British woman checked her watch and frowned. "I hope the bastard gets malaria."

After the plane touched down smoothly on the only runway in Zanzibar, I stood and collected my luggage. The British woman bit her lip. I then noticed that I was the only passenger getting off here.

Oddly, I didn't feel very important, but at least customs were hassle-free and cabs to Zanzibar Town were abundant. Rooms in town however, were not. The first three guesthouses on my list were already overbooked. That was the first sign that I was not the only visitor on the island.

The cab squeezed onward down the narrow streets until we happened upon a place called "The Narrow Street Hotel." A sign behind the front desk warned me to "dress and act modestly." It went on to explain subtly that Muslims are easily offended by standard tourist behavior.

Given the fact that Zanzibar is ninety-nine percent Islamic, I wondered if there were any bars in town. My dated and unreliable guidebook reported that there were three on the island. I decided to set out and find at least one.

Exploring the old Stone Town is a challenge for people who are accustomed to neat city blocks because right angles do not exist here. Streets curve and veer and defy most common laws of geometry. The buildings are the same; walls lean, floors and ceilings slant. Look skyward from any lane and you'll feel that the whole town will collapse upon you at any given moment.

The buildings are ancient, but seem very much alive. They crowd one another and refuse to stay in a straight line, forming dark corners and crevices that would be ideal for muggers, assassins and the like. A hotel clerk had warned me about such people, and advised me not to walk alone at night.

However, walking alone at night, or any other time, is nearly impossible. The streets are the center of local night life: Children play soccer or squabble over counterfeit Game Boys, men gather around their cars and gossip, women sit with their babies on the steps of coral-rag houses, and hundreds of hungry cats prowl in the shadows. Everyone kept a watchful eye on me. They knew I was lost.

I ran into a group of teenagers hanging out in front of a mosque and asked for directions to the Africa House Hotel. They didn't even attempt to explain how to get there. Without any discussion, one of them said he would take me. It was a twenty-minute walk through a labyrinth of winding, broken stone lanes. He asked for nothing in return. Escorting lost visitors around town is a matter of common courtesy. Only children expect money for this service, but not more than a hundred shillings (twenty cents).

The bar at the Africa House Hotel has a view of the ocean that is most astonishing at sunset. Unfortunately, the place is packed with tourists at that time and all the beer is gone by dusk. I arrived shortly after ten only to find a bored and lonely bartender. He told me to try the bars on Shangani Street, less than half a mile away.

I found a few bars there, all rather quiet, if not vacant. The few patrons I did see were either sleepy drunks or wide-eyed prostitutes. It was a refreshing change from Tanzania's capital city of Dar es Salaam, where hookers clambered into my cab. A guy who'd witnessed me kicking them out quickly seized up his crotch and offered it to me for the low, low price of twenty shillings.

But I quickly grew tired with the subdued nature of the bars on Shangani Street. So after downing a local pilsner, I left in search of yet another bar. A small white sign on an unnamed street pointed the way to the Spice House Bar and Restaurant. I followed a trail of these signs for half an hour until I found three policemen armed with AK-47s. They were freezing the assets in a shop owned by an Indian family who allegedly swindled six million dollars from the People's Bank of Zanzibar. Still, the police were happy to point the way to the Spice House, just a few doors down.

The restaurant was full of loud, whiny German tourists and their whiny children. At one table, a middle-aged woman screamed at her waitress: "Crab, *nein*! Lobster, *nein*!"

At the bar, a group of Dutch tourists were celebrating their last night on the island. One was trying to convince an Islamic bartender that Muslims were better than Christians in Africa. "Everywhere I go, Christians always want to save me," he said, slurring passionately. "I never met a Muslim who tried to save me."

The rest of the barflies were cliquish but friendly locals and expatriates. I sat next to one of the locals, a bug-eyed fisherman named Macho (which means "eyes" in the local dialect). He asked me what I thought of Zanzibar.

"Not what I expected," was the most polite reply I could offer.

"Oh? And what did you expect?"

"Something a little closer to the End of the Earth," I replied. He didn't seem to understand, so I added in a low voice: "Fewer tourists."

He laughed. "Tourism has been booming in the last four years. You should go to Uzi Island. Or better yet, Mafia Island." He raised both his voice and his beer. "No tourists at all there."

I'd actually heard of these places before. A friend in Dar told me that if I wanted to stay on Uzi Island, I would need to bring a tent. And as for Mafia Island, it's only for rich Tanzanians who enjoy sport fishing, though some tourists stop there en route to Kua on nearby Juani Island. In the early 1800s, raiders from Madagascar sacked the town of Kua and devoured all of its inhabitants. That sounded appealing enough, but then Macho told me that the next boat to Mafia didn't leave for another week.

"Try the east coast of Zanzibar," he suggested. "It's not The End of the World, but it's close enough."

Macho told me that a little Indian Muslim named Mr. Mitu could guide me anywhere on the island, so the next day I signed up for one of Mitu's Spice Tours. It began as a tour of the historic sites around town, with a brief stop at East Africa's first Anglican cathedral, constructed on the site of the Old Slave Market. According to local legend, its altar stands on the site of the whipping post. However, Mr. Mitu dismissed the story as anti-Arab propaganda. "It was not possible to have a whipping post because Arabs never carried whips," he argued. "They only carried swords."

Mitu's tour buses, which resembled Filipino jeepneys, delivered us out of town. The paved roads ended abruptly, but the buses continued grinding up the rutted roads through the countryside, where barefoot children in every village chased us, screaming, "Mitu! Mitu!"

He showed us inside the bat-infested ruins of the Kidichi Persian Baths, telling us Sultan Seyyid Barghash built them for his wife. He shepherded us through the grounds of the Maruhubi Palace, telling us that Barghash built it as well, but neglecting to mention that he did so for his ninety-nine concubines.

Mr. Mitu often invoked the Taj Mahal to describe these structures, but the comparisons seemed generous in light of the fact that all remnants of Omani opulence had fallen into ruins, and nobody was making any effort to save them.

I sensed a growing disenchantment among the tour group when one asked if we could see the Mangapwani Slave Caves, where Arabs continued slave trading after the British abolished it in 1897. Yet Mr. Mitu refused, claiming that no Arabs sold slaves from Tanzania after the abolition. "Other tour groups will take you there and show you the holes in the ground and tell you they are slaves caves!" he declared. "But I will not do that because I am not a liar! Those holes are not slave caves, only simple water wells!"

The tour improved as it evolved into a safari for the nose and taste buds. At first it seemed silly—trudging through the semi-wilds of Africa, stalking the not-so-elusive papaya—but it was more rewarding than any wildlife safari on the mainland. Each new plantation provided us with a different taste treat. Mitu allowed us to pick our own food: jack fruit, star fruit, pineapple, cashews, licorice, cocoa, mangoes, bananas, and grapefruits the size of bowling balls. I stuffed my face until I noticed the local children following us from a cautious distance. They anxiously puffed on cigarettes as they waited for our leftovers.

I regained my appetite while we hiked around spice plantations. We whiffed nutmeg, cinnamon and cloves until we were nearly stoned. Mitu then explained all the medicinal and cosmetic values of other nearby plants. Malaria medications, constipating alkaloids, nail polish, lipstick, pain relievers, hair dyes, laundry detergents and soap—it was a virtual drugstore growing on the land around us.

However, hop-scotching around farmlands under the equatorial sun can be a grueling task. And surprisingly, nature's drugstore doesn't stock any sort of sunscreen, unless, of course, you can weave palm fringes into sun hats, which is exactly what the local children do. Unfortunately, the hats are not for sale. Apparently, these little socialists haven't yet realized the market potential of their craft.

The tour concluded with lunch under a thatched shelter at the edge of a spice garden. We removed our shoes and sat on straw mats, while the drivers brought in enough soft drinks to drown a hippo. Then the food arrived: Steaming bowls of curried kingfish, dhal, rice, chapati, coconut danishes and spice tea. We stuffed our faces once again.

By the end, I was so full I could hardly breathe. But Mr. Mitu seemed to be anxious to leave. As we drove away, he told me why: "An opposition leader is coming this way. He will be dining in this area soon."

"Is that a problem?" I asked.

"Not at all," he replied, forcing a smile. "Only, it is better that we are not here when they arrive."

Several minutes later, we passed the opposition's entourage: Two jeeps overstuffed with uniformed men in black motorcycle helmets with smoked face shields, black neck braces, black gloves and large black batons. Evil clones of the Keystone Cops.

Opposition seems like dangerous business in Zanzibar. Though the shortest war in history occurred between England and Zanzibar in 1896 (Zanzibar surrendered after thirty-eight minutes), power rarely changes here without significant bloodshed. Last time this happened was in 1964, when Tanganyika's Afro-Shirazi Party revolted against the Sultan of Zanzibar. They succeeded in overthrowing him and massacred most of the Arab population in the process.

So I wasn't clear on the significance of this opposition party, also known as the Civic United Front. In Tanzania, the only legal political party was the socialist *Chama Cha Mapinduzi* (CCM, Party of the Revolution). And while Zanzibar operated on a semi-autonomous status, free to elect its own parliament and president, the CCM ruled Zanzibar as it did in mainland Tanzania.

However, that would change within a year. During the Zanzibar elections in 1995, the CCM youth wing engaged in a campaign of widespread intimidation and violence against CUF supporters. Still, the CUF would go on to win many parliamentary seats and fail to gain the presidency only as a result of rigged votes.

The CCM, still brandishing the bulk of Zanzibar's political power, would then spend the next three years imprisoning and torturing CUF supporters. According to Amnesty International, hundreds of these supporters were dismissed from their jobs, their homes were demolished, their children were refused education, and many fled to the mainland for their own safety.

I suspect now that those evil clones of the Keystone Cops, which Mr. Mitu had pointed out as the opposition, were actually members of the CCM on their way to greet the opposition.

Oblivious to the impending political crisis, I reveled in the Mr. Mitu's hospitality. I was so impressed with his Spice Tour that I immediately signed up for a trip to Jambiani, a village on the east coast. Soon after, I ran into Mr. Mitu near the Cine Afrique. He bought me a cup of coffee and I told him about my next trip.

"I'm leaving tomorrow morning," I said, showing him the ticket.

He took the ticket from my hand and turned it over. "Take it back to the office," he said in his rich Arabesque accent. "I want you to have free snuggling."

"Free what?"

"Free snuggling," he repeated. "Take this ticket back to my office and have them write, 'Free snuggling by Mr. Mitu.'"

"Thank you," I said, "but that really won't be necessary."

"You do not want to snuggle?" he asked in disbelief. He stood and puffed his cheeks, stretched his hands out toward me, then slowly spread his arms as if he were parting window curtains.

Suddenly, I understood: "Free snorkeling!"

"Yes!" he replied, clapping his hands together. "Free snuggling!"

The road to the east coast turned from fresh tarmac to dust and dirt. As the van slowed to straddle the ruts, a snake slithered out of our path. The driver said it was a mambo, also known as the two-step snake: If it bites you, you have enough time for two steps before you die. We also spotted a couple of Sykes blue monkeys, agricultural pests that are considered the most destructive animals on Zanzibar. I was disappointed to see they were grayish-brown—not blue by any stretch of the imagination.

Less than a minute after the snake encounter, the driver stopped and announced our arrival at the Jozani Forest, home of the red colobus monkey. Oddly, I was the only one in the tour group who wanted to venture into the forest.

Thick briars and tall grass obscured the path. The only clue that it was there was a thatched shelter and a sign with all but the word "reserve" peeled off. Under the shelter, I found the forest ranger: A very old man who was seriously lacking in the tooth and toenail department. He woke with a start, struggled to his feet, lurched to his left, then took a few steps to right himself. He reeked of Konyagi, Tanzania's version of gin.

He insisted that I lead the way, and we set off into the forest until we were up to our armpits in ferns. Every few steps seemed to stir up an animal in the undergrowth. I kept looking back to see if I was going in the right direction. He didn't seem to care where I was going, but he was having a hard time keeping up.

Suddenly, I heard a heavy thud directly behind me. I spun around. The ranger was gone. I retraced my steps a few feet and found him sprawled face down on the ground. I tried to help him up, but he fended me off, groaning, "*Sawa, sawa.*" (It's okay.) He pulled himself to his feet, but from then on he didn't take another step without first grabbing hold of something—a branch, a fern, a leaf—anything to steady himself.

He paused every five minutes or so to point at the treetops. I didn't see anything up there, and after fifteen minutes I was sure he was hallucinating. Worse yet, something in the underbrush was stinging my legs, and red welts formed on my ankles as if I'd steeped them in a vat of jellyfish.

Just as I was ready to abort this mission, I heard three heavy, log-crunching footsteps not more than fifty feet away. The ranger glanced in the direction of the sound, decided it was not a hallucination, then quickly and quietly led me off in the opposite direction. And for the next five minutes, he seemed completely sober.

I tried to imagine what indigenous animal could create such a terrifying noise, and could only imagine that it was an elephant bird or some other monstrous creatures not sighted in the region since Marco Polo asserted their existence in his famous book travel fables.

Time dragged by, and just as I suspected that red colobus monkeys belonged to the same family of mythical beasts, we found a tree full of them, at least two dozen in all. All small, listless monkeys with tails two to three time the length of their bodies. They were dull monkeys, but gazing up at them, I recalled two facts that made them seem worth the trouble:

1) There are only 500 of these monkeys left in the world.
2) The Jozani Forest is their last remaining sanctuary.

The road turned from dirt to sand, and the last five-mile stretch took about forty minutes to cross. When we arrived at the beach in Jambiani, the tide was so far out I couldn't see the ocean.

The hotel, however, was right on the beach—literally. Sand surrounded the building and filled the courtyard. Nevertheless, it seemed to be a clean, sturdy, bug-free hotel. Brilliant murals adorned its walls. Arched doorways added a touch of elegance. It didn't seem to matter that its fifteen or so guests had only three single bathrooms to share. Nor did it matter that Jambiani had not enjoyed electricity or running water for quite some time. Paradise here was simple. And for a moment, it felt like the End of the Earth.

Then I met the desk clerk. He looked exactly like Michael Jackson; that is, the late-seventies, *Off the Wall* version of Michael Jackson. He told me the hotel was full at the moment, but that someone would be checking out in about an hour. In the meantime, I could fill out all the necessary paperwork and pay for the room: six bucks a night, U.S. dollars only. Tanzanian shillings are not acceptable in most Tanzanian hotels.

Still, Jambiani is not a place for the Pina Colada crowd. Having fun can take some real effort, unless you enjoy lazing on a beach, eating fresh papaya and drinking milk straight from a coconut, both of which children sell at fifty shillings. They also sell dried fish and seashells. One child thrust a dead squid in my face and said in a timid voice: "Want to buy?"

Early the next morning, the ocean retreated out of sight again. Two Peace Corps volunteers and I hiked across the murky sands, climbed in an outrigger dhow and waited for the tide to come in and carry us away. A crew of three fishermen followed us, carrying our snorkel gear. They unfurled the sails, which had been stitched from bags labeled, INDONESIAN RICE. Soon after, four large, loud Europeans joined our expedition. Then as the ten of us set sail (ideally, the boat would accommodate four), I asked the Europeans where they were from.

"Denmark!" one proclaimed.

"We are Vikings!" cheered another. "The largest tribe in the world!" And they all broke into a boisterous Viking ditty.

I envied them. Many times during my travels in Tanzania, people asked what tribe I was. Even hotel registrars required my name, nationality and tribe. I tried several answers—Democrat, Southerner, Tar Heel—but none was acceptable. To avoid confusion, I learned to reply, "Cherokee." And while it has been rumored that I have a few drops of Cherokee blood in me, I don't consider it enough to bestow the honor of that title upon myself. Instead, I was forced to accept the fact that I was a man without a tribe. And as the Vikings broke into another Viking ditty, I secretly loathed them.

Or at least I tried. Their energy and enthusiasm was infectious. They were on their second round-the-world journey and they never ceased to be amazed by the smallest things. They rejoiced in everything. *Yay squid*! And soon I found myself singing along with their Viking ditties, even though I couldn't understand a word.

I even shared their enthusiasm for the sparse marine life this part of Zanzibar had to offer: Starfish bigger than my face, blue as the sky with blood-red spikes, and a bright orange whelk shell with yellow eyes on pink stems peeking out. As I picked up the shell, an inch-long barb crept out of one end. At once, I dropped it and the barb snapped against the shell where my thumb had just been. I dove to retrieve it, but the barb snapped again.

I left the menacing whelk and swam after a spear fisherman. He showed me how to probe the sand for sea slugs. He dug one up and squeezed it until white gunk shot out. Then he handed me the deflated slug. It felt like crushed velvet. He took it back and stuffed it in a bag labeled INDONESIAN RICE.

From the same bag, he withdrew an octopus the size of a basketball and handed it to me. It's tentacles clung to my arm and something gooey oozed into my palm. Immediately, I tore my hand free. Underwater, it sounded like velcro. The fisherman laughed so hard his mask filled with water. He raised his head above the surface, removed his mask and asked, "*Nini?*" (What is it?)

"Octopus," I answered.

"Octopusi," he repeated, and he stuffed his hand inside the octopus as if it were a glove.

By noon, the tide had returned, but the boat crew insisted on leaving the boat where we found it. We had to hike back to the beach, this time in waist-deep water. The heat of the sun turned brutal; and as we neared the shore, the shallow water began to scald my legs. I was in serious pain with more than 200 yards to shore. It was a scary feeling, being broiled simultaneously by the sea and sky with no place to take refuge. Even the Vikings stopped rejoicing.

But I made it back to the hotel without collapsing. The Michael Jackson desk clerk took one look at me and said, "You changed colors."

That night I was too tired to read or write, so I just sat on the front porch and watched flies feasting on the open sores and tropical ulcers on my feet. I was too tired to shoo them away. By 9:30, I managed to drag myself to bed, but I was too hot to sleep. My flesh had absorbed so much sun that now the heat pulsed throughout my entire body—a heat that would remain for the next three days and keep me warm in freezing rain in Amsterdam.

It was a stifling, breezeless night. The mosquito netting around me seemed suffocating, airtight. I tucked it aside and slept at risk of contracting a new strain of malaria that had reached epidemic proportions on Zanzibar.

I woke at dawn. Sweat had welled up in the hollow of my neck, and as I rose it streaked down my chest. A wet imprint in my mattress suggested that I had been sleeping on my back the entire night. The odd thing was, it was a bright red imprint on an otherwise white sheet.

I'm sweating blood, I thought.

Underneath the sheet, however, was a red mattress cover. My sweat caused the dye to soak into the sheets. It probably soaked into my skin as well, but I was so sunburned that it didn't make a difference. It was a puffy burn, the kind that makes a grain of sand feel like a razor blade. I never wanted to see the sun again.

But then I staggered outside, and there it was. A great ball of fire rising out of the Indian Ocean, streaking the sky with colors I never knew existed. I sat there and stared at it until I thought I would go blind.

That same day, back in Zanzibar Town, I sat in Jamituri Park waiting for an equally magnificent sunset. Vendors lined the sidewalks, selling sugarcane juice, smoked octopus and shish kababs right off the grill. Dozens of children and teenagers dived off the seawalls, twisting and somersaulting before splashing down, scrambling back up and doing all over again. Dhows drifted across the harbor, their triangular sails appearing like enormous shark fins. Behind them, orange thunderclouds rolled across the horizon. They stole the sun's fire and put on a furious display of lightning. Bolts reached across the sky and stabbed the ocean like skeletal claws and devils' pitchforks. Yet the sky above town remained perfectly clear, and a full moon rose above the former sultan's palace, the Beit-el-Ajaib (House of Wonder).

Darkness set in and the air stilled. The spiced smoke from the shish kabob grills swallowed the park, and rows upon rows of kerosene lanterns shined through like streetlamps in London fog. I gazed at seven minarets spiked against the moonlit sky and thought, Zanzibar is not the End of the Earth, but it's close enough.

Ghosts of Africa

TANZANIA: 1994

Tamora called me on a hot October afternoon in 1994. She just picked up a phone in Arusha, Tanzania, and compulsively dialed my office number in Chapel Hill, North Carolina. The connection was clear, and I knew immediately something was wrong.

I had not heard from her since I left Arusha at the end of March, but I thought of her constantly. I wasn't worried so much about her safety. As a Rwandan expat in Tanzania, she should've been relatively secure.

But there was this incident one week after I left: The presidents of Rwanda and Burundi also made their final departure from Tanzania. Difference is, their plane was shot down. Accusations and power grabs sparked off a civil war between the Tutsi and Hutu tribes in Tamora's homeland. Close to half a million Rwandans, mostly Tutsi, were already dead.

I asked about her family, meaning her parents and sisters who still lived in Rwanda, but she answered, "My daughters are fine, and I'm going to have another baby soon."

"That's great," I said. There was a pause. I braced for the news on the rest of her family.

She said, "Roman has been shot. I think he'll be all right. I brought him back to Germany to recover."

It had nothing to do with the crisis in Rwanda. Just your everyday Tanzanian bandits broke into their home and demanded money. When they threatened Tamora and the children, her husband fought them back, so they shot him in the face.

I wondered if I would have been so brave.

When she said the bandits fled with her Land Rover, I suddenly thought of her driver.

"Alec is fine," she assured me, sounding pleased that I remembered him. "He asked about you the other day. He wants to know when you're coming back."

I told her I couldn't anytime soon. My girlfriend and I were going to Korea. We had a contract to teach there for a year.

I could swear I heard her gasp. She asked if I missed her. I said, of course. Just hearing her voice reminded me how much I missed her. It was deep and echoed of London, like a West End girl with an East African lilt, though prone to sing in Swahili or growl in German without warning.

She said, "Please come back to Africa."

I continued to hear her voice long after I set down the phone. I sensed profound sadness in it, and one phrase continually came back to haunt me: "I'm going to have another baby soon." I caught myself counting back the months on my fingers. Impossible, I thought, but later that night I scoured my journal for evidence to the contrary.

A hundred miles or so southeast of Arusha, the Lutheran mission stood in the shadow of Kilimanjaro amidst a thousand acres of banana plantations. I was there to attend a conference on AIDS and women's health. Roman, a German doctor who worked in bush clinics near the Rwandan border, had been invited to share his expertise, but declined due to an overwhelming caseload. Instead he sent his wife and coworker, Tamora.

She arrived at night, during the first of many power outages. I greeted her in the reception hall. Her face evaded the candlelight, but she carried the intoxicating smell of jacaranda and her voice melted me.

"Excuse me for saying so," I told her as I hoisted her bags, "but you have the most amazing accent."

She thanked me as if she'd heard that a hundred times before, and explained that she learned much of her English in London. Coincidentally, we soon learned, we'd attended the same college at the same time. We squinted at each other through the darkness. "You wouldn't recognize me," she said. "I had less hair then." She combed her fingers through her braided, midriff-length extensions.

I volunteered to show her to her room, and struggled under the weight of her luggage. When we arrived, she effortlessly relieved me of all but the briefcase and invited me to return later for a beer. I told her there was no beer on the compound, warning her that it was forbidden. She lit a cigarette and casually announced she'd sent Alec out for a case.

Alec proved himself resourceful in locating tremendous amounts of Heineken and Konyagi, the Tanzanian version of gin, and I returned to her room night after night. He often stayed to drink and talk with us. Tamora's flawless translation of my English and his Swahili kept the conversations lively.

One night, as Alec and I prepared to leave her room, she asked me to return after it seemed everyone else had gone to sleep. I stupidly agreed. Half an hour later, I skulked back and tapped on her door. She didn't answer. I let myself in and found her in the bathroom wrapping a towel around her head, her bathrobe slightly parted. "So soon," she said in mock surprise.

A few more drinks put her jovial mood to rest, and soon she began lamenting European attitudes toward Africans in Europe and Africans attitudes toward their own European-educated folk, especially those who married Europeans. Her tone was not self-pitying, but seething in anger. I got the feeling that she had kept these feelings bottled up for years, unable to share them with either Europeans or Africans, that only an American ear would hear her out.

She also bemoaned her husband and his all-consuming dedication to the clinics. She smoked incessantly as she shared her feelings of neglect and her desire for another baby.

"But Roman, oh no. He doesn't have the time for it." She gnawed at her thumbnail and muttered something in German.

I listened with no advice to offer for consolation, which was probably for the best. She needed to vent, and then she needed a hug. I patted her on the back and she returned a powerful embrace. Eventually, I pried myself loose. She apologized for her behavior. "I have a horrible temper," she warned, blaming it on her Tutsi heritage. "We can be awful at times."

When I snuck back up the following night, I found her in much better spirits. The power had gone out again, but she could see by candlelight that I looked tired. I was, not only from staying up so late the night before, but because of the Mefloquin, anti-malarial pills that inspired absurdly colorful and vivid dreams, and made me loopy in general.

She offered a massage. I accepted, flopping back on her bed. She unbuttoned my shirt and rolled me over. Then, squeezing my shoulders slightly beyond my pain threshold, she started up on Roman again. I was too tired to hear it. I sat up at the edge of her bed and told her I should get a full night's sleep.

"Please don't go," she said, grabbing my hands.

Red flags rose in the dusty fields of my mind. If I'd learned anything in college, it was that gorgeous women find me irresistible only if they suffer from manic depression. I watched her for a moment, looking for familiar signs of instability, particularly the jerky smile that cracks the mask of invulnerability. But admiring Tamora's deep dark eyes and the hard edges of her face, I saw a woman too strong to fall apart.

She leaned in to kiss me. I impulsively bit her nose.

"What was that?" she demanded.

"We can't kiss," I told her apologetically. "You're married."

She huffed, nostrils flaring, but she never let go of my hands.

"And I've got a serious girlfriend."

"How serious?" she challenged.

"I've known her longer than you've known your husband."

"And you never once cheated on her?"

I freed one hand and grabbed a beer. "Once. In London."

"It could've been with me," she joked. "Maybe it was and you just don't remember."

I squinted at her. "Maybe. How many times have you cheated on your husband?"

She became indignant. "I have never cheated on Roman.

Never." The name got her going again. She pressed her head against my neck. Her shoulders heaved back quiet sobs. "I swear to God I'm going to leave that man."

This business of skulking about the Lutheran mission well past the midnight hour reckoned me back to the thrill of similar escapades in my junior high years; and yet for the same reason, I felt enormously silly doing it night after night. I had certain responsibilities now, commitments to the conference that were going neglected. Shame shadowed me in the dark corridors.

That's when I caught Dr. Mbisi—one of Tanzania's leading gynecologists—sneaking out of a nurse's room. We bid each other good evening, but avoided eye contact.

He seemed an entirely different man, I thought, considering what he had reported to the conference board: "When you make love to an African woman, you can wear a sheath, but you are not protected. Because you will see when you are done that she has made you wet from your knees all the way to the top of your chest. So I am telling you, one way or another, you are going to need a body bag."

I wanted to tell Tamora about the encounter in the corridor, but when I arrived in her room, she told me to leave. "I don't want to see you tonight," she said. She cried over a tall glass of Konyagi. "I don't want to see you ever again." Her cigarette ash curled toward the floor.

"What's wrong?"

"Just go."

"Tell me what's wrong."

She turned her face away. "I love you," she said. "I know I shouldn't, but I do." Melodramatic words like that would have tumbled off anyone else's tongue like so much cheese, but in her voice they were lyrical. "Why do you love me?" she asked repeatedly. I never said I did. "What do you see in me?"

I didn't know where to begin. "Everything."

She stood, marched up to me and thumped her fists against my chest, shoving me toward the door. "Go!" she insisted. In the quiet night, her voice carried like a shout.

I knew if I left then, I could not come back. Nor would she ask me to. Risking another outburst, I curled my hand behind her neck and softly hushed her. She tilted her head for a kiss and whispered, "Don't be afraid."

And so we kissed. Her full lips and tongue felt thick enough to make mine seem insignificant. Her embrace adjusted my vertebrae. All the fear we felt inside translated into a passionate energy that carried us through the night.

And yet, all we did was kiss.

Dust devils spun along the highway between Kilimanjaro and Mt. Meru, and the red capes of Maasai cattlemen burned against the vast empty plains. With the conference behind us, Tamora and I sped toward Arusha with further plans for Zanzibar. Alec passed the time cracking raunchy jokes that made Tamora groan. She didn't want to translate them, but Alec and I insisted, and he laughed again at punchlines he no longer understood.

In Arusha, she secured three rooms at the Golden Rose Hotel. I sighed in relief, thinking at last I might get a full night's sleep. However, she later explained that the third room, mine, was for the sake of decent appearances. "Alec knows about us, of course," she explained, "but we don't have to rub it in his face."

I spent the day's fading hours mustering the courage and excuses on why I should sleep alone that night. *This is wrong. I need sleep. I have diarrhea from the goat we ate for lunch. I'm hung over. The Mefloquin is giving me sea legs and mild hallucinations. I think I'm coming down with malaria.*

All except that last one were true, but Tamora wouldn't hear any of it. "If you leave my room, I'll tell Alec to take me home right now," she threatened. Then she offered me a drink. I knew then that a few beers would put me out cold. Nothing short of heavy drinking was going to get me through the night.

I have a vague recollection of a single bulb hanging from the ceiling and a comment I made on how it looked like an alligator egg. I remember how we sat close on a bed no bigger than a cot and the way the mosquito netting around us seemed to breathe on its own. I felt as if a ghost had swallowed us whole.

I can recall part of the conversation, how she railed against Roman for denying her another child. And then that glint in her eye when she said my name.

She said, "Ausherman. *Aus Herr Mann.* You're German."
"Oh please. Most of my family is from the Netherlands."
"That's close enough."
I didn't like where this was going.
"How would anyone know?" she asked.
I looked for a delicate way out. "Does it strike you as, I don't know, ironic? Considering something like this right after an AIDS conference?"
She backed away. "You're not HIV positive, are you?"
"Of course not. I'm just saying it seems a bit hypocritical to—"
"*Scheisse!*" Her eyes narrowed. "You're afraid that I have the HIV."
"No. I would bet my life that you don't have HIV. But I wouldn't bet my girlfriend's life any more than you should bet your husband's—"
She slapped my face and snapped something in German that I understood as: "Get out!"
But I know I couldn't have left the room without her that night.

The reasons escape me now, but we did get kicked out of the Golden Rose Hotel. I think it had something to do with an argument she started with another guest. It didn't seem serious to me at the time, no more intense than, say, a heated discussion between fans of rivaling high school football teams, but it went on for hours and ended when the guest, a slightly built man with narrow eyes, abruptly excused himself to his room.
"What was that about?" I asked.
Tamora remained still on her bed, quietly seething. "He is from my village," she said. "But he is Hutu. I recognized that as soon as I saw him."
"You don't like the Hutu?"
"I have many Hutu friends," she replied in a convincing manner. "My mother's best friend is Hutu. But you know, in Rwanda, there are problems." Then to my bleary, vacant look of ignorance, she said, "You have no idea what is happening in my country."

This was shamefully true, but she would patiently explain. Exactly what she told me, I don't recall, and even if I had been in my most coherent and alert state, which I certainly was not, I don't think I would have fully grasped the problem. I mean, she was telling me about two tribes in conflict for 600 years. No, conflict isn't the word for what they did; that much can be illustrated in a few select years in the recent histories of Rwanda and Burundi. Take 1959: 100,000 Tutsi butchered. Or 1972: 1000 Tutsi killed and 200,000 Hutu slaughtered in retaliation. Or 1988: Estimates up to 24,000 dead, both Hutu and Tutsi.

Now, in March of 1994, Rwanda was home to some 6.5 million Hutu and 600,000 Tutsi, all crammed together in one of Africa's poorest and smallest nations, a dinky chunk of land that had long exhausted its ability to sustain agricultural demands. One idea was already taking root in the minds of too many people: that the most efficient way to reduce competition for limited land and resources was genocide, and that centuries mutual hatred made this a viable option.

All that was needed to begin the campaign was an excuse, a catalyst, a spark to set off yet another mass slaughter. Tutsi rebels were already on the offensive, and President Habyarimana's attempts to achieve peace with them enraged Hutu extremists.

Habyarimana and Burundi's President Ntaryama were on their way to Tanzania in search of a democratic plan to avert chaos. Meanwhile, the French were equally busy shelling Tutsi rebel positions in Rwanda and denying any involvement.

There were too many variables to consider, too much information to comprehend. But I got this much: What Tamora was telling me that night was something bad was about to happen. Whether she said that it would begin within weeks or that the death toll would exceed all previous massacres combined, I'm not sure. I'd like to believe that I'd never forget a warning like that, regardless of my state of mind. But there are so many things I don't remember, and yet so many things she couldn't have known.

I do remember moving into the Arusha Resort Centre, where Tamora gave up on the pretense of a third room. I remember the morning we spent cruising along the lowland swamps of Arusha National Park. We brought along Tamora's niece, a child named Kamikazi, which means Small Princess. We stalked warthogs and dik-diks around Tululusia Hill, then kicked back for lunch at Momela Lodge, a prominent fixture in the John Wayne movie, *Hatari!* Later, out on a barren savannah, Tamora dared Alec and I to get out of the Land Rover and approach a herd of buffalo. We took turns, advancing as they retreated and retreating when they charged. It was not the brightest game, but Kamikazi found it hilarious.

The day faded away long before we were ready to leave. Alec grew nervous as the sun neared the horizon. He sped toward the gates, but a herd of giraffes wandered into the road and sauntered along in our way. He screamed at them, "*Twende, Bwana Twiga!*" (Let's go, Mr. Giraffe!) and I feared he might try to drive between their legs.

It was well past the sundown curfew when heavily-armed rangers caught us a hundred yards or so inside the gate. Both Alec and Tamora tried to reason with them, blaming our lateness on belligerent giraffes, but to no avail. I sat back, quietly wishing that they would just lower their rifles. Ultimately it was Kamikazi who convinced them that we were not poachers. She didn't have to say anything, only batted her big six-year-old eyes and the spell was cast. I never before appreciated a child as much as her.

Tamora and I thrived on days like that. And on tamer nights we danced and laughed and felt more alive than we'd ever known. Our only disagreement resulted from the songs they played. While I preferred the indigenous *muziki wa dansi* (dance music), she insisted on dancing only to cheesy songs like that ubiquitous Ace of Base ditty, "All That She Wants (Is Another Baby)". We held a mutual disrespect for each other's taste in music, but easily got over it.

I felt enormously happy. This was my fourth trip to Africa, I realized, and never before had I seen it this beautiful.

She was beautiful, especially when we kissed. We kissed late into the night. I kissed her mouth and her ears. I kissed her breasts and her back. But when I kissed her down there, she abruptly stopped me.

"Do you remember the joke Alec told about African women?" she asked, averting her eyes. "About how orgasm makes us urinate? Well, it's true."

"That's absurd," I scoffed, but I had to wonder if this is what Dr. Mbisi meant by African women leaving you wet from knees to neck.

"No, I'm telling you," she insisted.

"So you never allow yourself to orgasm?"

She reached down and thumped my head. "Of course I do. Just never like this."

I curled my hands around her thighs, telling her, "Don't be afraid."

After her moaning stopped and her trembling stilled, I saw that the sheet beneath me was soaked beyond the span of my elbows. I inhaled deeply then crawled up to kiss her lips.

She turned her face away.

"That wasn't urine," I assured her.

Still she wouldn't kiss me.

Later, as she slept, I sat on the front porch and shared my last cigarette with a security guard. He was Maasai, and he patrolled the resort grounds with a bow and arrow. I wanted to talk to him, but we understood almost nothing of each other's language. I wanted to tell him how horrible I felt for cheating on my girlfriend, for my hypocrisy over risking infection, for allowing myself to love Tamora and for all the things we did.

And yet, I told myself, all we did was kiss.

Tamora announced over breakfast that she was going home. She said that she felt ill and didn't have the strength to continue on to Zanzibar. I figured the exhaustion that had plagued me earlier finally caught up with her. She apologized. I told her it was for the best.

The last time I saw her was at the airport in Arusha, where I boarded the plane for Zanzibar.

The last time I heard her voice was in October 1994.

Several months after the phone call, on a hot summer day in Seoul, I received a letter from her. She explained more about Roman. Doctors had to remove part of his brain, but after a year of rehab he seemed to be doing well. She had the baby. She and Roman then went back to her village in Rwanda to look for her family.

Of that trip, she wrote: "My father had been killed in our house. My mother had been killed by her best friend and thrown in Lake Kivu. My other relatives had been killed in the field but many were killed in the church and buried in mass graves . . . ." It went on.

I couldn't begin to imagine her torment, but I caught glimpses of the crushing misery it must have inspired in Roman as he stood beside her, trying helplessly to absorb away her grief. Given a choice, I think I would've rather taken a bullet. He accepted both, and yet Tamora emptied her heart into a letter, repeatedly declaring her love for me and begging me to come back to Africa. It consumed me with guilt, that I was the object of her misplaced affection, stealing love from a man who endured so much pain for her sake.

I might have felt half as much guilt for what I'd done to my own relationship, except that nothing changed. My girlfriend knew as well as I did what happened over there. She read the letter.

Tamora and I maintained a correspondence for another year or so. Each of her letters sounded a little more desperate than the last, always begging me to come back to Africa. The last one, sent November 1996, misquoted part of a Kate Bush song I once played for her. I briefly recoiled from the adolescent practice of referencing pop tunes in pining letters, but the lyric chilled me.

It went, "There's a ghost in our home, just watching me without you."

I imagined that ghost as Roman. And then as her mother. Or perhaps her baby. But truth is, I'm not sure what she meant. It's a strange song, and some things are best left unknown.

Honeymoon in Caracas

VENEZUELA: 2001

It's one of those things on my list of 101 Things To Do Before I Die. Somewhere toward the end, it reads: Honeymoon in South America. That's pretty vague. And that's where the problem begins.

Betsy and I got married in the summer of 1999. That wasn't on my list, but it was a necessary step towards crossing out the Honeymoon in South America entry. We'd never been to South America. Unable to decide on a country we roiled with indecision for more than a year before we settled on Venezuela. It was October, and I was reading about their President Hugo Chávez in *Newsweek*. In talking about the revolution in his country, he said, "It's like love. You have to make love every day in many ways."

¡*Viva la revolución!*

Imagine a country where the president commands his people to make love not just every day, but in many ways. I thought, now there's a country we should visit. But what were we supposed to do when we got there? I mean, besides the Presidential imperative.

Our uncertainty causes us to approach La Isla Margarita with diminished enthusiasm. Maybe we'd feel better about coming here if we knew about two dozen other tourists bound for the same island on the same day. Their flight goes down in flames shortly after takeoff, incinerating everyone on board. We arrive safely, uneventfully.

True to our old travel habits, we stray past the popular ports of call, bypassing the Hiltons and discos and duty-free shopping, and press on to El Agua, a town where traffic and electricity are sporadic.

We check into the cheapest hotel in town. Far from the beach and secure behind iron gates, the Hostería El Agua smells of drenching, day-old piss. The odor is heavy in the air—more notably, in the towels and pillowcases—and it grows stronger as the day warms.

Our room lacks the requisite screens and netting, and mosquitoes drift by in erratic flight patterns. Betsy and I are not protected against malaria or dengue fever. I leave her in the room to unpack while I get a brief orientation from the desk clerk downstairs. He conveys all essential details about the town—the best restaurants, the areas best avoided at night—with a crudely drawn map and patient Spanish.

I return to the room and find a thick haze that smells of gasoline and citronella. Betsy has fogged our small, enclosed sleeping quarters with half a can of mosquito spray designed to protect a large, open campsite. Mosquitoes are stuck to the walls, and the floor is slick with an oily film. This will not be conducive to the Presidential imperative.

Betsy wants nothing more than to move out of the hostería and into a resort near the beach. The one she has in mind is Hotel Le Flamboyant, an all-inclusive resort with fountains in the swimming pool and scarcely a guest under fifty.

I'm fiercely opposed to the very idea. Lounging in a resort does not qualify as real travel. We should be spending our time on hikes through rainforests and mangrove swamps, I argue. And besides, we are not the resort type. We are veteran travelers who recognize and appreciate the romantic aspects of roughing it in the Third World.

That night in our room, the ratio of bites to kisses is approximately 34:0. The mosquitoes are literally masticating the romance out of our honeymoon, leaving me no choice but to secure a room in Hotel Le Flamboyant before Betsy so much as sits down to breakfast.

The resort—with its cool tile floors, its soaring viga ceilings, its air-conditioned rooms, its wafting scents of jasmine and cilantro—everything about it mocks my rugged traveler sensibilities. The cloying serenity of this faux-Eden compound makes me edgy, as if the manicured hedges and Spanish tiles are closing in on me, hermetically sealing me off from the country I traveled so far to experience. And the purple plastic bracelets that identify us as Flamboyant guests are particularly offensive, though I must admit their subtle fragrance—sort of like Luv's Baby Soft—stirs up memories of a fifth-grade crush.

That night after dinner, Betsy is charmed with how frequently and passionately I kiss her hand, when in fact I'm snorting her wrist.

After a restless night, I wake determined to abandoned this Caribbean island for an exploration of El Oriente, the coastline east of Caracas. More specifically, I'm interested in a fifty-mile stretch of coastline between Barcelona and Cumaná, but I'm not sure why. Maybe I've been seduced by superlatives: El Oriente is where Columbus first set foot on the mainland. Cumaná is South America's oldest Hispanic city, and the site of the fiercest native resistance that early Spaniards would face in the New World. If it were home to Venezuela's biggest ball of wax, I'd probably want to see that, too.

Superlatives are sorry excuses to travel, Betsy warns as I rush her out of the resort.

At the ferry terminal, I fight my way to the front of the ticket line and shout broken Spanish through bulletproof glass until the ticket agent figures out that I want to go to Cumaná. Tickets in hand, we wait on wooden benches in a chainlink cage, watching other passengers arrive and depart on schedule.

Once they're gone, I notice that the only other waiting passengers are five weary Italian travelers and fewer Venezuelans. Then there's the usual assortment of dockside inhabitants, and they seek us out every half hour. The same jewelry vendor, candy vendor, sunglass vendor, half-starved child beggar, half-crazed adult beggar—they're all thinking maybe we've changed our minds since the last time they asked us for money. They're thinking, maybe this time we've come to our senses and realized how much we really do need sunglasses, a rosary, and a piece of gum the size of a yardstick.

What they don't know is that I am a more persistent nag. Every half hour, I seek out someone—anyone in uniform—for the status of the ferry. They tell me it's running late, but assure me it will be departing within the hour. I notice one of the Italians doing the same thing. Equally uncertain of our Spanish comprehension skills, we meet to compare notes on what the men in uniform might be telling us. We concur that they are in fact telling us that the ferry is running a bit late today.

I occasionally stray from the cage and wander the bulkhead, watching children splash around on the littered beach below. The belly of a fish breaks through the oily surface, then sinks. Further down the road, three children are fighting over something in a garbage barrel, and not one is tall enough to reach it without falling inside.

The day is heating up fast. Sweat becomes more noticeable as it wakens thin cuts on my shoulders, back and buttocks. These I incurred the night before from the sharp edges of the purple plastic wristbands. Each sudden shift under the embrace of Betsy's left arm resulted in a mini incision in my flesh, and I am just now beginning to feel the sting. The pain isn't so bad. Far more pleasant than a mosquito bite. Besides, it's for the revolution.

I return with my report on the world outside the cage. Betsy sighs and says she's starving.

I tell her I didn't see any restaurants out there, but the liquor stores on the other side of the fence do carry chips, and the kiosk next to those is selling pollo asado. She reluctantly leaves her post at the gate to inspect the chips and chicken. The half-crazed mendicant follows her at a distance. She wants to know if I think the chicken is safe. It's been sitting out half cooked for the better part of the day. I tell her, at this point it's safer than staving off hunger with greasy chips.

The ribby madman watches us pick through our suspect chicken. I encourage Betsy to dig in, despite its suspiciously pinkish meat. I tell her that I watched the chef thoroughly roast the whole bird on an open flame, but fail to mention at least two points of potential cross-contamination between the grill and the plate. It doesn't matter. She can't compete with the onslaught of flies. She can't choke this dead fowl down, not under the watch of the madman and two whimpering dogs that are near bursting with tumors.

We pick over the plate one last time, nibbling at the peppery meat, then drop our forks. Before we can so much as stand upright, our wild-eyed friend descends on our table and whisks away our plate. He follows us back to our cage, finds his seat on the floor in front of us and gnaws on bones we deemed unfit for our own consumption. Far from showing appreciation for our leftovers, he keeps a steady scowl on us. Then, midway through his meal, he stands and yells at us. I can understand just one word—*rico*. It's the nickname he's picked out for every traveler who has refused to give him money. The rest of what he says is incomprehensible, but he stands there repeating it, as though demanding an answer from us, until a Venezuelan traveler explains to him that it's no use, that we can't understand him because we're English. That's what bugs me about this place. Everyone here mistakes us for English or German. The madman doesn't care. He slams the rest of the meal in the trash barrel next to Betsy, prompting a child to dive in after it.

In the commotion, our ferry has come and gone, but all the passengers are still here. A man in uniform patiently explains to me that the ferry needs repairs. If we still want to go to Cumaná, we can take the next ferry to Puerto La Cruz.

Abutting Barcelona, Puerto La Cruz is a destination for reveling tourists and unrefined petroleum. It's also a hub for buses and por puesto taxis that can deliver us anywhere in El Oriente, including Santa Fe and Cumaná.

However, the man in uniform explains that the ferry there will cost us another ten dollars and an additional four-hour wait on the docks. The exasperated Italians collectively throw up their hands and storm out of the cage. Betsy folds her arms across her knees and slowly thumps her forehead on her wrists. A man with an armful of rosaries offers one at a special discount. All I can think is: This day is shot. No amount of preparation could have avoided it and there is nothing I can do to change it.

That is what I hate about travel. It's not travel when you're stuck in transit. True, many great travel stories revolved around getting stuck (*Alive, Into Thin Air, Titanic*, etc.), but there is absolutely nothing to say about waiting ten hours for a ferry that will never arrive.

We board a ferry bound for a place we never wanted to go. One hour out to sea, the frustration of it all catches up with Betsy. Every decision about our honeymoon was mine to make, and this one drove her to tears. I knew then we would not heed the president's imperative that day, not in any way. She's still starving. She's reminiscing about the dinner buffet at Le Hotel Flamboyant like it was her last meal before a prison sentence that commenced years ago.

The ferry is equipped with a café and a restaurant. Problem is, since we incurred a few unexpected expenses—the pollo asado, the difference in ticket prices, a bit of last minute duty-free shopping in the liquor store—we are down to pocket change in the local currency. We dine on the breakfast bars I packed in case of emergency. Running out of cash during a ferry delay was not the kind of emergency I had in mind. When I packed them, I was thinking along the lines of getting lost in the Amazon or getting abducted by Colombian guerillas or both. Sitting here on a boat with a lounge that's air-conditioned to the point of refrigeration, with about 600 seats to share among maybe sixty passengers, with bootleg copy of *Coyote Ugly* playing on multiple screens, with Venezuelan pop pumping out of an adjacent bar—with all this, it hardly seems like the kind of crisis that might warrant the consumption of our emergency cherry cobbler breakfast bars.

The ferry slows to navigate its way along some of Venezuela's most spectacular islands. Picuda Chica, Cachicama, Quirice, Chimana del Sur. I squint to make out their silhouettes against the moonlit sea and the lights of Puerto la Cruz, and I try to imagine the magnitude of beauty shrouded in the darkness. I'm tempted to jump overboard and swim to their uninhabited shores. It's not a serious consideration, but I back away from the railing just in case.

Upon arrival, we take a cab to the Hotel Caribbean and pay the fare with a handful of coins, some worth less than three cents, and a few crumpled US dollar bills. A doorman hurries us off the sidewalk in into the empty, candlelit lobby, all the while warning us how dangerous it is to be outside in this part of town.

The Presidential imperative, I surmise, has already been shot.

You would think I learned something that night, that success or failure in the Presidential mission greatly depends on the price of our accommodations. Yet each night in a new town, we bunk down in a budget posada, and each morning we examine each other's bodies for bites. One morning, I discover three round welts in a line on her ribs and four more on her inner thigh. She finds a few on my belly and a series of knotty bites on my knuckle. This proves to be our most intimate moment in days.

We spend hours a day making lists of activities, then fail to accomplish most of them due to an overwhelming sense of inertia either on our part or that of the local tourist guides.

When did we begin to rely on tourist guides for anything?

I look back through my notes and find pages describing our hotels. I never used to write about hotels. When did I pick up this bad habit?

What are we doing wrong here?

Old habits are hard to break. For fifteen years, my strategy was simple: Find the cheapest place to crash. I would pride myself in hunkering down in the most abysmal conditions. Deprivation of the most basic comforts adds much to a sense of adventure. Lacking five-star insulation from a foreign environment allows you to commune with it and more fully appreciate the people who live there. And, by removing the temptation to sleep in, it forces you out into the world you've come to experience.

When Betsy and I traveled Asia between 1994 and 1996, we adhered to this basic principle and held up well. Whether it was in a frigid Korean *yogwan* or under a suffocating mosquito net in a thatched hut on a remote Philippine island, we had sex and lots of it.

But toward the end, after a series of sleepless nights that culminated in a longhouse village in the jungles of Borneo, (or maybe it was two nights later when monkeys raided our cabin,) something changed. Travel no longer felt like an adventure when we spent the days sleepwalking through forests and markets and temples. Worse, we stopped making love on a daily basis.

We began to wonder why we were there at all, and realized then that we had no purpose. We went to Borneo because we completed our teaching contract in Korea and we weren't ready to go home. Our point of being in Asia had expired and we simply invited our souls to continue wandering.

We're doing the same thing here, and I'm wishing that we stayed at the Flamboyant until we bled through a thousand cuts from those purple plastic bracelets.

Weary, but not yet defeated, we push onward to Santa Fe.

Santa Fe is located about halfway between Puerto la Cruz and Cumaná, and is locally regarded as a safe haven for criminals from both cities. However, its fledgling tourist industry is driving out the bad elements and beginning to draw the world to its beach.

To get there, my wife and I hire a taxi from Puerta la Cruz. Our driver seems to know his way around Santa Fe, but hasn't heard of the Playa Santa Fe Resort, the hotel we've selected from the guidebook.

He cruises down the town's main street, two lanes of busted asphalt divided by a littered, weedy strip of dirt. We're in the only car on the road, the only functional car, anyway. A rusting hulk of a Buick with cracked headlights rests askew of the gutter. Homes along the way look abandoned for their darkness and state of disrepair. A closer look reveals the residents tucked back in the shadows of enclosed front porches. The beach is nowhere in sight.

The driver asks five different people where the Playa Santa Fe Resort might be and they point in five different directions, the last of which leads us down a narrow dirt alley walled in by off-white stucco. We're in luck. The lettering under the mildew stains clearly reads: Playa Santa Fe Resort & Dive Center. The entrance gate, however, is secured under a rusted lock and chain, and a heavy shag of weeds indicates how few have passed through in recent months. Our optimistic driver reverses his car out of the lane and continues backward down a beach access road. He promises us that the entrance is on the beach, just four houses down.

Under the weight of our luggage, Betsy and I trudge through smooth white sand, while local children run free and screaming along the water's edge. Their parents watch from their posts. Coolers, inflatable sea creatures, umbrellas and chairs are arranged around them like bunkers set to repel a naval invasion. Pelicans loiter on wooden skiffs bobbing ten yards offshore. Music blares out of the crowded, key lime café behind us, while the samba carnival rhythm of roving drummers and whistlers sounds to be nearing from the other direction.

A cluster of pale, topless Europeans seems to indicate the general whereabouts of our next hotel. A sign behind the iron gate confirms it, adding that members of AA and NA are most welcome. I wonder if we are, what with all the duty-free booze I'm packing.

We enter anyway, following a red tile walkway through a garden that seems impossibly lush this close to the ocean. More gardens adorn the central courtyard. Signs of guests are not in evidence.

I leave my bag with Betsy in the foyer and explore the rest of the hotel. The library and kitchen are dark, but tidy and well stocked. The upstairs veranda and balconies are breezy, affording spectacular views of the sea. Rooms are spacious and come equipped with mosquito netting, several fans and a small refrigerator, the kind designed for medical labs. This hotel seems to have everything but an attendant.

A neighbor is sleeping on his front porch. He's an American who no longer works at the resort, but nonetheless pries himself out of his hammock and finds us a room key. He tells us not to worry about criminals in Santa Fe, assuring us that the worst of them have either been locked up or gunned down. "Just look out for Jorge," he warns us. "He'll try to sell you a boat tour and he doesn't even have a boat."

A recent article from Caracas' *Daily Journal* confirms his assurances. Conspicuously framed and mounted on the lobby wall, the clipping reports on American and European proprietors of beachfront posadas who have successfully recruited their local counterparts into a campaign to keep the beach safe and clean. Trash is collected daily. Streetlights have been installed. Security watches are in effect. Palm trees lost to seasonal storms are continually replaced and nurtured.

The program is a success. Santa Fe offers one of the few beaches—perhaps the only beach—on coastal Venezuela where you can safely walk at night, swim without fear of pollution, and dine on a patio café so close to the sea that you could fish from your table, if you were so inclined. In short, it's a world apart from the Santa Fe we drove through to get here.

At nightfall streetlights flicker on, bathing the sand in an orange glow that extends well out over the water. A mugger here would need scuba gear to sneak up on you, and even then you'd spot his bubbles fifty feet away. The beach is also spotless. Not so much as a shell interrupts its surface. Whoever came through to pick up all the Sunday picnic debris did so with the efficiency of the tooth fairy in hockey season. Nothing remains but the palm trees and the boats. The only sound comes from ankle-deep waves folding on sand and receding with a slight hiss. Betsy and I listen for it while sipping Polar beers at the Siete Delphines Café. Our enthusiasm is returning, and in a giddy whisper we discuss tomorrow's plans to tour the islands.

Antonio is our guide to the islands. At ten on a Monday morning, we climb aboard his boat along with a young German couple and an American girl. The latter, Megan, is enjoying her first trip abroad and traveling solo. I'm impressed with her bravery, but can tell by her burnt and perforated skin that she doesn't know much about sunscreen and mosquito repellant.

Pelicans glide alongside our boat. Megan remarks on how they look like pterodactyls. I'm thinking ravens, but only because it suddenly occurs to me that my favorite NFL team played in its first Super Bowl yesterday. I ask if anyone knows who won. They answer with a round of shrugs.

The pelicans begin a series of kamikaze dives. Antonio cuts the engine and drifts toward their point of splashdown. A dorsal fin breaks through the surface ahead and disappears in one fleeting moment. Two more pop up ten feet starboard. Soon dolphins are circling the boat. The water is clear enough to spot them five feet beneath the surface, giving me about a half second head start on aiming my camera. The German guy hasn't caught on yet. He's busy snapping pictures of the little whirlpools they leave behind.

We circle around two white stone islands that look like a cubist's rendering of a cat chasing a mouse. Antonio announces their names: El Gato and El Raton. The boat continues to the next island, Arapo, where he drops anchor.

We bail out in hip-deep water and wade to a deserted palm-fringed beach with thatched gazebos.

I'm the first one back in the water. I grab a mask off the boat, spit in it and strap it on. Visibility is good, about thirty feet, but there isn't a whole lot to look at. Most of the antler coral is bleached and broken. Deeper clusters of lumpy coral are holding up better, but the fish around them are small and scarce: a few schools of skittish neon blue minnows, the occasional parrotfish, and not much else. I paddle around for about half an hour before deciding the island itself might make for a more interesting exploration.

Betsy and Megan paddle for shore as well, but unwisely take a shortcut through shallow coral. Betsy winds up with a few scrapes, while Megan incurred several open cuts to go with her burns and bites.

I sit them both on the stone wall of the gazebo and tend to their wounds. As I'm lecturing them on all the nasty infections they can get from coral abrasions, I catch movement out of the corner of my eye. Something is creeping down the steep, densely vegetated embankment at the edge of the beach. Something big and reptilian. Another one is following. Soon two iguanas slither out onto the sand, each as big as a dachshund. A third runty lizard scampers up behind them.

Megan pulls a banana out of her backpack and breaks off a piece. The iguanas charge her. She panics and spastically tosses the banana bit in the sand. The iguanas race for it and engage in a battle that rivals the finest in Japanese monster cinema.

The Germans swim ashore. Careful not to stumble in their flippers, they walk backward up the beach, just as they probably learned as a safety tip in a scuba class. Both are scowling about the sickly coral, so I invite them to explore the island with me.

The five of us skirt around a rock jetty to another deserted beach, then continue on to find a third beach positively crawling with Venezuelan teenagers.

Now, it's said that two things dominate the hearts and minds of young Venezuelans: baseball and beauty pageants. However, nobody on this beach seems interested in baseball. Clearly they're all in beauty pageant mode, some striking swimsuit calendar poses, others trying to appear as if caught off-guard, throwing a surprised looks that say, *Who is that sneaking up behind me?* Or, *My, but that's a big camera.* They're flipping their hair and losing their tops and looking coyly over their shoulders, all the while dozens of pocket cameras are clicking in every direction.

A recent consumer survey searching for the vainest people in the world declared Venezuelans as the runaway winners, and the folks here are living up to their victorious results. I half expect them to take root at the water's edge and relive the legend of Narcissus.

I depart from the camera carnival to further explore the island. The beach ends at a wooden dock with a café built into the hillside above it. From there the shoreline corners around and drops straight into the sea. The only way to avoid a spot of rough surf is by scaling across the wall of rock above it, then dropping down on yet another beach. This one holds a small fishing village, the entire population of which apparently consists of watchful roosters and mean dogs. Climbing up the steep hillside through iguana-infested thickets seems like a safer bet, and I'm rewarded at the top with a spectacular view of the island.

After three hours on Arapo, Antonio rounds us up and shuttles us to another island, La Piscina, named for the swimming-pool qualities of its surrounding water. The island itself is scarcely bigger than a baseball diamond, but perched high on its one big rock is a white concrete house. Like so many structures on the beaches and islands around here, it was abandoned long ago, perhaps even before it was finished. Such buildings seem like relics of a tourist industry that began to die out before it ever fully flourished.

The reefs surrounding La Piscina share a similar quality, though I find it difficult to inspect them closely as the wind is whipping up waves that fold around the island from both directions and knock visibility down to twenty feet at best. Betsy and I feel up to the challenge of this new sport, what we call surf-snorkeling, or snurfeling, but it soon exhausts us. Lacking flippers, we kick and claw our way through the current, back to shore. The Germans follow close behind. Again we're amused by their diligent practice of walking backwards, but then I suppose there's no graceful way to walk in flippers.

That evening, a Dutchman at the resort offers to take us on an open water dive, enticing us with stories of a shipwreck near a thermal vent. Since he seems uncertain of its precise location, we choose instead to explore a village up in the hills: Los Altos de Santa Fe.

We know of six outfits that run tours up to Los Altos and its nearby attractions, such as the bathing pools on the Rio Neveri, and the San Pedro and La Toma waterfalls. Yet for reasons still not clear, none are willing to take us. Furthermore, we learn that no taxi, *por puesto* or bus leaving Santa Fe will go to Los Altos de Santa Fe. There's only one way to get there, the drivers insist. Go to Puerto La Cruz and catch a jeep from there. All I can gather from their frantic gestures and breakneck Spanish is that their vehicles are not fit to handle the road to Los Altos.

The road is indeed tortuous, rising from sea level to 3000 feet in a winding ten-mile drive, but it's well paved all the way up to the village, and the "jeep" is actually nothing more than an elongated Toyota Land Cruiser. We bail out at the far end of Los Altos and start our search for Casa Quini.

Everything I know about Casa Quini comes from a brief notation in an unreliable guidebook: It describes accommodations as "very pleasant," says the food is healthy, and mentions that tours are available.

The quest begins with a pleasant stroll up a residential side street. The homes seem freshly painted in rich Caribbean colors and their yards are densely foliated, but well groomed. Casa Quini is the last house on the left. A smiling man wearing nothing but denim cutoffs greets us at the gate. He speaks no English, but he's patient with my poor Spanish and tells me that we can find Quini at a place called Tai, which is in the center of Los Altos, a few miles back the way we came.

We have no idea who Quini is, only that we need to find her. Despite the rarity of traffic in town, we soon manage to hitchhike back to Tai. It's an old plantation house with immaculate grounds and a pottery barn. There we find Quini, her hands full of clay.

A native of Caracas, Quini speaks near flawless English. And to our astonishment, she's willing to drop everything to take us on a tour of her adopted hometown. "You really need a full day to see everything," she tells us, checking her watch. It's getting on one p.m. "What can I possibly show you in just a few hours?"

I tell her anything will be fine.

We hop in her jeep and speed back to Casa Quini. In addition to creating brilliant pottery and ceramics, Quini runs a guesthouse and a popular pet-sitting service. Pottery seems to be her main priority, leaving her husband, the man in denim cutoffs, to the bulk of responsibilities at the house in her name. We stay there just long enough to pick armfuls of tangerines from its Edenesque garden.

Back on the road, Quini explains the history of Los Altos de Santa Fe. For centuries it marked the halfway point in a two-day journey along the mountainous Camino Real from Barcelona, capital of Anzoátegui state, to Cumaná, capital of Sucre state. Los Altos developed not only as a popular stopover, but also an important trading center, as coffee and cacao plantations sprang up in the surrounding area.

By the early twentieth century, the government recognized a need for more efficient transportation between the capital cities. They soon built the National Road, now called Highway 9, which effectively diverted traffic out of the hills to the fifty-mile coastline below. Like Route 66 in the post-Interstate era, the Camino Real withered away. Following a collapse in the price of coffee, most plantations were abandoned and Los Altos was eventually left for dead.

Today passage along the Camino Real takes a machete, a burro and an adventurous spirit. Los Altos de Santa Fe, however, seems on the brink of a renaissance, with galleries that feature local painting, woodcarving, metalwork and papermaking. Quini takes an active part in the revitalization projects.

No easy feat. For one, she would like the village to drop Santa Fe from its name. "Too many people associate Santa Fe with criminals," she says, referring to the lower town's reputation as a bandito hideout. She's also having a difficult time persuading locals that attracting tourists is a good thing. "They like their quiet way of life here. I don't blame them for that. I don't like what happened to other towns. But I know there is a responsible way to develop. And I look around and all I see is the potential."

The more we drive, the more I see it, too. The jeep bumps and grinds up a rock-strewn road approaching verticality, and the forest is closing in. Branches slap at the windshield and scratch at the doors. Then the road turns bad. Quini backs into a small clearing and tells us we must walk from here. We follow an old burro trail through the remains of an abandoned coffee plantation. The forest has since reclaimed so much land that we don't notice the hundreds of coffee plants until Quini picks a bean and offers us a taste.

She also points out the plants that can do us serious harm. Grassy clumps of *cortadera* grow along the trails edge. Its raspy underside is well suited for grabbing bare skin and tearing it loose. Brushing up against these can result in open wounds that take weeks to heal. The less pervasive *guarito*to, a fuzzy purplish plant, also threatens exposed skin with its rash-inducing toxins. It's embarrassing to think of the damage we could suffer from casual contact with a couple of pernicious weeds, but without Quini's watchful guidance, we certainly would not emerge from this forest with our legs fully intact.

Far less threatening is the animal life; or rather, its absence. Quini says the forest is crawling with snakes of all venomous sorts, but we're safe as long as we stay on the burro trail. Far smarter than their North American counterparts who are fatally prone to stretch out on asphalt, snakes here have long since learned to avoid paths beaten down by the hooves of burros. Sloths are a more common sight along the trail. Unfortunately, we don't spot any during our hour-long hike. We do catch glimpses of a number of falcons, along with several species of parrot ranging in size from those typically found on the shoulders of pirates to one just slightly larger than the average hummingbird.

We continue through the tunnel of foliage, constantly uphill. At a break in the treeline, Quini makes us promise not to look to our left until she says so. Averting our eyes is easy, as we're fixed on stepping over ever-larger patches of cortadera. At a precise location, high atop a grassy hill, she tells us to look. We turn to see the whole of the Costa Azul and the islands of Mochima National Park, all in one breathtaking view.

"I did not want to bring you here because I thought it might be cloudy," Quini tells us. "But look! Just look how perfect!" Her hand gestures seem to indicate that she's offering us the view as a gift. If so, it is one of the finest we have ever received.

I open my guidebook to a map of the park. From this we are able to identify the islands below, including El Gato, El Raton, Arapo and La Piscina. On the previous page are a few descriptive lines about Casa Quini. I show it to her.

"It's me!" she gasps, clutching the book. Her eyes widen as she reads aloud the high praises her house has received. "This is wonderful!" she says, reading it again. I feel as if I've just offered a small gift in return.

The forest dims as the sun slides low in the sky. Quini hastens our hike back to the jeep, warning us of the puri puri that come out at dusk. These invisible insects have a bite like a mean pinch, and the little black dots they leave on skin itch far worse than mosquito bites. They also scoff at DEET-heavy sprays. Only thick clothing or a goopy layer of baby oil will keep them from biting. We have neither.

Back in town, Quini points out a number of *bahareque* homes, a centuries-old style of building similar to adobe homes on pueblos in the American Southwest. The technique is still in use today, and a fresh coat of paint is all that's needed to disguise a hundred-year-old house as one built last week. Quini seems determined to continue this tour well past sundown. We would happily follow along were it not for a dinner engagement at the resort.

The bus drops us at the edge of Santa Fe hours after dark. The streets are far more active now than at any hour of daylight. Children race by two to a bike. Bars are overflowing. And at the town's one working payphone, the line is nearly a block long. Late for dinner, Betsy and I keep the pace up, navigating the dark streets by following the stench from the fish market. From there it's just a quick dash down a narrow lane that leads back to the beach.

We see familiar faces at the beachside cafés: Canadians and Italians we met days before on Isla Margarita. The American and the Germans from our snorkeling tour. England, Poland and France also have representatives here.

The world is converging on this beach, and yet nobody seems to have any current knowledge of it beyond this perimeter of sand. It's Tuesday night, and still nobody can tell me who won the Super Bowl.

Certain that Quini broke our Venezuelan curse, we set with confidence to Cumaná. Since its first settlement in 1506, Cumaná has been like a spastic geek who seems to invite bullying. Caribe and Cumanagoto Indians repeatedly assaulted the town before Spanish, Dutch and French pirates and slave traders took turns roughing it up. It also took a beating in the Wars of Independence. It faced successions of hurricanes and tidal waves. Worst of all, it suffered through at least five devastating earthquake, the first in 1530 and the most recent in 1997.

Fascinated with its colorful and convulsive history, Betsy and I find a hotel in the historic center of town. Bubulina's is a newly renovated colonial building with the charm of provincial Spain. Historic maps and documents adorn the walls, and each room has a name instead of a number. We're assigned to one named, ominously enough, *Alacran*. Scorpion.

After a lunch in their empty restaurant with a hyper-attentive waiter, we enjoy a leisurely two-hour stroll (read: we're lost) through crowded plazas, noisy markets and perilously busy city streets. We eventually return to the hotel, where I immediately recruit the front desk staff into finding a guide who speaks English.

We're desperately seeking another Quini.

What we get is Beatris.

Beatris arrives at eight pm, two hours after her appointed time, which is fine because we've been stuffing ourselves stupid with octopus, pan-fried fish, and a lomito steak the size of a human heart, smothered in cheese. We're also sampling an assortment of Chilean wine and local liquors, so we're in a pretty good mood despite her tardiness.

Beatris, she doesn't drink. That's one of the first things she tells us. She also tells us about a diet she maintained while living in Washington, D.C. Her Baskin-Robins diet, in which she limited herself to four scoops a day. She wants to know if they still have thirty-three flavors.

She takes us on a night tour, showing where things were prior to the 1997 earthquake. She points out the neighborhoods where you never have to lock your doors and alerts us to the streets where you never walk after dark. (Our hotel is in the latter group.) She cruises past the Toyota factory to show us their Christmas decorations. Sadly on this last night of January, the Nativity scene has been dismantled. But we're in luck: Santa and Mrs. Claus are still happily waving from a Toyota truck perched high upon a post.

"How about that!" Beatris remarks. "How about that!"

She shuttles us out to the airport to help us purchase tickets to Caracas and reconfirm our flight to Houston. Unfortunately, no one at the airport is able to handle either task. The trip isn't an entire bust, though. She meets a friend who has been stranded there for hours, unable to find a ride home. Beatris cheerfully offers her a lift.

Back in the car, the conversation turns to politics. Like every Venezuelan who has broached this subject with me, Beatris is adamantly opposed to President Chávez, this revolutionary leader who advocates making love every day in many ways.

She can't articulate her reasons, but I gather from her sentiment that she's suspicious of his revolution: It panders to the lowest common denominator, the poor and uneducated. That's not a bad strategy in a nation with an appalling eighty percent poverty rate, where one in ten children fail to finish primary school and half as many complete secondary education.

But instead of focusing on viable solutions, Chávez often takes a defensive stance. His oft repeated motto is: "Whoever isn't with me, is against me." His rhetoric tends to rant against the evils of unions, capitalism, privatization, and globalization. And many of his critics complain that he's beginning to sound a lot like his comrade, Fidel Castro.

Beatris asks me, "Have you heard what he is doing to our schools?"

I have, it's in all the papers, and I don't know whether to be amused or frightened. He's sending oil to Cuba in exchange for teacher-trainers and educational materials. To head the National Education Project, he's selected Carlos Lanz, a former Marxist guerilla who spent seven years in prison for the three-year kidnapping of an American businessman. He's also appointed several more veteran guerrillas to revise school curriculums and textbooks. Pre-military training is now compulsory at the secondary level, and every student will be indoctrinated with the principles of his revolution. I wonder how teachers will handle his carnal commandment.

I also wonder how Chávez could be perceived as anything worse than his opposition, the former oligarchy of larcenous businessmen that effectively drove this oil-rich nation into crushing poverty. And while Chávez might be cruising for a dictatorship, at least he didn't resort to nepotism and a rigged election to win the presidency. Nor does he burble out Bushisms like, "The education issue ought to be discussed about." And, "Rarely is the question asked: Is our children learning?"

I tell Beatris, as I've told many other Venezuelans, I would gladly trade presidents. She says she would gladly accept such a deal. "Bush is such a handsome man," she says. "And he speaks so eloquently. Oh, all the Venezuelans love Bush."

Quini doesn't love Bush. Quini firmly declined my offer and suggested a counteroffer: "Just stick them both in a blender and grind them up together."

I miss Quini.

I ask Beatris' friend, with Beatris translating, if she supports President Chávez. Her answer is succinct: "*Claro.*" Of course. She won't say why.

After Beatris drops her off, she informs us in a conspiratorial tone: "That was the governor's wife."

I ask, incredulously, "Someone forgot to pick up the governor's wife from the airport?"

Beatris nods. "Someone is in a lot of trouble."

Deep in the night, in Alacran, our windowless room, something stings me awake. I stagger into the bathroom and examine my right hand. Finding nothing, I deliriously conclude that the pain there, this hot needling sensation, is the result of a bizarre dream.

In the morning, Betsy tells me that she, too, was awakened. Not by pain, but by something crawling up her torso. She described it as lighter than a mouse, but much bigger and heavier than any cockroach, and too soft to be a scorpion. Something more along the lines of giant tarantula in size, weight and texture.

Beatris soon shows up to give us a tour that includes marching us through a squalid market that sells hammocks and ceramics, live chickens and long-dead fish. She insists that we buy her lunch there, which seems fine as I wrongly assume the food will be cheap. As we're waiting for it to arrive, I peruse stacks of bootleg CDs on what looks like an ice cream cart fitted with a bone-rattling stereo system.

I'm listening to a sample from what sounds like a compilation of samba rhythms when Beatris says to Betsy: "How about that! Stephen likes the nigger music. How *about* that!"

When I return to the table with the CD, she looks at it and tells me: "You know, Venezuelans are all born with a little nigger inside us, and when we hear this music, we awaken the nigger within and just start to move." She raises her hands above her head and sort of scooches her butt on the bench. Nothing about her indicates that she has any African bloodlines. "It brings out the nigger in all of us. Even little babies, they start to move like the niggers."

What happens next is hard to explain. I have a fork in my hand, along with the perfect opportunity to stab her in the forehead. Unfortunately, I can't follow through. It's sad, I know, denying this poor woman the frontal lobotomy she so desperately needs, but I just can't do it, and Betsy is equally paralyzed with repulsion.

So we tolerate her blather for another hour or so before she finally returns us to the scorpion room with the promise to meet us at the same time tomorrow. As soon as she's gone, Betsy and I flee Bubulina's and check ourselves into another hotel on the far side of town: The Hotel Bordones, with its unhappy staff and its faint whisper of the exotic resort it was in the 1970s, before the earthquake and hurricanes and economic depressions.

It sinks us into a deep depression. It has the charm of a putt-putt golf course gone bankrupt. Among the decapitated palm trees are lighting fixtures cleverly disguised as polka-dotted mushrooms, but they have lost their ability to illuminate. Astroturf on the bridge over the pool suffers from mange, and the level of the water below is about a foot short of the skimmers along the wall. On the gazebo, cracked speakers rattle out the Kansas tune, "Dust in the Wind." Three waiters lean against an empty buffet counter and stare at us, perhaps wondering why we appear to be beckoning them to our table.

A half mile inland, and in plain view of Los Bordones, is the spankin' new resort, Nueva Toledo. We looked into it before deciding on Los Bordones. We saw its inclusive bars and buffets, its cool fountains, its international coterie of concierges. We noticed that fact that its immaculate swimming pool took up more square footage on God's green earth than our house and yard. It was a mistake to look at all that before checking into Los Bordones.

First thing Friday morning, we haul our bags that half mile, check into the Nueva Toledo, and strap on the red plastic bracelets that identify us as a guests of the resort. Betsy wants to know why I keep sniffing my wrist.

It's our last full day in Cumaná, and yet we spend most of it rolling in the sheets. I am struggling with the guilt of wasting our final moments here, but this resort is smothering any inclination to go out and explore the city.

But then, suddenly, the city comes to us to present the Carnival Queen of Cumaná.

At ten p.m., the invasion commences. Camera crews and guests of the Queen swarm our bars and poolside. Soon after, the festivities begin. It's a parade of song and dance numbers involving three-foot headdresses and half-naked bodies, painted skin and leopard-print loincloths. All this just to introduce the losers of the Carnival Pageant, all twenty of them, all wearing bikinis and high heels, and walking as if their hips are disjointed.

Betsy and I start to fade around midnight. Our bodies sting from dozens of little slashes inflicted by those red plastic bracelets. We try to ward off sleep for a few more hours with a late buffet and a pot of coffee, but it's no use. By the time they get around to introducing the Queen, we're tucked away, crashing headlong into sleep—despite the thundering drums and shrieking whistles. The samba rhythm echoing throughout the resort, it's just rocking us to sleep.

Saturday morning, our heads hurt too much to think, and we're itching at our sliced-up hides. Over a buffet, our sixth since checking in twenty-four hours earlier, I propose a plan that might validate our trip to Cumaná. President Chávez is scheduled to appear in the Parque Ayachucho to commemorate the failed coup he led nine years ago.

My plan is this: We should meet him.

I can't imagine what he could have to say about that incident. Back then, he was an unknown army paratrooper who thought it would be neat to overthrow President Pérez. So, at midnight on February 3, 1992, he and three other officers led 15,000 soldiers on a progressive junta. They shot up the presidential palace and ran a tank into the front door.

The door remained in place, and therefore so did the Pérez administration.

Caught in an awkward position, Chávez nonetheless appeared cool on TV as he told stunned viewers that he had failed "for now."

Betsy and I arrive at the Parque Ayachucho at 9:30. Busloads of marching bands and school children trudge down the few streets that aren't blocked off. Armed soldiers in jungle camouflage fatigues wave them on, while soldiers in desert camouflage fatigues slump on the handlebars of their racy Yamaha motorcycles. Vendors tout flags and sombreros bearing the colors of the Venezuelan flag. We pace through the accumulating crush of patriots, stupidly asking when the President will arrive. The answer is always the same: At ten o'clock, with a shrug.

Shortly before eleven, bands assemble around the podium and stumble through their warm-up scales. Half an hour passes. Local camera crews roll in and unpack their gear. I realize then that nobody expects Chávez to be on time. I would wait here all day if we didn't have a plane to catch.

At the airport, camera crews loiter in the parking lot. The President's plane idles on the tarmac, but televisions in the terminal reveal he hasn't yet arrived at the park.

Still, I'm convinced that he'll breeze in any minute. I've got my camera out. I've got my questions ready. (Must you truly make love every day in many ways? Or can you double up some days and let others slide, like, say, when you're having a bad day in a really crappy hotel?) I'm watching the reporters and the cameramen and the soldier guarding the plane. Every time one of them so much as shifts his weight, I'm on my feet looking for the Presidential caravan.

A school bus roars up. Fifty armed soldiers disembark. They march upstairs to the cafeteria and order lunch. No sign of Chávez.

We're called to board our plane. I've still got the camera out as we cross the tarmac, passing within inches of Chávez's plane. Any second now, I'll get a picture of him. That's all I want. One picture to justify this trip.

As we taxi away, I get one snapshot of his empty plane.

"I hate Chávez," I tell Betsy.

"You have no reason to hate Chávez," she tells me.

"I can think of plenty." I stump thoughts through my brain for a few minutes before coming up with this: "The sick bastard pens encouraging notes to Carlos the Jackal."

It's true. Chávez practically admitted a crush on Carlos the Jackal, aka Ilich Ramirez Sanchez, the Venezuelan terrorist who is serving a life sentence in France for murder and who has called on his supporters to kill one American or Israeli for each day he remains in prison.

Chávez has an unhealthy infatuation with guerillas and terrorists. That's reason enough to hate him. But what really pisses me off is the fact that I listened to him at all. It's not that I put so much faith in his words, but rather took his statement as a sign. It was a desperate grasp at a guiding light in a moment of critical indecision. If I had read a horoscope suggesting we surf the Amazon, we would have done that. But no, the sign I got came from an interview in which the President of Venezuela commanded everyone to make love every day in many ways.

It was not a valid reason for coming here. I'm not even sure what he meant. Maybe it was a reference to his idol, "El Libertador" Simón Bolívar. The revolutionary, though diminutive general allegedly celebrated his victories over the Spaniards with passionate sex, and he was known to broadcast his enthusiasm via shrieks from his bedroom. What he lacked in size he compensated with noise, often depriving his officers of sleep.

I still don't see how making love works as a metaphor for revolution, but the comparisons between sex and travel are as plentiful as they are cliché. Sex, like travel, is an adventure. Exploration leads to wondrous new experiences blah blah

blah. The truest of all is this: Done right, sex and travel are exhausting. That's why they don't mix well. It takes too much energy to do both. Eventually, one has got to give.

Or maybe Betsy and I are getting old. It's a scary thought considering we're only thirty-four. But it's been sixteen years since we started dating and eleven since we started living together (against her parents' wishes, as I recall. When they came to visit, I hid out in Africa.)

Travel has always been an integral part of our relationship, one I nearly destroyed early on when I fled to London and shared a flat with another woman. And I didn't fully win Betsy back until after I suffered through a celibate year in China.

It all seems so long ago. We have loved each other for nearly half our lives. Maybe growing old isn't such a bad thing, provided we do it together.

And this resort fetish we've cultivated, this guilty pleasure in holing up in a fake paradise and blocking out Third World squalor, it's entirely new to us. Maybe it should count as a valid travel experience.

We hold hands as the plane takes off. High above Costa Azul, I peer down at seven pinpricks of brilliant pink soaring over solid green mangroves. They're flamingoes. I watch them as long as I can, until we're over the darkening blues of the Caribbean. It's all so beautiful, such stark contrast to our destination.

Caracas is so ugly that I feel guilty for taking pictures of it. We're looking for a quiet place to sit, but the cafés are locked in some sort of competition to determine who has the loudest stereo system. On a side street, we find an Arabic café with relatively small speakers. To make up for the low volume of music, a steady stream of folksingers practice their craft on guitars slightly larger than ukuleles. The tip I offer to the first untalented young singer amounts to little more than a dollar, and he seems perturbed.

The second singer, an elderly man with a gimp, is considerably better. Betsy handles the tip on this one, emptying her purse of all coins and bills worth less than a quarter. We've accumulated gobs of this small change along the way, and I figure, shortly after his elated departure, that she's just tipped him something in the neighborhood of ten dollars.

I'm in the middle of berating her generosity when I see the old man again, this time accompanied by his hunchback wife rather than his guitar. I figure they're coming to sing a duet for us, but they shuffle past our table and head straight for the pharmacy next door. The owner won't allow them in his store, but he does accept their money in exchange for a small bottle of pills. The old couple passes us again, hugging and giggling.

I jokingly suggest it's Viagra, but I'm thinking it's something more serious than that. The image sticks with me throughout the night and the following day. It haunts me and elates me in turns, depending on how my mind interprets it at any given moment.

During the flight home, I attempt to suppress all thoughts on the old couple by beginning a new list. A list of all the places in the world where Betsy and I can take a real honeymoon. It soon blossoms into a six-page amendment to my list of 101 Things To Do Before I Die. I think, I hope, it'll take us forever to accomplish them all.

Nothing Will Kill You

IRELAND: 2003

Ticks in the Burren

The Burren is Ireland's version of the badlands. Its hostile terrain seems to discourage most activities of the living. In 1651, General Edmund Ludlow surveyed the land for Cromwell and reported back that there was "neither water enough to drown a man, nor a tree to hang him, nor soil enough to bury him." The latter was so scarce, he noted with typical anti-Irish sentiment, that residents stole dirt from one another.

What he saw as plentiful was rock, with more rocks stacked upon it. The placement of rocks in this region suggests a collective case of obsessive-compulsive disorder that has persisted for 6000 years. They've stacked rocks into dolmens and ring forts, and so many walls that, if combined into one stretch, might dwarf that great one in China. They've assembled piles and cairns, castles and famine cottages. Cathedrals and abbeys survived Viking plunder only to fall to Cromwell's fury. The tower of Kilmacduagh still stands, albeit leaning, as the tallest in Ireland. And yet there remains rock strewn everywhere, some of it good for throwing at other rocks, but most of it immovable.

Unlike the vast swaths of ancient lava I've come to know in New Mexico's badlands, the Burren's rocky land is the remains of a gazillion sea creatures that died sometime in the last 350 million years. Crushed under the pressure of the sea and scoured by Ice Age glaciers, their shells and skeletons appear today as massive limestone pavements covering 250 square miles some 2000 feet thick. It is a land fragmented into grikes and clints—slabs of rock and cracks between them. It is not terrain especially well suited for hiking.

Betsy and I set out on a warm June afternoon to climb Mullaghmore, a 600-foot hill terraced like a staircase for giants. We hopscotch the grikes, carefully minding our footsteps not only to avoid stepping into a clint, but always vigilant for the vipers that would be cozy in such crevices. We're well aware of the absurdity in watching out for snakes in Ireland, but this cautious habit is too deeply ingrained into our American psyches to break now. Both Betsy and I have a sharp eye for reptilian skin, no matter how benign or well camouflaged, which helps explain how we manage to spot the head of a lizard hiding under a rock five paces in front of us.

After scrambling up a series of ten to twenty-foot cliffs that buffet each terrace, we reach the summit and find—surprise—a huge pile of rocks.

Our alternate route down the hill takes us to higher cliffs that shelter dense strips of ash and silver birches. We descend into these damp woodlands and blaze trails through ferns and fungus, emerging once again in the stony desert. The terrain often changes like that, with quick and unexpected microclimates. At one moment, it might be an expansive grassy meadow, the next we might lack a place to step for fear of treading upon on rare orchids, the next we're wallowing in marshy muck or skirting a crystalline lake.

By the time we return to the main road, a paved lane that jags throughout the Burren, we're sunburned and dehydrated. Worse, we're positively crawling with ticks, some the size of sesame seeds, others scarcely bigger than pinprick. They're creeping up our shins and burrowing into our thighs and we're dreading to think how high some might've climbed. And as we're perched on a high, flat rock, stripped down to our shorts and grooming each other like tender monkeys, a cyclist happens by, the first human soul we've seen in several hours. He stops to observe, as though to interpret the behavior of these primates he's encountered, and seems both awed and mystified when we call out hello.

An Irish Blessing

That evening, having scrubbed ourselves down with the obsessive vigor of Lady Macbeth, we crawl the pubs of Ballinderreen, a village just north of the Burren. It doesn't appear on most maps, but it has a catchy motto: "Don't be mean. Keep Ballinderreen clean." And it seems complete as villages go, containing one church, one school, one grocery that doubles as a post office, and two pubs.

The pubs function as community centers, with tykes crawling underfoot and scaling barstools and generally capering about, while their parents gossip and the younger adults hustle the pool room. They're curious about our presence and not shy with questions.

In exchange for several generous offers of Guinness and Smithwick's, we gush over the endless and exaggerated beauty of the Ireland, the same land where centuries of backbreaking toil often resulted in famine, and where those who stayed to endure it, those left behind during the great migrations, they would become the ancestors of the friendliest folk we've ever met.

For them we detail our foray into the Burren and our mounting of Mullaghmore. To our surprise, no one else in the pub has bothered to explore that bit of rugged land. I tell them of rare and exotic flora, and of ephemeral lakes with waters as clear as the Caribbean. And when that fails to interest them, I mention that I spotted a snake near the top of Mullaghmore.

The blasphemous remark hushes the room. A college student with a scraggly goatee informs me: "We have no snakes in Ireland."

I laugh it off, nervously amidst the stares and chilling drop in mood. "Of course. I was only kidding. But we did see a lizard. A fat little brown one."

The student, getting the joke, flashes a quick *fuck you* grin as he reminds me: "You understand that, right? No snakes in Ireland."

Sure, St. Patrick rid the land of serpents, but anyone who eliminates an entire genus from a national environment hardly deserves reverence. All the same, I'm not about to announce that their patron saint was an ecological terrorist. So I change the subject to ticks, and our temporary infestation of them, asking if they might carry any of the parasitical diseases of their American counterparts—Lyme, or perhaps Rocky Mountain Spotted Fever.

He assures me that Irish ticks are completely free of such nastiness. "Don't worry," he tells me. He lights a cigarette and adds emphatically: "Nothing in Ireland will kill you."

His last statement, that proclamation of invulnerability, would stay with us throughout our travels in Ireland. That was important to our plans here. We began considering the lore of Ireland, particularly St. Patrick's rash act and its ecological repercussions—remove a link from the food chain and Nature will curse your land forevermore—and we concluded that's what brought misery to Ireland. I mean, besides the British.

But misery and Nature are the father and mother of poetry, which helps explain why Ireland gave birth to so many great poets. We intended to explore that theory here. We would spend the first week in the rural South, traveling the counties of Galway and Clare hoping to absorb the landscape that had inspired centuries of timeless verse. We would gaze over the Cliffs of Moher, where recently a forlorn man from Doolin leapt from the 540-foot precipice into the turbulent sea below, which pitched his body against the rocks for four days before a rescue crew could retrieve it.

We would consider the legendary poverty of Ireland so well explored in most works of Irish literature. Ireland is still poor in some respects. In terms of poverty rates in the western world, only the United States ranks worse. But we would discover that's scarcely in evidence in these rural areas.

Still, with few exceptions, we would discover Romantic inspiration everywhere we turned, Nature so obscenely stunning that it appeared as the creation of a Disney animator tweaked out on ecstasy. We would gorge ourselves on this bucolic scenery until words failed us, or until pastoral smells overwhelmed us and drove us to the urban North—Derry and Belfast, in particular. There we would explore the other half of Irish poetic inspiration, the political despair and rage that fuels a poet like so many rivers of sticky black stout.

And perhaps, we mused, we would still be so infused with that southern Romance in the stormy North that we might skip about, hand in hand, my wife and I, a Catholic and Protestant respectively. And perhaps we could wear badges that identified us as such as we frolicked along in contempt of the Troubles and the marches and the hatred in general. It was to be a mission of peace and goodwill, but it could also be construed as a suicide mission as well. So it helps to keep that statement in mind, that blessing of immortality: Nothing in Ireland will kill you.

The Long Road North

Betsy and I met in 1985 at Elon College, home of the "Fightin' Christians." Our mascot was an Amish man with his fists raised, (a design ripped off from Notre Dame's Fighting Irish mascot,) and our athletic teams regularly battled the Quakers of our nearby rival, Guilford College. Back then, Christians fighting Christians seemed little more than an unfortunate joke. But that was North Carolina and this is Ireland. It's not so funny now.

We're heading North as they're nearing the height of the marching season, that time of year when British Loyalists, in what must now be considered the longest victory dance in history, celebrate William of Orange's 1690 trouncing over King James at the Battle of the Boyne. These marches began about 200 years ago as a tribal demonstration of Protestant dominance and have since grown in excess of 3500 parades per season. Most are considered innocuous celebrations, but up to 300 are regarded as flashpoints that invite retaliation in the form of a lot of shouting and throwing stuff like rocks and petrol bombs.

The most contentious of these marches takes place in Portadown. On the first Sunday in July, members of the Protestant Order of Orange march from their Orange Lodge to Drumcree Church. After a brief service, they continue their march back to their lodge, as tradition dictates, following a shorter route that takes them across Drumcree Bridge and down Garvaghy Road.

Historical accounts and descriptions of the original parade route vary, but the general consensus seems to agree that the march on Drumcree went uncontested from 1807 until the late 1960s. But then, in one of the worst known acts of civic engineering, someone decided to build housing estates for Catholics along Garvaghy Road. Throughout the early 1970s, the area developed into a strong nationalist community, the members of which resented the annual parade of Orangemen, what with all their noisy drums and accordions and "triumphalist taunting."

Catholic protests and Protestant intimidation escalated over the years, but the real violence didn't kick in until 1995, when Royal Ulster Police stopped the Orangemen at Drumcree Bridge. That year and almost every year following it saw the annual parade disintegrate into rioting and mayhem.

The police, usually with the aid of British security forces, tried to halt the parade for seven years straight (1995-2002), but succeeded in about half of their attempts. What happens this year is now a matter of speculation, but all sides seem to agree that it will be an ugly scenario. Not exactly the stuff of poetic inspiration. Yet Betsy and I agree to add Portadown to our list of destinations, in part because we're growing disillusioned with the whole poetry angle.

Poetry in Ireland, we surmise in our first week here, is dead. At Thoor Ballylee, the stone tower where W.B. Yeats lived and worked, the great poet's name now endorses a diverse line of crappy merchandise, from velcro wallets and change purses to retractable tape measures, calculators, and yo-yos. In Galway, once the urban poetic forum of western Ireland, open mic poetry is a fad that didn't take. And a quick survey of local chapbooks reveals that few Irish poets today can write a poem without employing words like *bitterness* or *foggy* or *juggernaut*, or without invoking pastoral images of unremitting drudgery, such as that of Da cutting peat from the bogs. And if that doesn't sound the death knell for poetry, then Seamus Heaney dropped the bomb on it when he recently lauded the lyrical prowess of American rapper, Eminem.

If a Nobel Prize-winning Ulster poet can't tell the difference between a master wordsmith and an anemic bigot with Tourette's syndrome, then yes, it's safe to say that poetry in Ireland is overdue for a eulogy. Too bad those capable of writing one are just as dead.

These are my sentiments as we begin our long drive north. My disappointment with the Irish poetry scene is almost as intense as my despondency over the American dollar, which is taking a beating from the Euro and is sure to fare worse against the British Sterling. We're feeling impoverished, and it's poetically uninspiring.

Still, we're excited about entering Northern Ireland, even though we're not sure where the border is. It doesn't appear on the roadmap, and there's no checkpoint. Our first clues to crossing over are slightly better roads, and white road signs with red edges, in stark contrast to the Republic's cautious yellow signs.

We had trouble with the roads in the South. Even in our Nissan Micra rental, a vehicle slightly bigger than a bumper car, streets seemed too narrow. Most major highways wouldn't qualify as country roads in Alabama, and country roads resembled bike paths. We shared these tracks with tour buses and petrol tankers and heavy farm equipment. We never saw a tractor working a field, but we followed more than we care to remember down many a long and winding road with stone walls hemming us in on both sides.

To further complicate matters, road signs often displayed cryptic messages like AUTOMATIC LEVEL CROSSING and EXPERIMENTAL TRAFFIC CALMING and RIVER SUCK and STOP THE CARNAGE.

But one heartwarming sign appeared at the entrance to each city, town and village, a sign that announced and welcomed Special Olympic athletes from the respective nation it hosted. The games dominated the nightly news throughout Ireland with reports that regularly neglected scores in favor of manipulative, tear-jerking fluff. Slow-motion victory moments, mournful violins to console the losers. These short features often highlighted the bonds formed between these foreign Olympians and their Irish hosts, and it was all I could do to keep from crying like a sap every time I saw one. Hell, I got misty when we drove into Enniskillen and saw the sign that said they hosted the Netherlands.

Enniskillen, our first stop in the North, is a perfect small Irish town, complete with a lough, a quay, a castle, and a charming Gaelic subtitle: *Inis Ceithlean*. It boasts gorgeous institutions of worship, a cathedral and two churches, each within a block of the others, a schematic that belies any conflict.

The William Jefferson Clinton Peace Center is a new feature in town. Erected on the site where an IRA bomb killed eleven people in 1987, this monster of modern architecture houses a youth hostel, café, and art gallery, but offers very little in explaining its role in peacekeeping. A small bronze plaque tucked away in a vestibule is all that identifies the building, and its art gallery merely displays the scribblings of local elementary school children who show unintentional promise in abstract expressionism.

At a pub called Horseshoe and Saddlers, we get our first lesson in Catholic-Protestant relations. The bartender there is a ruddy-cheeked lad with a strong build and short blond hair. He looks like the kind of guy who plays middie for a prep school lacrosse team. He's got alert eyes and is generous with smiles, but not in that fake way like you might expect from a waiter at Applebee's. Reckoning him too young to get terribly offended by sensitive questions, I spill my curiosities early into the conversation.

"So how do you tell the difference between a Catholic and a Protestant?"

He shrugs. "I dunno." He pauses as though anticipating a punchline.

If there were one, it might be: *Then how do you know who to throw rocks at?* But that seems inappropriate at this stage. Instead, I ask him, "Which one are you?"

"Protestant," he say, indifferently. "And yourselves?"

"Same," I tell him.

"Catholic," says Betsy.

Our nefarious alliance doesn't faze him one bit. I continue peppering him with questions on recent pipe bomb attacks and the bitter rivalry between Armagh and Dublin in the All-Ireland football final, but he seems oblivious to troubles of any sort. So I let him ask the questions, all the ones we've been asked a hundred times already, including the destinations left on our itinerary.

I tell him Derry, Belfast, Portadown, Dublin.

"Portadown? Why?"

"To see the march."

"Oh my God," he says with a nervous giggle. He calls another young bartender over and tells him: "They're going to Drumcree."

That bartender cracks a smile as he warns us: "You really shouldn't go there."

Sunday Bloody Sunday

Two days are all we need to take in the attractions around Enniskillen—the Marble Arch caves, Cole's Monument, the Portora Royal School where Oscar Wilde and Samuel Beckett studied—and soon we're off to Derry. Signs along the way bear the alliances of local vandals. Nationalist graffiti artists have painted the LONDON out of LONDONDERRY, while Loyalists have added it where it was omitted.

Also along the way is Omagh, best known as home to the worst single atrocity in the history of the Troubles. In 1998, the Real IRA, a breakaway faction, planted a car bomb that killed twenty-nine people and injured 200 more. Now a memorial garden grows alongside a busy street a few blocks from the city center. Nothing there explains what happened or who died. It simply reminds visitors not to forget. Heavy traffic drowns out any hope for quiet contemplation, and among the litter strewn throughout flowers and shrubberies is a page torn from a school handbook advising students on how to deal with bullies.

By contrast, the Bloody Sunday Center in Derry is housed in a former bank within the downtown Derry Walled City. It's a moving and informative, if somewhat heavy-handed testimony to the events on that last Sunday in January 1972, when British paratroopers gunned down fourteen of the 20,000 Catholics who attempted to march out of their Bogside neighborhood in protest of internment without trial. Photos, displays, and a slide show thoroughly explain how the soldiers turned heavy artillery upon a "peaceful demonstration" and effectively blew away a civil rights movement in its infancy.

Interpretations of the massacre are the subject of movies, books, songs, and poems. Now it's also the focus of the Saville Inquiry, also known as the Bloody Sunday Inquiry, the longest legal inquiry in British history. Its belated hearings began at Derry's Guildhall nearly thirty years after the event in question.

The Guildhall is a Gothic wonder in sandstone and red brick, with spirelink pinnacles and an imposing four-faced clocktower. Its main chamber houses a pipe organ, stained-glass windows, and cascades of burgundy draperies. A sacred aura permeates the room, despite modifications for the trial.

Where you might expect a sacrificial altar is the presiding table for a three-judge panel. Wooden carrels and lecterns accommodate the sixty lawyers involved and at least that many desktop computers. Every square foot of congregational space is reserved for the press, families of the victims, and any other curious onlookers who happen to wander in.

Betsy and I traipse in to find the trial in progress, but the hall near empty. The panel has called for the testimony of the soldiers; but since they're afraid to return to Derry, the proceedings have moved to London.

A live, closed-circuit feed transmits the trial back to the Guildhall, where it appears on several large television screens suspended from the oak-beamed ceiling. Some screens reveal barristers' questions and the witnesses' responses; others exhibit charts and graphs, grainy photographs, and virtual reality tours of the Bogside, circa 1972.

This combination of Gothic design and advanced technology has the ambience of a modern-day Frankenstein's laboratory. It's what you might imagine if NASA installed a command center in the Notre-Dame cathedral.

Betsy and I take a seat on a creaky pew in the balcony. One panoramic screen displays highlighted text. On another, Barrister Brian McCartney, appearing for the majority of the victims' families, is questioning Soldier 10. But as McCartney details an incident when a rubber bullet was fired into an apartment living room, Soldier 10 interrupts his examination with uncontrolled laughter.

In response, a volley of disapproving murmurs rises up from a press box hidden beneath the balcony. The Guildhall is not as vacant as we thought.

Meanwhile, tribunal chairman Lord Saville appears on screen. He is not amused.

Waterloo Haiku

The police station across the street from our hostel looks like a federal prison with all its watchtowers, cameras, and razor wire. Similar security measures surround a nearby unemployment center, as well as a program center for the handicapped. Half this city, it seems, is caged. Cameras monitor every street corner and sidewalk in town, and heavy-gauge wire mesh protects windows, street lamps, traffic lights—anything that can be broken with a well thrown rock.

Vandals have evidently launched paint bombs at military installments, effectively turning at least one watchtower into a Jackson Pollack masterpiece. They've also tagged walls and bridges with pro-IRA slogans, but the bulk of graffiti is aimed against our president and the invasion of Iraq. Within the walled city, a ten-yard exclamation in blood-red letters reads: BUSH IS NOT WELCOME IN DERRY.

The Bogside is refreshingly free of mesh and cameras. Instead, reminders of the Troubles are illustrated in twenty-foot murals that depict, among other things, hunger strikers, political prisoners, and a schoolboy with a gas mask and a petrol bomb. Murals on the frontline of flats are in pristine condition. Those deeper in the neighborhood are peeling beyond legibility.

This is what they call Free Derry. Activities here are monitored from a tower in an army camp within the walled city. The streets are heavily littered, but don't see much traffic. A rottweiler sleeping in front of a booking office earlier in the day scarcely shifts when we pass by again on our way to a soccer match that night.

The match ends in a draw, and four young men with red crew cuts and green Celtic jerseys follow us out of the stadium, all yelling in a drunken brogue so thick we can't tell if they're ecstatic or outraged.

One catches up with us and asks what we think of Derry. With knee-jerk diplomacy, Betsy answers, "It's beautiful."

"Are you fucking mad?" he shouts, stabbing a finger at his head. "Have you lost your fucking mind?" His hand sweeps up toward the army tower on the hill.

"Yeah, well *that*," she says, trying to recover from her baldfaced lie.

"Hey, don't worry about it," he says. "Welcome to Derry. Are you up for a pint?"

We've planned on going to a quiz, a pub game where a quizmaster calls out trivia questions and teams write down their answers in the given amount of time. Our Celtic friend, we'll call him Danny, knows just the place for a good quiz: the Dungloe on Waterloo.

Along the way, he tells us he's "hardcore IRA," but he doesn't say what that means, even when we press him for an explanation. (Or if he did, we lost it in the accent and dialect.) Betsy is somewhat apprehensive about him tagging along with us, but we figure we're relatively safe during daylight hours. It's well past nine p.m. The sun won't set for another two hours. Cloud cover and a misting rain mute the city down to a wash of gray. A chill in the air and wafts of burning coal evoke nostalgia for I don't know what until Betsy says, "Smells like Seoul." And suddenly I'm hungry for kimchi.

Danny doesn't respond to her remark. He seats us at a table near the door and goes to the bar to fetch us a round. Returning with two sixteen-ounce bottles of ale, he tells me my Guinness will be along shortly, but the quiz won't start for an hour. In the same breath, he tells Betsy: "Don't worry about the open bottle. I didn't drug it. I'm not that kind of guy, you know? I spent some time in prison, yeah, but that doesn't mean I go putting poison in your drink."

Betsy smiles and nods, unable to decipher a word through his accent and the loud music.

"I'm just trying to be nice and make you feel welcome," he continues. "But you Americans are so stupid—" The bartender catches his eye. "Hang on a moment, I'll get your Guinness."

When he returns and we finish our toast, he continues his train of thought on the U.S.A. He says he was sent to America after his father died. A family in New Jersey took care of him, and as a testament to American stupidity, he describes a day when the stupid American mother took him to the stupid American cinema. "She took me to see *Snow White*. You tell me, how stupid do you have to be to take a twelve-year-old boy to see stupid shit like that?"

"Shameful," I say, but my mind is warming up for quiz mode. I figure that he saw Snow White on its fiftieth anniversary release, and I do the math from there. "So you're twenty-seven now?"

"Twenty-six," he says. And then he wants to know how old we are, what we do, where we're from, who we voted for, why we're here, where we've been, and where we're going next. As soon as we're done answering that round of questions, he asks, "What the fuck are you going to do in Portadown?"

"I need to write a story about Drumcree."

He ducks his head as though someone threw a bottle at it. "Keep your voice down when you say that."

"What? Drumcree?"

He hunches down over the table. "Don't go there. You don't want to be there when the Orangemen are marching." He casts furtive glances around the bar. "They're like the fucking KKK. Imagine the Klan marching through the blackest neighborhood in Alabama. That's what the Orangemen are doing on Garvaghy Road." He slumps back in his chair and snarls. "God, I hate the English."

"So you think it'll be dangerous?" I ask.

He looks dead at me and replies: "Just make sure when you get to the barrier, you're not on the Protestant side."

"Why is that?"

"Stay with the soldiers. You'll be safe there." Then he leans in and says in a conspiratorial tone, "Or better, go to . . ." He says something that starts with *Cor*, ends in *agh*, and has about five syllables in between. "You might see some of my friends there," he adds with a wicked grin.

"Cor- *what*?"

Betsy, not getting it either, nor much of the rest, rummages through her purse.

He points a finger at her and shouts: "Hey! Hey! Turn that off!" Now neither of us understands what he's talking about. He says, "I don't want you recording what I say. Turn it off now!"

She holds up her hands, her purse in one, Chapstick in the other. "No tape recorder," she says.

I hold up my camera bag and shake out my jacket. "None here, either."

"Don't take my picture. Don't use my name. And stop recording what I say." It sounds like his final warning. He drinks down the rest of his bottle and says, "I hate the fucking English."

"We're not English," Betsy reminds him.

"Do you have any Irish in you?"

"On my father's side," she says. "The McCarthy's from Cork. But that was generations ago."

His face brightens a bit, and he asks me in a hopeful tone: "What are you then?"

"Dutch, mostly. My mother was born in Holland." And I already know how he'll react to that, because William of Orange, the king who conquered the Irish, was a Dutchman, too.

"Fuck! You're an Orangeman! You're not going to write a story about Drumcree. You're going to march, you fucking Protestant Orangeman."

I can't tell if he's serious. "Hey, give me half credit. At least I married a Catholic."

He glares at her. "What the fuck did you marry him for?"

I'm waiting for her answer, but she doesn't have one ready. It's a bad sign, because the quizmaster is ready to begin and she'll need to come up with answers faster than this.

Danny buys us another round, but leaves the table before we can finish it.

Once he's gone, I tell Betsy: "From now on, if anyone asks, we're both Mormons."

After a grueling two-hour quiz, the quizmaster announces that Team America took second place, but everyone in the pub knows we did so only by enlisting two Irishmen who helped us with questions on World Cup Soccer and British celebrities.

"Not bad," Betsy says. "I mean, for our first quiz."

Our quiz partners are surprised to learn we don't have quizzes in pubs back home. I tell them we have poetry slams instead. Then I have to explain what a poetry slam is.

Their response to this novelty concept is: "Come on then, let's hear some poetry."

I can't recite poetry on command. I just can't. But they're insistent, so I offer up my best haiku:

Sometimes when I'm sad
I throw rocks at my neighbors
and that cheers me up

They don't get it. Maybe because they don't know what a haiku is. Maybe because they're more attuned to limericks. Or maybe because throwing rocks at neighbors here is just a common cure for the blues. Either way, it doesn't strike them as the least bit funny.

Belfast Poetics

One of my primary goals in Ireland was to read poetry in public. I'd feared that reading poetry to the Irish might be akin to preaching patience to Buddhists, but that concern faded as all my leads on open mic venues turned up nothing more than quizzes and cover bands.
Until Belfast.
In Belfast, just south of St. Anne's Cathedral, I found a café bourgeoning with poets. It was open mic night at the Arcadia Coffeehouse, and there I read my sad little poem, "Dance Craze."

If you have lived, you have danced
a square dance, slam dance, break dance,
belly dance or tango.
But few remember the sad dances,
in particular that one
expression of soul-crushing misery,
the Dance of a Thousand Tears.

It began, I recall, in a dark tavern back east,
on the south side of town,
that place where the workers went to drink
when the factories shut down,
where the coal miners would mourn friends
lost in a collapsed shaft,
where gathered the widows of sailors
after a deadly storm.
And the mothers who lost sons in the war,
they would come, too.

They would come to drink and sigh.
That was all.
Until that one bleak night,
deep in a February freeze, a Frenchman arrived.
He was missing a leg,
but he had an accordion and the saddest song
anyone had ever heard,

*a dirge about a lonely Frenchman who had lost his leg,
and now wandered the coldest nights,
playing sad songs on his accordion.*

*And despite his missing leg, he could dance.
He had choreographed steps,
something between a funeral march and a solo waltz.*

*And the people learned to dance this way.
The unemployed factory workers, the surviving coal miners,
the widows and grieving mothers, they all danced.*

*They danced with tears,
and their cries amplified their sadness a thousand times,
and even those with cold,
callused hearts could feel their pain—
pain like the blinding sadness
you feel when you have to shoot a pony,
or when you find kindergartners caught in your bear traps,
and they're gnawing on their little ankles trying to get out.*

*You might mistake it for the despair
you see in an orphan's eyes
when you tell him that his parents
traded him for an old hairbrush and an ashtray,
and that to this day they still believe it was the best
deal they ever made.
But no, the dance was much more dismal than that.*

*It was the sadness of betrayal like you haven't felt
since the first time your mother punched you in the mouth,
or when the woman you've been stalking for seven years
falls in love
with the man who's been stalking her for six days.*

*It was the sorrows of the Troubles
and the Plague and the Depression
all bound in convulsive motions.
This was the Dance of a Thousand Tears,*

and to witness it filled you with such gothic melancholy
that your heart might break and your soul could snap
like the bones of an old dog under a great rolling rock,
and you might leap out a window or rub salt in your eyes
to relieve you of the miserable sight.

And yet the dance spread to dance halls,
even to upscale clubs,
where rich folk with nothing to mourn
succumbed to this tragic ballet.
Such poseurs.
They ruined the sad dances.
Sold them out and sucked out the marrow of emotion.
Same as what happened when white folk
took up singing the blues.

It killed. I can't be modest and say otherwise. The audience went wild and demanded more. I read three more. I did not read my haiku, but I did mention my novel. They bought every copy that I'd brought with me and wanted to know where they could buy more. They crowded around our table as I signed autographs. They shared their wine and, later, in a pub across the street, they bought us beer, all the while bubbling up wondrous verses amidst the craic.

Even when we brought up Drumcree, the response was poetic. A young woman with explosive red hair and dressed like retro-Madonna, with the black leather and fishnets, she climbed upon the table, crawled over to me, and spake a metaphor of a time bomb: "Tick tock tick tock tick tock . . . ."

After the pubs closed, one guy offered to drive us back to our hotel. We crammed ourselves into the backseat with three girls who for the duration of the ride rhapsodized over their favorite bisexual experiences. It was all very eloquent.

Belfast quickly became and still remains my favorite city in all of Ireland. Poetry is alive there, as proven in the way they deify living poets. Even the bad ones are treated to more ego stroking than we deserve.

• • •

Eve of the Orangemen

A tower of black smoke leans over Portadown. It's visible from the b&b on the outskirts of town. "The bonfire isn't until Sunday night," Maureen tells us as she serves up tea and biscuits in her living room. Knickknacks and gewgaws abound, but everything is dust-free and orderly as though recently unwrapped and meticulously set into place. She allows smoking in her house, is a smoker herself, but every room still smells of country morning wildflowers and grandma's potpourri.

Maureen has straight hair, too blonde for her age, but she's pretty in a latter-day Katherine Hepburn kind of way. "It must be a practice bonfire," she says. "They must be burning the wee bits that fell off the pile."

The wee bits, I reckon from the size and density of the plume, must include a wee car, or at least a few tires.

Portadown doesn't offer much in the way of accommodation, and we're lucky to get a place just a fifteen-minute walk from Drumcree Church. Maureen agrees, saying, "It's best you stay on this side. Maybe for once a reporter will tell our side of the story."

She tells me that in recent years, journalists paid upward of 300 pounds a night to sleep on a floor in a home in a Catholic neighborhood. "Homes so dirty," she explains in a fiery eloquence also reminiscent of Hepburn, "I wouldn't sleep in one if you wrapped me in plastic." She catches herself, considering for a moment what our religious background might be. "Well, I don't know what you two are. I don't care, really. The point is all those reporters want to know is how much those poor Catholics are suffering. Well, no one ever asked me if I'm stressed. I've got paratroopers crawling around in the fields behind my house. Wouldn't you think that might be stressful?"

I turn my gaze through the bay windows. Tall grass wavers as far as the eye can see, interrupted only by a hidden road whereupon a solitary tractor putts.

Stress does show as cracks in Maureen's British composure. So for a more pleasant change of subject, I ask her which nation Portadown hosted for the Special Olympics.

"We didn't," she replies. Then, in a moment of recollection, she adds: "I saw some African boys downtown. Black as your boot, they were. But they didn't stay."

For the record, I've never worn black boots. Still, I get what she's saying.

I tell her that we're going out to scout the town, and ask her if she can help us find a certain place on the map. "A young man in Derry told us about it," I explain. "He said we should be there."

"What was he?"

"He described himself as 'hardcore IRA.'" I show her a page in my notebook where I tried to spell out the multisyllabic destination.

"Look at this," she huffs as she snaps my notebook. "This is nonsense. Those people can't even write. I mean, did he hold the pen in his toes?"

I suppose now I should've told her that it was my own penmanship after a few pints in a dark pub, but I didn't want to undermine my credibility as a journalist.

The air is still and quiet as Betsy and I stroll down to Drumcree Church. The road narrows as it slopes down between the cemetery walls and a weedy berm at the edge of a pasture. At the lowest point is Drumcree Bridge, scarcely wider than a country lane, with stout stone walls on each side to prevent motorist from driving off into the creek below. I hardly noticed it, wouldn't have recognized a bridge at all were it not for the enormous yellow-and-black striped barrier constructed upon it.

A couple of elderly gentlemen stand in the middle of the road, hands clasped behind their backs. "Smaller barrier this year," one notes with a tone of disappointment.

"Yes, but it's more robust," his friend remarks.

Soldiers sandbag the stream and pump more water into it, presumably to make it deeper and more difficult to cross, though anyone who managed that much would still face a zigzag fence of barbed wire, loops of razor wire, concrete blocks, and armed troops in full riot gear.

More soldiers on the Drumcree side clear away rocks and other debris that might be used as projectiles. I approach a soldier on a cigarette break and ask him, "Where's the safest place to observe tomorrow's events?"

"Belfast," he tells me.

We scout out the rest of town with Brian, a New York Times correspondent who's covered the march on Portadown for more years than he cares to recall. He drives us along the first leg of the parade route. Perspex barriers have been erected at St. John Church at the top of Garvaghy Road to allow onlookers a view of the parade while preventing any physical interaction with the marchers. More barriers and armed troops stand at the entrance to all side streets leading into the Garvaghy area. On the other side of the road, a Protestant mural depicts a Red Hand Commando unit—men in ski masks brandishing assault rifles. And while this painting is on the same scale as those in the Bogside, its artist employed a primitive technique, an unintentionally childlike rendering of this terrorist squad, that makes it far more intimidating.

To the left flies the Union Jack. I have to look twice to be sure, because at first glance, in a cognizant glitch, it registered in my mind as stars and bars, the flag of old Dixie.

In front of the mural are the remains of the practice bonfire, a charred heap the size of a pitcher's mound. Near that is a pile of wooden palates, tires, particle board, tree limbs, tires, folding tables, sofas, and easy chairs. This is the pyre for Sunday night's bonfire, and it's big enough to cover a baseball diamond. Imagine this junkyard burning in the night and St. Patrick's mission for reptilian genocide suddenly seems like a ecological misdemeanor.

A convoy of army trucks rumbles past, while an armored vehicle stations itself discreetly under an overpass. At every checkpoint, Brian hands over his press pass. The soldiers wave him through, but they're stopping other cars to take names.

He warns of soldiers hiding in the grass at roadsides, in the fields, anywhere trouble might unexpectedly stray. "You don't see them until you're right on top of one, and it can scare the hell out of you," he explains. "Look, there's one now." He points out a soldier not ten feet away, perfectly camouflaged to match a dappling of sunlight and foliage shadows on stone wall. Without Brian's keen eye, surely we would've missed this armed chameleon.

Choice of colors plays strange tricks in Portadown. The Orangemen love their orange, and display it proudly in the form of an orange sash. The Catholic communities, however, show no restraint when displaying their favorite color, which also happens to be orange. It's the color of their favorite football team, Armagh, who soon will battle their archrival in Dublin.

This is perhaps the only time of year when nationalist communities will lower their tricolors, the flag of the Republic, in favor of an orange one, and Catholic children play in the streets, all wearing bright orange jerseys. All this, ironically, on the eve of the dreaded March of the Orangemen.

Drumcree Sunday

Swallows, or maybe starlings, wheel through the air as we wait for the Orangemen to arrive. Loudspeakers posted outside the church rattle out a dirge about making your mother proud as she watches you from heaven above, or some such nostalgic drivel that sounds too much like country music.

I'm growing impatient, and worse, I've had too much tea at breakfast. I excuse myself to find a hedged orchard and a well-concealed spot at the edge of a thick stand of trees and thickets.

Moments later, as I'm zipping up, I hear something heavy shift in the scrub, and a metallic click that sounds not more than five feet away. I squint into the dense tangle of vines and briars, and see nothing but dappling sunlight and deep, dark shadows. I could just as well be staring into a Vietnamese jungle.

Upon my return to Brian and Betsy, I tell them, "I think I just peed on a paratrooper."

Clouds converge above as the crowd grows. TV crews set up cameras on the cemetery walls. The birds fly in frantic circles until one with faulty ailerons suddenly plummets into the road.

"That's a bad omen," I say.

"Yeah, and the music's just now stopped," Brian points out. The only sound that remains is a steady percussion from an army helicopter hovering over the church. Its narrow spike of a spire now looks like an anti-aircraft missile ready to launch.

Soon the parade arrives, a quarter-mile stretch of drums, accordions, orange sashes, swords, umbrellas, and bowler hats. It doesn't seem so much like a Klan rally, but rather a herd of Masons, or maybe just Shriners with an edge. They begin migrating into the church, but hundreds more choose to mill around the road to pass time until the confrontation at the barrier. Many gather in the cow field, kind of like at Woodstock, only without the music and goodwill for all. Others wait in their cars, bracing their nerves and fueling their rage with nicotine and alcohol in heavy doses.

Reverend Pickering's voice crackles through the loudspeakers, telling us that there's still plenty of seating available inside. No one takes him up on his invitation. Four young boys caper about in the field and on the cemetery walls. All sport crew cuts, one with Carolina blue highlights, another with a maroon Nike swoosh stripe painted on the back of his head. This pack of little ruffians apparently has a young alpha male. Betsy names him Jack, after the tribal usurper in *Lord of the Flies*.

They gather around her and ask where she's from.

"New Mexico."

"Where's that?"

"America."

"South America?" Jack asks impatiently. "Do you go around in massive white hats?"

Betsy keeps an eye on them as they confront other strangers in the crowd. She soon figures out their mischievous game: They're seeking foreigners who can teach them how to say 'fuck' in other languages.

After Pickering's forty-minute service, the same tolerable length of the Catholic service we attended a week earlier, the parade resumes for a hundred yards or so toward the bridge, then stops at a new barrier.

Parade marshals, Orangemen in bowler hats, have erected their own barrier, a strip of orange tape, to keep the rest of their tribe at least twenty feet away from the main barrier. It stretches out into the pasture to keep them away from the stream as well. And as an added precaution, they've positioned themselves behind the tape, about ten men in all, urging the crowd at all times not to break through.

Then the speeches begin, quick diatribes calling for the preservation of the British way and condemning those who seek to corrupt it. They voice their protest over the barrier at the soldiers they identify as traitors, demanding that they "remove this hideous wall." Their words are kinder than those used by the more vocal members in the crowd, who have a propensity for shouting "Scumbags!" and "Wankers!" at any given moment.

The end of the speeches marks the point, according to the new tradition, when the crowd is supposed to attack the barrier. But the speakers have left, the marshals remain, and no one is quite sure what to do. Only the children seem clear on the objective. They scramble about in the field digging up rocks.

"I've got a brick!" cries Jack. A brick, in the local vernacular, is just a rock that's suitable for throwing at an enemy. To be sure, he holds up a rock the size of his shoe. But the other boys are already in the process of throwing their rocks at the soldiers behind the wall. Problem is, they're standing too far away, behind the orange tape, and their wee little arms just can't launch a brick that far. Instead, they splash down into the stream, or worse, lose their trajectory on the near side of the barrier and graze the pants of oblivious Orange marshals.

One finally succeeds in striking a corrugated steel side barrier. The resulting crash alerts crowds on both sides in a familiar way that might be likened to, say, the crack of a bat on the first pitch of the season. It gets everyone's attention, but when they see the chief rioter is less than twelve, their hopes for a skirmish slump.

A marshal approaches the lads to tell them they are very naughty indeed. "Don't throw anymore bricks," he advises, wagging his white-gloved finger, "until we're gone."

Hearing that, a skinhead nearing his fifties demands to know who gave the parade marshals the authority to police the children and protect the barrier. "You're a traitor," he snarls at the marshal. "A bloody Lundy is what you are." (Lundy being the cowardly governor of Londonderry who fled the city during the siege in 1688.)

His sentiment is shared by diehard Loyalists throughout Northern Ireland. They resent this Local Orange Order's attempt to seek peaceful resolution. A compromise with the Catholics, they say, infringes on their right to walk the Queen's highway. And they are none too pleased with that.

This puts the Portadown Orangemen in a pickle. If they fail to march that seven-minute segment down Garvaghy Road, then they have been defeated in a sense. However, their rallying cry is: "Here We Stand. We Can Do No Other." It sounds ineffectual, but it's their motto and they're sticking to it.

If they bargain with the Parade Commission for permission to finish the march, then the diehards, in particular the faction known as the 'Not an Inch' brigade, will brand them as traitors for compromising Protestant rights. For this hardcore mob, the only possible solution is to repeat the skirmishes of previous years, which inevitably results in rioting for days on end, a lot of wrecking and breaking, multiple injuries and hundreds of arrests, and occasionally a few deaths.

This is what draws the media here, the enticement of that thug element. They stagger around in the pasture, working up a fury as they approach the front line. One thug plods into a cow pie like he doesn't know it from Shinola. By his side is a middle-aged woman with some good teeth in her head, and a purple T-shirt that reads in sparkly letters: FCUK ME. She says, "If President Bush were here, he'd get us through that barrier."

As the thugs move closer, the boys jubilantly tear down the orange tape. But that's as far as the confrontation goes. Rain sprays in like frothy spit from a chorus of ranting madmen, and the bulk of the crowd migrates over to a concessions van for deep-fried snacks. The tough ones stick it out at the barrier—a handful of desperate reporters and a seething, though pitifully small element that really has no business here but to turn a local dispute into a national circus.

And I start to wonder what I'm doing here. I've come to Ireland in part to meditate on its poetic inspiration, to glean that wisdom, gracious and otherwise, and apply it to an insightful chapter on how far I've come since my Carolina days. But now I find myself standing in a field full of redneck hatred and an overwhelming stench of cow shit, and that does not sit well with me.

I need to stop looking for trouble. I need to move beyond human misery and hateful cruelty as something to observe, that kind of travel that slips so easily from exploration to exploitation. I never expected that frolicking about with my Catholic wife would imbue the North with warm fuzzies, but I didn't anticipate getting sucked into all their ugliness either.

The crowd dissipates further, until all that remains in the cow pasture is a lone TV correspondent, his soundman and his cameraman. They're busy taping a news segment with the background intensity of a farm report. Closer to the church, a German correspondent gestures to Brian a pantomime of drinking and typing and more drinking as a way to illustrate the tedium of churning out copy for such an unnewsworthy event.

Back at the b&b, Maureen is both relieved and unimpressed with the peaceful conclusion. She believes the conflict is passing. Like most folks here, she hopes that one day all of Portadown may grow to realize there's a whole world beyond their hideous little wall, and that Drumcree will no longer stand for Protestant-Catholic antagonism, but come to symbolize the Christian spirit of reconciliation.

Or as she puts it: "They're building a mosque in town, so perhaps we'll find a new enemy."

Death of a Crusader

In Dublin, on the south side of St. Michan's Cathedral, storm cellar doors open to a cobwebbed crypt below. Down the dark vaulted hallway, against that back wall of the last chamber on the left, rests the mummified remains of a man believed to be a crusader. The telltale sign of his former occupation is in his burial position, namely with his legs crossed at the ankle. But because he was a tall man—at six foot six, exceptionally tall for the thirteenth century—he didn't quite fit in his coffin. To remedy the problem, his legs were snapped off at the thighs and crossed again.

He's holding up quite well for a corpse over seven hundred years old, as well as his three companions. The nun, the thief, and the stranger—all are several centuries younger than the ancient crusader, and yet he could easily pass as their brother. His nose is a bit mushed, like a boxer's whose cartilage is wearing thin, but his tongue is in place, his mouth open and silent as though nonplused with his arrangement. Oddest of all, his right hand is slightly raised. He seems to be reaching out of his coffin, almost beckoning me into his crypt.

I step over his friends and kneel by his side. The back of his hand looks and feels smooth as polished mahogany, though perhaps due in large part to the thousands who have come before me to press this very piece of desiccated flesh. It's said that shaking hands with him brings one good fortune.

However, I'm not sure how to rate his fortune. I mean, he's dead. And what's worse, he's not taking the traditional route from ashes to ashes, dust to dust. He is preserved for generations of tourists who, by gawking at this unmistakably dead man, must now consider their own mortality. Indeed, most who have done so have since experienced it, that final departure.

And yet the crusader stays with us. He resists the ravages of time, achieving what we mortals can only dream of, that something of our lives might still be recognized long after we're gone.

We don't know where he's been, if like other crusaders he spread terror, in the name of God, to Muslims, heathens and pagans far and wide. He speaks nothing of his past, and in his silence, he becomes a mystery to be unraveled through disquieting imagination, with all threads ending at the same final question: *Why is he still here?*

For me, the sinewy hand imparts not so much good fortune, but a strange sense of calm. I'd like to offer him a blessing in return, but the only one that comes to mind is this: Nothing in Ireland will kill you. It seems a bit late for that.

For Bram Stoker, a Dubliner who suffered through a sickly childhood at the lip of death's abyss, the crusader served as inspiration. It's said that he conceived *Dracula* in this very crypt. I can imagine how. I'm staring death in the face, holding its hand, as it were. And it's horrifically poetic.